JOHN WESLEY'S
EXPERIMENTAL DIVINITY

STUDIES IN METHODIST
DOCTRINAL STANDARDS

JOHN WESLEY'S
EXPERIMENTAL DIVINITY

STUDIES IN METHODIST DOCTRINAL STANDARDS

Robert E. Cushman

KINGSWOOD BOOKS
An Imprint of Abingdon Press
Nashville, Tennessee

JOHN WESLEY'S EXPERIMENTAL DIVINITY:
STUDIES IN METHODIST DOCTRINAL STANDARDS

Library of Congress Cataloging-in-Publication Data

Cushman, Robert Earl.
    John Wesley's experimental divinity.

    Includes index.
    1. Methodist Church — United States — Doctrines — History.
    2. Wesley, John, 1703-1791.   I. Title.

BX8332.C87   1989   230'.7   88-28475

ISBN 0-687-20446-1

With Glad Recollection and Esteem
Dedicated to Colleagues,
Inaugurators, Editors, Directors
of the
Wesley Works Editorial Project, Inc.
1959-1971:

Franz Hildebrandt, Albert C. Outler,
Bernard W. Anderson, Eric W. Baker, William R. Cannon,
Frank Baker, Philip S. Watson, Raymond P. Morris,
Charles W. Ranson, Gerald O. McCulloh,
and especially
Joseph D. Quillian, partner,
1960-1981

CONTENTS

I have . . . set down in the following sermons what I find in the Bible concerning the way to heaven, with a view to distinguish this way of God from all those which are the inventions of men. I have endeavoured to describe the true, the scriptural, experimental religion, so as to omit nothing which is a real part thereof, and to add nothing thereto which is not. . . . It is more especially my desire . . . to guard those who are just setting their faces towards heaven . . . from formality, from mere outside religion, which has almost driven heart-religion out of the world. . . .

—John Wesley, Preface to *Sermons on Several Occasions*

PREFACE

These essays seek to contribute to the ongoing study and exposition of Methodist doctrine in its first century. While they presuppose knowledge of the institutional history of the movement, their contribution is principally to the history of doctrine. In particular, the essays seek to investigate further the doctrinal commitments of early American Methodists in the years 1769 to 1816, or the era of Francis Asbury.

This inquiry is pursued on the supposition of a direct and immediate dependency of Early American Methodism upon the Wesleys, together with a reexamination of that supposition. At the same time, it recognizes that the influence of George Whitefield and the Great Awakening of evangelical interest throughout the eastern seaboard colonies during the middle years of the 18th century was truly contributory.

Our concern in the succeeding essays is, at least, threefold. It is, in the first place, an effort to rediscover and describe John Wesley's "experimental and practical divinity." Secondly, it is with the relation of this "divinity" to the emergent doctrinal understanding and preaching of the early American Methodists. In the third place, it seeks to adjudge the measure in which doctrinal standards, in contemporary American Methodism, are obligated to the historic tradition, responsible for it, or ought to be, and how.

Wesley's phrase "experimental and practical divinity" has for more than a century, and until very recently, been unattended if not all but unknown to most Methodist people and theologians. It appears infrequently but emphatically in Wesley's writings. In an important instance, as in the Preface to *A Collection of Hymns for the Use of the People Called Methodists* of 1780, Wesley refers to that very hymnal as "a little body of experimental and practical divinity."[1]

The word "divinity" in 17th century English usage is not synonymous with the word "theology," that is, a reasonable account of God. Rather, "divinity" is an account of God as he is known by way of his own self-manifestation in Jesus Christ as Lord and Savior through the illuminating and converting work of the Holy Spirit. Thus, according to English usage of the 16th and 17th centuries, "divinity" is a Trinitarian doctrine of God's salvation in Christ in which attention to the nature and way of human salvation, or the Gospel, is foremost.

Wesley was to rediscover that such usage was rooted in the distinctive doctrinal focus of the Church of England. Indeed had been the "divinity" of the Caroline Divines and their Anglican predecessors back to Latimer and Cranmer. It may be said that Wesley was educated in the Caroline tradition and stood in that succession. Yet it must immediately be added that he did so with marked deviations from it.

It will be the task of the following chapters to indicate that the important variation from the Caroline divinity is in great part Wesley's "experimental and practical divinity." I will attempt to show that it, too, is a doctrine of salvation that may perhaps best be summarized in the title of Wesley's sermon, "The Scripture Way of Salvation." This divinity denotes a doctrinal system best described as mapping the way of salvation. It entails a transformation of human existence that properly issues in "holiness of heart and life," or "Christian perfection." Its distinctive thesis is that the truth of Scripture and the "promises" of God to sinful humanity are, in the first case, confirmed and, in the second, claimed only by living experience empowered by the gracious working of the Holy Spirit. In this way doctrine comes to life, the creed is made incarnate, and humanity participates in the divine nature.

Concerning the second principal task of these essays, namely, the relation of Wesley's "experimental divinity" to the doctrinal commitments of the early itinerant Methodist preachers, a main contribution of these studies will be to probe their memoirs and surviving autobiographical documents. Here alone is it possible to recover the gospel preached by these astounding knights-errant of the Lord. Without question they were spiritual "giants in the earth": William Watters, Philip Gatch, Caleb Pedicord, Daniel Ruff, James Cromwell, John Tunnell, Freeborn Garrettson, John Dickens, Jesse Lee, Thomas Ware, et al. The surviving materials are few, and to let them again be heard, quotations in these essays are extensive. In this respect, these studies may in some measure serve as a source book of early Methodist doctrine.

In the third place, with reference to the question of doctrinal standards, these studies suggest that the regularly espoused doctrinal system of American Methodists from 1773 to the death of Asbury in 1816 was, without evident modification, precisely Wesley's "experimental and practical divinity." This "divinity" is the substance of

Wesley's soteriology or doctrine of salvation, and is rooted both in Scripture and tradition.

The tradition in Wesley's case cannot be separated from his exegesis and comprehension of the 1547 Edwardian Homilies of the Church of England. As confirmed by "experimental religion" or "experience," the Homilies, along with Scripture, provided the ground of Wesley's abridgment of the Thirty-Nine Articles of 1571. This abridgment, known as the Twenty-Four Articles, Wesley supplied to the Christmas Conference of 1784, along with the *Sunday Service*, his abridgment of the Book of Common Prayer. These together serve to signify the sum of the received doctrinal tradition which was acceptable to John Wesley and to which he regularly deferred.

At this point it must suffice to suggest that any discussion of the doctrinal standards of the Methodist Episcopal Church must acknowledge the role of Scripture, tradition and "experience." By experience, Scripture and tradition are confirmed in "living faith." This confirmation, we will find, denotes the role of "experimental religion" in the language of the early American Methodists, or the abstraction of it, namely, Wesley's "experimental and practical divinity."

To my knowledge, this study of Wesley's "experimental divinity" has, however anomalous this may seem, no predecessor. It appears to be the case that while several facets and themes of this "divinity" are repeatedly treated by Wesley in many of his writings — his *Journal*, the *Appeals*, the *Minutes* of his Conferences, as well as in numerous tracts, essays, sermons, and hymns — he nowhere gives a comprehensive and systematic explication of it. Nor is such an explication to be found in Richard Watson's *Theological Institutes* (1823), Thomas Jackson's essays on Methodism (1839), or William B. Pope's masterful *Compendium of Christian Theology* (1875). We will find it in a few American authors of stature such as Jesse Lee, Nathan Bangs, and others, but Matthew Simpson's *Cyclopedia of Methodism* (1876) has no entry for either "experience" or "experimental religion," nor does that volumous resource edited by John McClintock and James Strong, *Cyclopedia of Biblical, Theological, and Ecclesiastical Literature*.

Quite exceptional is the article on "Christian Experience" in the recent *Encyclopedia of World Methodism* (1974) by Gerald O. McCulloh. At some length it affirms the central place of the experience of saving grace and the witness of the Holy Spirit as integral to the Wesleyan teaching on justification. It regards "the emphasis upon experience as basic to Methodist epistemology"; and it states that "scripture, reason, and experience have been the grounds of authority for Methodism."[2] The latter statement, while distinctive, recalls another like it in Part

II, Section 1 of our current *Discipline* which asserts that, in 1808, "the Wesleyan appeal to the fourfold norms of Scripture, tradition, experience, and reason was so widely understood that it was taken for granted."[3]

This may very well be the case; but it is one of the curiosities of the history of this subject that the solitary critical work on "experimental religion," either in the 18th or 19th centuries, is a little known two-volume exposition by Thomas Williams entitled *An Historic Defense of Experimental Religion in Which the Doctrine of Divine Influences is Supported by the Authority of Scripture* (1795). By "divine influences" the author refers to the Holy Spirit; when carefully examined, his viewpoint is strikingly close to the Wesleyan schema. While the author refers to the Wesleys, he seems to identify with the Calvinist wing of the Methodists.[4]

While several 17th and early 18th century authors, such as Joseph Allein, Isaac Ambrose, and Richard Baxter, make way for the role of Christian "experience" in saving faith, only Philip Doddridge provides a coherent exposition of "experimental religion" as such in his widely read and often reprinted *The Rise and Progress of Religion in the Soul* (1745). The following year Jonathan Edwards' *A Treatise Concerning Religious Affections* (1746) set forth the view that the "affections," not the "intellectual faculties," are "the springs of action in all things religious." As Ola E. Winslow observes, "the emphasis shifted from outward manifestations to inner certainty" so that "Jonathan Edwards and John Wesley stood together in their insistence on the inner witness, not of the mind, but of the emotions."[5]

Wesley's *Journal* for October 8, 1738, indicates the high approbation which attended his reading of Edwards' *A Faithful Narrative of the Surprising Work of God in the Conversion of Many Hundred Souls in Northampton, etc.* (1737). To Winslow's statement of their unanimity, however, it should be added that any acknowledgment of a role of emotion in Christian experience would have been understood by both Wesley and Edwards as concomitant to an effectual working of the Holy Spirit. This alone was, for both of them, sufficient reason for the onset of an "inner certainty."

My major professor in philosophy, Cornelius Krusé of Wesleyan University, to whom I remain indebted, gave me wise counsel as I began teaching. Successful teaching, he thought, "was closely allied to the fine art of useful repetition." Accordingly, I ask but one thing of the reader, in addition to attention, namely, to observe that each of these essays deals with the same subject from a particular perspective, and that all are, like a compass, galvanized by the same gravitational field, that is Wesley's doctrine of "experimental religion."

With some hesitation, these essays are offered as "tracts for the time" for interested Methodists and others entertaining the slightest doubt regarding the survival value of Protestantism in America. Parts of the essays were first presented as lectures under the title "Doctrinal Standards in the Wesleyan Tradition" to the Society for Wesleyan Studies of the Virginia Annual Conference at Randolph Macon College, Ashland, Virginia, in February, 1986. This was on the invitation of the President and Vice-President, respectively, Rev. Jeffry P. Mickle of Alexandria, and Rev. Prof. James C. Logan of Wesley Theological Seminary, Washington, D.C.

It was evident that the subject matter was proposed because of a keen interest of the Society membership in the then pending quadrennial report on Methodist doctrinal standards under preparation by a Commission deployed by the General Conference of 1984 and scheduled for presentation to the forthcoming General Conference of April, 1988. Since I shared this interest, the invitation was welcome, and more so, since I delighted to renew conversation with former students, ranging over four decades, of my years at Duke Divinity School. Likewise it was a gracious occasion to be presented and heard by the dedicated resident Bishop of the Richmond Area, Dr. Robert M. Blackburn, with whom I had had heartening association in the years of his episcopal leadership of the North Carolina Conference.

As readied for publication, the original six lectures have become thirteen essays, some of which retain much of the style of public address. An unsuccessful endeavor to see the whole published prior to the 1988 General Conference was encouraged in part by Bishop Earl G. Hunt's request for the original lectures and his circulation of the same in the Spring of 1987, through the Secretary, to the Quadrennial Commission of which he was Chairman.

Of the thirteen chapters of this study, the introduction and chapters 1 and 2, and parts of chapters 3, 5, 9, 10, and 11, are carried over from the lectures, while chapters 4, 6, 7, 8, and the epilogue are additions. For readers who wish the shorter course, I judge that the "prospectus" of the introduction is essential, along with chapters 1, 2, 3, 5, 6, 10, 11, and the epilogue.

For timely assistance in bibliographical research I am indebted to the resourcefulness of Ms. Harriet V. Leonard, Reference Librarian of Duke Divinity School Library. To Professor Kenneth E. Rowe of Drew University Library, I express thanks for photocopies of materials from his indispensable Union Catalogue and of J. J. Tigert's *Doctrines of the Methodist Episcopal Church in America*. For assistance with manuscript preparation, I am grateful for the veteran secretarial service of Mrs. Vivian Efird.

Likewise, I am most thankful to Mrs. Gail Chappell, member of the Divinity School secretarial staff, whose services as a word processor provided indispensable supporting assistance in the winter and spring of 1987, and, again, in aid of publication at years end. And to both Mrs. Frances Parrish, staff supervisor, and to her excellency, Mrs. Clara Godwin, Administrative Assistant to the Dean, I remain ever indebted.

Finally, I am under particular obligation to two longtime colleagues of Duke Divinity School: to McMurry S. Richey, Professor of Theology and Christian Nurture, retired, for both helpful warnings and encouragements; and to Stuart C. Henry, Professor of American Christianity, also retired, for tailoring of "pre-wrinkled" garments with felicity. Finally, I wish to express my thanks to any to whose published works I may, by oversight, be tributary without acknowledgment.

Robert E. Cushman
Duke University Divinity School
May 28, 1987

INTRODUCTION

"IF GOD DOES NOT ACKNOWLEDGE ME. . . . "

The intent of these essays is to reexamine in historical perspective the doctrinal standards of American Methodism during its formative period, the final quarter of the 18th century and the 19th century to the death of Francis Asbury in 1816. These doctrinal standards continued to provide the *animus* of Methodism well into the 19th century, during which the Methodist movement came of age in the flood-tide of an advancing frontier and the domestication of a continent.

By the 1760s, Methodist "local preachers" from Ireland or elsewhere who had some previous connection with John Wesley appeared in the American seaboard colonies as spokesmen of the Wesleyan revival in Great Britain. Their names are all but legendary. There was the Irishman, Philip Embury of New York; Captain Thomas Webb of Albany, Long Island, and Philadelphia; Robert Strawbridge in Maryland where, according to Francis Asbury, the first society in America was formed, possibly as early as 1763, either at Sam's Creek or Pipe Creek.[1] Shortly thereafter the names of Robert Williams, Richard Wright, Abraham Whitworth, John Owen, and John King appear as earliest itinerant preachers in the colonies. By 1769, Richard Boardman and Joseph Pilmore were located alternately in New York and Philadelphia, the first of Wesley's designated "Assistants" to be sent to the colonies with explicit mandate to supervise Methodist doctrine and discipline in the American societies.

Francis Asbury arrived in Philadelphia on October 27, 1771, with the explicit authorization of John Wesley. Although at first he was subordinate to Richard Boardman, by October 10, 1772, a letter from Mr. Wesley to Asbury required "a strict attention to discipline" and, reports Asbury, "appointed me to act as assistant."[2] This was the prelude to Wesley's appointment of General Assistant Thomas Rankin, along with George Shadford, as delegated emissaries the succeeding year, with authority to supersede Boardman and Pilmore and to convene a conference of all "preachers in connection with the Reverend Mr. John Wesley."

This organizing conference of American Methodism, which took place in Philadelphia, July 14–16, 1773, will be discussed in chapter 1, in order to consider properly the bearing of Conference organization upon early Methodist doctrine and discipline in the closing decades of the 18th century and onward into the post-revolutionary era. As Methodism moved northward from New York into New England and on to Maine through the work of Jesse Lee and others, it also marched westward across the Appalachians into the Ohio and Mississippi valleys and into "the southwest" — as it was known in the first quarter of the 19th century — through the Louisiana Purchase to the French settlements along the "Father of Waters."

The "formative" period of early Methodist doctrine and discipline may be proposed as the period which coincides with the long and varied "superintendency" of Francis Asbury, from his instatement as Assistant under Wesley in 1772 until his death in 1816. Within that space of forty-four years are to be found the landmark events formative of American Methodism. Asbury had accepted his assignment to America by Wesley and the Bristol Conference on August 7, 1771. On October 27, 1771, he landed in Philadelphia, was received by Francis Harris, a prominent Methodist layman, and was welcomed by Joseph Pilmore at St. George's Methodist Chapel that evening. There Asbury preached his first sermon in America the following evening, October 28.[3]

On his way to America, Asbury had written in his *Journal*: "If God does not acknowledge me in America, I will soon return to England. I know my views are upright now; may they never be otherwise."[4] To be "acknowledged" by God in his teaching meant for Asbury that the truth of the doctrine he preached would be known by its fruits in renovated lives. For an early Methodist to know and to say that his mission and message was "owned of God" was his sufficient reward. Such language occurs constantly in the memoirs of the early itinerants. On departing England, Asbury had bid farewell to sorrowful parents, family, and friends. He was twenty-six years old. He was never to go home again. Without question, he was, more than any other human being, to visit and become intimately familiar with the American wilderness and frontier from Maine to Georgia, and west to the Ohio. Our most knowledgeable witness, Thomas Ware, fifty years an itinerant Methodist preacher of intelligence and great gifts, stated that "Next to Mr. Wesley, Bishop Asbury was the most unwearied itinerant the world ever saw."[5]

As Francis Asbury himself received warm welcome from Joseph Pilmore in 1771 in Philadelphia, so in turn he was to welcome, on June 3, 1773, General Assistant Thomas Rankin and George Shadford, sent by Wesley to regularize the work of the Methodist societies in the colonies. This regularization was inaugurated at the Philadelphia Conference of 1773 under Rankin's presidency.

After the lapse of eleven years, which embraced the Revolutionary War, Francis Asbury received Thomas Coke on November 15, 1784, at Barratt's Chapel, Delaware and, with Coke, proceeded to the Christmas Conference, which was hastily scheduled to meet at Lovely Lane Chapel in Baltimore, December 24, 1784. There the Methodist Episcopal Church was established, and Asbury, with the unanimous approval of the native American preachers, was inducted into holy orders; he was made deacon and elder, and was ordained to the "superintendency" of the newly established church. The ordination was performed by Coke and two elders themselves newly ordained by Wesley, Richard Whatcoat and Thomas Vasey, who were joined at Asbury's request by Philip Otterbein, a German "Presbyterian" minister.

For thirty-two years Francis Asbury was occupied with this arduous superintendency, exhibiting an endurance well beyond that of most men; he was principled, devout, and seemingly tireless in his self-giving of a soul dedicated to the family of God. With his passing, early Methodism experienced an ever enlarging geographical outreach. In the midst of cultural and social change of the early 19th century, Methodism participated in the large-scale migration and settling of the Midwest. Methodism in this period also faced the hardening of forces over the slavery issue between North and South, and the growth of cities and American industry in the northeastern and north central states.

By mid-century a process of accommodation to culture was already at work in the churches, and American Methodism was showing strain and lapse at the point both of its General Rules and of the evangelical discipline which had nurtured its "classes" and given vitality to the earlier societies. Its educational program, however, was enriched in the local church, so that home and world missions became an increasing challenge for Methodism in the later 19th century. Moral causes for social well-being were a regular topic of the Methodist pulpit throughout the nineteenth century, and in the North this included an increasingly articulate indictment of slavery as well as strong support of the temperance movement. An enlarging awareness of responsibility for the struggle between capital ownership and rights of laboring classes was finding a place in Methodist forums before the turn of the 20th century. The *Social Creed* of Methodism, promulgated in 1908, was to become a model of churchly response to the increasingly embittered struggle. Prior to 1914, it was adopted by the Federal, and later by the National Council of Churches of Christ in America, after having passed through recurrent revisions by the Methodist Churches.

By the early 20th century American Methodism in its several branches — including black Methodism — had become the leading progressive Protestant force in North America. The momentum in conciliar leadership was to continue, reaching high-tide with the reunion of the principal Methodisms of the United States in 1939, which were then predominantly white, and the formation of The Methodist Church.

In due course, jurisdictional Methodism — as the controversial vehicle of reunification — developed a regionalism which was subsequently further accented by a generation of insurgent minority rights and claims movements within as well as without the church. The era of jurisdictional Methodism witnessed the decline, if not displacement, of creative episcopal leadership; the espousal of "the managerial revolution" in church governance; the attendant burgeoning of church bureaucracies with the permission of the General Conference (especially since 1972); the shaping of policy by the "quota system" through boards and agencies since 1968; the uniform programming of church vision, aspiration and function; and the externalization of religious consciousness. Apart from the quadrennium 1968–1972, this era has not been a period of doctrinal interest or inquiry. However, both charismatic and liturgical renewal as well as resurgent evangelical concern have had continuing manifestation within the United Methodist Church, as Gallup and other polls have shown.

With this abbreviated synopsis of American Methodist history as background, we turn to the question of Methodist doctrinal standards.

SOME GUIDELINES FOR INQUIRY

For our present inquiry, two questions especially need to be answered. First, why, from 1792 until 1968, was our *Discipline* always called *The Doctrines and Discipline of the Methodist Episcopal Church*? Second, why does the famous First Restrictive Rule of 1808 prohibit revocation or change either of "our articles of religion" or "establishment of any new standards or rules of doctrine?" In these successive phrases I discern two matters. Although "standards" and "rules" are plurals, they were conceived as inseparable and are, in historic fact, co-implicates of one another. For the Wesleys and for the early Methodists in America, doctrine was of little worth unless it was verified in experience and became more and more radiant in a Christian life. Asbury and his colleagues agreed that this alone was the mark and sign of the Divine approval.

This proposition is the clue to the 18th century revival under the Wesleys and the inception of American Methodism. Another way of stating the matter is that with the Wesleys "doctrine comes to life."[6] In considering Wesleyan doctrinal standards, one cannot without distortion separate the *doctrine* irradiated in Christian lives from the *discipline* which is indispensable to its embodiment, nurture, resurgence, or recapitulation. Therefore, the earliest American Methodists were compelled to state their case in terms of *both* doctrines *and* discipline. Pertinent to the point are the words which Francis Asbury wrote in his *Journal* on his way to America in 1771:

> The people God owns in England, are the Methodists. The doctrines they preach, and the discipline they enforce, are, I believe, the purest of any people now in the world. The Lord has greatly blessed these doctrines and this discipline; they must therefore be pleasing to him.[7]

It is true that the word "discipline" frequents the Book of Common Prayer, especially in the ordinals for deacons, elders, and bishops. But until 1784 there was little ecclesiastical precedent for such title as *The Doctrines and Discipline* of the United Societies or of the Methodist Episcopal Church. Obviously, this title is itself a major clue for any inquiry regarding doctrinal standards in early Methodism.

To comprehend the premise that, for the Wesleys and the early American Methodists, doctrine is of little worth unless it is verified in experience and becomes radiant in Christian life, some grasp of an extended historical context is needed. It is also necessary to explore Wesley's personal story, using his *Journal* and his published works as the main sources. Often, moreover, one can be surprisingly helped by study of the Wesleyan hymnody in its several editions. In the Preface to *A Collection of Hymns for the Use of the People Called Methodists* (1780), Wesley speaks of that hymnal as "a little body of experimental and practical divinity."[8] If we understand the terms "experimental" and "practical" as they are used here, we are on the way to discovery of his basic doctrines of salvation.

It is also essential to understand the rationale of the Wesleyan societies in 18th century Britain and America. Despite the 1784 founding of the American Methodist Episcopal Church, the *Doctrines and*

Discipline of that body kept on speaking of "our United Societies" throughout most of the 19th century.[9] Indeed, the stated duties of a "preacher in charge" were "to preach; to meet the *societies, classes, and general bands*; to visit the sick; to preach in the mornings where he can get hearers."[10] Until 1888, the Methodist Episcopal Church retained a surviving self-understanding as that of "the United Societies" transferred to American soil with the blessing and authorization of "our venerable friend, who, under God, had been the father of the great revival of religion now extending over the earth."[11] Without doubt, all were aware of the words of the "Large Minutes": "A Methodist preacher is to mind every point, great and small, in the Methodist discipline!"[12] Such discipline is the prescribed way in which doctrine may come to life and become radiant in it.

PROSPECTUS: A SUMMATION OF WORKING THESES

1. What is a doctrinal standard? It is living faith as we find it in church history from the New Testament onwards, which regularly discloses itself in an unfolding progression of characteristic utterance. It starts with doxology: praise and thanksgiving, adoration of God with thanks for his blessings, both of creation and redemption. It is followed by public confession in the *ecclesia*, the cell church. In the New Testament this was called *homologia*, confession of agreement with the common mind of the assembled group; it could take the form of "hymns, psalms, and spiritual songs" (Col. 3:16-17; Eph. 5:19) as well as that of prophecy, exhortation, or preaching.

In *The Apostolic Preaching and Its Developments*, C. H. Dodd states that the declared faith in the New Testament initially takes the form of *kerygma*, proclamation, and that the Petrine proclamation in Acts, in effect, supplies doctrinal norms. The same is true of the gospel that Paul preached.[13] Without these, Christian doctrine would lack foundation. In 1881, Nathanial Burwash, a Canadian Methodist scholar and theologian, in a volume entitled *Wesley's Doctrinal Standards*, anticipated Dodd's views. He held that the Apostolic church conveyed the substance of the Gospel not by way of creeds, however implicit these might have been, but as "the preached word," the *kerygma*.[14] Burwash attributed to Wesley an explicit recognition of such a form of Christian affirmation and confession and claimed this recognition was Wesley's reason for the "Standard Sermons." Whether this is the case or not, it is true that for Wesley the Homilies of the Church of England took precedence over the Thirty-Nine Articles as the standards of the doctrine of salvation. Evidence of this fact is visible throughout Wesley's writings.[15]

2. The witness of "living faith," to use Wesley's recurrent phrase, unfolds further in the action and the prayers of the liturgy. Here, common affirmation finds public expression as a *consensus fidelium*, a consensus of the faithful, which finally issues in the "rule of faith." This "rule" gives voice to the common mind and thus supplies the worshiping group with its self-identity.[16] And, by this, a rule obtains for distinguishing between saints and strangers. Gradually, the rule takes on an agreed articulate substance and form; and shortly "living faith" attains to its expression in creed. At this point we have reached the far end in the progression of faith's unfolding. Here, objectification of the living faith occurs: the *credo* — "I believe *in*" — becomes "I believe *that*": doxology becomes "It is so!" In the form of the creed, living faith seems to become an object of public knowledge and deceptively offers itself for public subscription, appraisal, or critique.

3. Where the gospel is preached and heeded there can be a working consensus among the faithful. When the consensus has been declared there can be a "rule of faith," a *regula fidei*, among believers; this becomes a measure for determining who rightly belongs in the group and who does not. Such was the case in the Apostolic Sees of the second and third Christian centuries. The "rule of faith" was, at first, largely an internal yardstick, a crosier, for shepherding the sheep of the flock and protecting the sheep by warding off the "wolves," that is, the heterodox.

Such were the *General Rules of the United Societies* under Wesley, which were first formulated in 1738, elaborated in 1739, decisively sketched in 1743, and enlarged from 1744 to 1789.[17] The *General Rules*, as also the *Minutes of Several Conversations*, presupposed a soteriology or a way of salvation; hence the *General Rules* and the *Minutes* were enjoined as a regularized way of advancing toward the end-in-view on the part of all. For Wesley, salvation, while it necessarily entails renovation of life, is a disciplined process of redemption that is continuous to the end and is manifest in its fruits.

In the view of Wesley and his early followers, including Coke and Asbury, the *way*, i.e., the *General Rules* and the *Minutes*, was instrumental to the *end-in-view* and therefore, the end and way were inseparable. Together, they were the "rule of faith" in the sense that together they supplied the distinctive reason for early American Methodism to continue to exist under the name of "United Societies." That rationale is summarized in the *General Rules* and the Wesleyan *Minutes of Several Conversations* (1744). The *General Rules* were retained by the early

Methodist Episcopal Church and have appeared in every edition of the *Doctrines and Discipline* since 1785:

> Such society is no other than "a company of men having the form and seeking the power of godliness united in order to pray together, to receive the word of exhortation, and to watch over one another in love, that they may help each other to work out their salvation."[19]

It is of no small importance that it is immediately added:

> That it may the more easily be discerned, whether they are indeed working out their own salvation, each society is divided into smaller companies called *classes*. . . . [20]

Salvation, then, is a communal endeavor, as well as an objective:

> There is one only condition previously required in those who desire admission into these societies, — a desire "to flee from the wrath to come, to be saved from their sins": But, wherever this is really fixed in the soul, it will be shown by its fruits.[21]

This is the foundation upon which American Methodism was established. Without affectation or abashment Thomas Coke and Francis Asbury could therefore declare, in their inaugural "Address to the Members of the Methodist Episcopal Church," that "We humbly believe that God's design in raising up the preachers called Methodists, in America, was to reform the continent, and spread Scripture holiness over these lands."[22] This declaration was obviously derived from the "Large Minutes":

> **Q.3.** What may we reasonably believe to be God's design in raising up the Preachers called Methodists?
> **A.** Not to form any new sect; but to reform the nation, particularly the Church; and to spread scriptural holiness over the land.[23]

In 1784, however, the case stood differently. A sect was installed with the title of a "church," a wholly voluntary institution standing in its own right. Its purpose, or "design," was not to reform the Anglican establishment, but to *be* the reformed church and "to spread Scripture holiness over" the new lands of America. The story of American Methodism in the 19th century was to become a story of whether and how the United Societies would become a church of this kind, or would lapse into more conventional versions.

American Methodism began, in 1784, as a sectarian movement in the form of a church. The reason for this is primarily to be found, not in its doctrine, but in its discipline. Yet, its discipline was integral and inseparable from its doctrine, and both together, in tandem, supplied what we call today its doctrinal standards. This view was expressed by

Joseph F. Anderson, Secretary of the Central Pennsylvania Conference, in his *Methodist Dictionary* (1909): "The Twenty-Five Articles and the General Rules constitute what might be termed the confession of Faith in the Methodist Episcopal Church."[24] Anderson's understanding was clear enough and his memory long enough to be apprised of Methodist history.

One final consideration offers itself for clinching the tandem relationship of doctrines and discipline in original American Methodism. We are dealing with the *regula fidei*, the rule of faith as the internal working consensus distinctive of earliest Methodism — i.e., what Methodist preachers believed among themselves, not as a creed, but as working principles of preaching and of action leading to the end-in-view. That this internal working consensus was ruling doctrine in the life and work of William Watters, one of the earliest native American itinerant preachers, is quickly evident to all those who are privileged to read his autobiographical account of his "Christian experience and ministerial labors."[25] Herein is eloquent and instructive witness to the "heart religion" and experience of saving faith which impelled and empowered the living witness of this cultivated and devoted Methodist itinerant.

When American Methodism established itself as the Methodist Episcopal Church, its self-understanding as a church derived from two sources, both of which were supplied by Wesley. One was the definition of a Wesleyan Society in the *General Rules* of 1743 as quoted above, which was already axiomatic as a given deposit with the Annual Conferences since 1773. The other was the Article XIII, "Of the Church," of the Twenty-Four Articles. This was supplied by Wesley as his abridgment and emendation of Article XIX of the Thirty-Nine Articles of the Church of England in 1784. Wesley missed nothing. As the definition of a society in the *General Rules* of 1743 was, in effect, an emendation by Wesley of the Anglican Article XIX, so Article XIII of the Twenty-Four Articles was to supply the basic doctrine which Wesley had always assumed and emphatically affirmed as an Anglican churchman:

> The visible Church of Christ is a congregation of faithful men, and women, in which the pure Word of God is preached, and the Sacraments be duly administered according to Christ's ordinance, in all those things that of necessity are requisite to the same.[26]

Whether Wesley expressly believed that the "United Society," as defined by the *General Rules*, was a *bona fide* explication of the phrase "in all those things that of necessity are requisite to the same," I do not have a text to prove and shall not argue.[27] I simply observe that the indications are clear that the 1784 foundation of American Methodism carried with it a doctrine of the church which combined the Article "On the Church" with the definition of a society in the *General Rules*. Such language persisted into the sixties of the 19th century. At a most crucial point, therefore, doctrines and discipline were yoked together as a distinctive source of Methodist doctrinal standards. For this reason, it appears, that the *Form of Discipline* of 1785–1791 became in 1792 suitably entitled *The Doctrines and Discipline of the Methodist Episcopal Church in America*.

Prior to 1792 there had been seven annual editions of the *Form of Discipline* under the title *A Form of Discipline for The Ministers, Preachers, and Members. Now Comprehended in the Principles of the Methodist Episcopal Church in America. Considered and Approved At a Conference Held in Baltimore, in the State of Maryland, on Monday the 27th of December, 1784.* It is of the first importance to observe that this *Form of Discipline* was for the ministry and members alike — a clear indication of the prevailing societal conception of the new church. Such also is the clear indication of the episcopal "Address to Readers" by Coke and Asbury, republished for near one hundred years in every edition of *The Doctrines and Discipline* through 1888.[28]

These facts serve to confute the astonishing position taken by Abel Stevens, in his *Centenary of American Methodism*, that only the *General Rules*, not doctrine, were obligatory upon members as well as preachers.[29] So far as I know, Stevens was the first publicly to divide doctrine from discipline, while at the same time discounting the former. This was at once reflective of pragmatic attainments of Methodist organizational strength by the 1860s together with an emerging sentiment in favor of the ethical imperatives of the gospel for the world.

The 1792 entitlement of the *Discipline* remained until 1968. What this meant is surely indicated in an "Address of the General Conference" of May 1840 at Baltimore. It was in response to the "Address of the British Conference to the Bishops and Members of the General Conference" on the subject of slavery. The message was conveyed by fraternal delegates. The American response declared: "In our *General Rules* (called the 'General Rules of the United Societies,' and which are of constitutional authority in our Church) the buying and selling of men, women and children, with an intention to enslave them, is expressly prohibited. . . ." This address of the General Conference is signed by Bishops R. R. Roberts, Joshua Soule, Elijah Hedding, James O. Andrews, Beverley Waugh, and Thomas A. Morris, the first of whom had been younger contemporaries of Francis Asbury.[30]

The constitutional status and authority of the *General Rules* and their substance is illuminated accordingly. This incident may well have prompted the movement which followed, first, in the Methodist Episcopal Church, South, in 1846, and then in the *Doctrines and Discipline* of the northern church in 1848. In both, the *General Rules* of the United Societies were placed immediately following the Articles of Religion whereas, before, they had preceded the Articles. Thus, they now conformed to the long-standing tradition as to their correlation.

Thus, the way of salvation described and prescribed by the *General Rules* since 1743, which had been from that time constitutive of the societies, was openly and explicitly mated, as it always had been in practice by the American societies, with "doctrine" as defined by the Articles of Religion. The documentary evidence of the Methodist *Form of Discipline* from 1787 onward proves this, whereas an editorial alteration in 1846 and 1848 simply confirms it. The public declaration by the Bishops of the church in 1840 of the "constitutional" status of the *General Rules* voiced the long prevailing common understanding. And this, in turn, was expressly reasserted in 1851 in connection with the question of the condition of church membership by an informed and judicious student of these matters, Moses M. Henkle.[31]

On these grounds we begin to see light as to how and why in 1808 the First Restrictive Rule spoke, however imprecisely, of a twofold ground of the doctrinal standards of Methodism. The concept rested upon an unprecedented and uniquely Wesleyan comprehension that doctrine, especially soteriology — the *way* of salvation — required mating with "method" by which its end or consummation might normally become effective and radiant in human life. Wesley summarized the religion of a Methodist this way: "He thinks, speaks, and lives according to the method laid down in the revelation of Jesus Christ."[32] These words are charged with meaning long since lost from common Methodist understanding, so that we shall need to recall what that soteriology was. We shall also need to discover that both it and its way of implementation in the *General Rules* and the *Minutes of Several Conversations* were an integral and constitutive part of the Methodist Episcopal Church in America. If this were not the case, we would have no idea of how Methodism was to advance the difference between "the *form* and the *power* of godliness," as Wesley hoped, or why, in the 19th century, Methodists continued to justify their "design" as "to spread Scripture holiness across the lands."[33]

25

CHAPTER 1

DOCTRINES AND DISCIPLINE IN EARLY AMERICAN METHODISM

Informed attention to the earliest solid history of American Methodism — including its societies and organization, as well as doctrines and discipline — recalls the names of Jesse Lee, John Emory, Nathan Bangs, and Moses M. Henkle. Lee's *Short History of the Methodists* appeared in 1810, Henkle's manual in 1851, while the works of Emory and Bangs fall in the third and fourth decades respectively of the century.[1]

In the 1880s, about a century after the founding of the Methodist Episcopal Church in 1784, there appeared scholarly historical studies, both constitutional and doctrinal, associated with the following names and in the indicated chronological order of succession: Moses M. Henkle, John Atkinson, Holland N. McTyeier, John J. Tigert, Thomas B. Neely, and James M. Buckley. McTyeier, Tigert, and Neely all became bishops of the Methodist Episcopal Church, South; the latter two, together with Buckley, retain to this day the rank of chief constitutional historians of American Methodism. Even now, a century later, all further scholarly inquiry and treatment of the subject matter must presume, as a deposit, findings which their searching and rather simultaneous endeavors attained.

The greater part of the work of these scholars was done before the close of the 19th century, when memories were longer than ours are now, and before the traditional doctrinal consensus of American Methodism was either eroded or exploded in the 20th century. One can get a taste of that consensus in Bishop E. R. Hendrix's *The Creed of Ecumenical Methodism: Where Can It Be Found?*[2] Or, as we shall have occasion to observe, in such a manual of Methodist doctrine, usage and ecclesiastical order as Hilary T. Hudson's *The Methodist Armor*, which went through nine editions from 1882 to 1921.[3]

My competence for the tasks of this essay is plainly inferior to such a scholar as John J. Tigert. Nevertheless, in the matter of doctrinal standards of Methodism, it is conceded by Part II of *The Book of Discipline* that the tradition is to be consulted.[4] Accordingly, I shall try by reexamining the now little attended early history of our *Doctrines and Discipline*. It was so entitled from 1792 until 1968.

THE *MINUTES* OF THE EARLY AMERICAN CONFERENCE, 1773–1784

At Philadelphia in July, 1773, the societies which had sprung up under Strawbridge, Embury, Webb, and others in the seaboard colonies, acting as a corporate body in Conference, and by unanimous consent of those present and voting, received their status as a United Society "in connection with the Reverend Mr. John Wesley." The offer of such authorization had been conveyed by Wesley's delegated agents, Thomas Rankin and George Shadford. Thereafter, until December, 1784, the official and corporate actions of the Methodist Societies were recorded as *Minutes of Some Conversations Between the Preachers in Connection With The Reverend Mr. John Wesley*.

The first complete published record of the actions of the Conference appeared in 1795 as *Minutes of the Methodist Conferences Annually Held in America, From 1773 to 1794, Inclusive*.[5] It is of some importance that John Dickens, the publisher of this volume, was the authorized chief publisher of Methodist literature of the period and founder of the Methodist Book Concern. He offers the volume as a compendium "wherein may be seen the growth and spread of infant Methodism to the manhood of twenty-two or twenty-three years."[6] He is mindful of no discontinuity in doctrine intruded by the Christmas Conference of 1784, between the beginnings in 1773 and the maturity of 1794. In 1773 it was agreed that "the authority of Mr. Wesley and that conference" should "extend to the preachers and people in America, as well as in Great Britain and Ireland."[7] Further, it was agreed that "the *doctrine and discipline* of the Methodists, as contained in the minutes, [shall] be the *sole rule* of our conduct who labour, in the connection with Mr. Wesley, in America."[8]

Several features of this agreement call for comment. First, it is to be noted that the constitution of the Methodist Society in America was a mating of two realities. The Methodist Society came into existence by voluntary concurrence with the authority of John Wesley as represented in certain "minutes." Second, these "minutes" were recognized to be "doctrine and discipline," and as such were to be "the sole rule" of all endeavor — we might say, ministry — of those concurring in the 1773 agreement. Third, in the voluntary concurrence of the Conference as a corporate body of like-minded persons, the Conference was, in fact, declaring its own doctrinal as well as its disciplinary standards. They originated with Wesley, but they were voluntarily espoused.

There is every reason to suppose that this threefold consensus was to be recapitulated eleven years later at the Christmas Conference of 1784 with a significant addendum — also supplied by John Wesley — namely, the episcopal order of governance. There were to be ordained elders, deacons, and superintendents, promptly called "bishops." There was also to be a liturgy of common prayer and sacraments and a doctrinal base, supplementary to the already acknowledged "doctrines and discipline" subscribed in 1773, namely, Wesley's Twenty-Four Articles of Religion.

Let us return to the inaugural Conference of 1773. By common consent of the preachers assembled at the agency of Wesley's delegated representatives, Rankin and Shadford — with Francis Asbury, also a delegated Assistant under Wesley, present — a formal and mutually agreed upon "connection" with Mr. Wesley was established. The public charter of agreement was certain "minutes" of Wesley's authorship. These were recognized and acknowledged by all present as "doctrines and discipline," for the *Minutes* of 1773 name them such. It was unanimously recognized by the 19th century scholars of Methodism that the "minutes" referred to in 1773 should be identified with the so-called "Large Minutes," the full title of which is *Minutes of Several Conversations Between the Rev. Mr. Wesley and Others; From the Year 1744, to the Year 1789.*[9]

The *Minutes* of the American Methodist Annual Conferences through the period of the Revolutionary War are continuous, with no special reference to or alteration of the "doctrines and discipline" of the inaugural Conference. In the years 1777–1780, there was much agitation in Virginia and Maryland to introduce the usage of the sacraments by Methodist preachers — the resurgence of a practice exercised by Robert Strawbridge well before 1773.[10] Although it was reproved by Rankin and Shadford and steadily opposed by Asbury, it could not be completely repressed, partly because in the later seventies Asbury was rather out of circulation as Wesley's Assistant, keeping a low profile in Delaware due to his presumed Tory sentiments.

At the Baltimore Conference of April 24, 1780, the first question put to the Conference was: "What preachers do now agree to sit in conference *on the original plan,* as Methodists?" It was a question pursuant to the reaffirmation of the terms of union affirmed in 1773. Twenty-four preachers answered this question in the affirmative, with Francis Asbury heading the list. No dissenters are listed.[11] The fact is that the dissenting preachers of Maryland and southward were not in attendance. Meanwhile, the Annual Conference held on May 20, 1777, at Deer Creek, Maryland, was the last conference presided over by General Assistant Thomas Rankin. In 1778 he departed for England, followed later by George Shadford, leaving Francis Asbury, *de facto*, the chief surviving Assistant to John Wesley with the American brethren and societies.

Because of his loyalty to and authorization by John Wesley — a published opponent of the Revolution — Asbury's leadership, while acknowledged and uncontested, could, in the situation, hardly be honored unambiguously by many Methodists caught in the rising tide of revolutionary sentiment in the colonies. Coincident with these realities was an increasing demand among Methodists in both Maryland and Virginia for access to the sacraments of Baptism and the Lord's Supper — especially as the parish ministers of the Church of England in Virginia and the Carolinas were abandoning their parishes and departing for home. By the end of the war, hardly a third of the original ministers of Church of England remained.

At the Conference held on April 16, 1781, at Choptank, Delaware, the first question was formulated to rally firm consent to the original charter of Methodism as defined by the 1773 Conference in the presence of Wesley's agents, Thomas Rankin and George Shadford. The question was this:

> What preachers are now determined, after mature consideration, close observation, and earnest prayer, to preach *the old Methodist doctrine*, and strictly enforce *the discipline*, as contained in the *notes*, *sermons*, and *minutes*, as published by Mr. Wesley, so far as they respect *both preachers and people*, according to the knowledge we have of them, and the almighty God shall give, and firmly resolved to discontinance [*sic*] a separation among either preachers or people?[12]

The answer to this question is affirmative for a total of forty persons whose names are supplied, with that of Asbury heading the list. The implication of the question is that the integrity of the United Societies rests upon fidelity to "the old Methodist doctrine" and "discipline" deriving from Wesley as the charter of the constituted Society, the substance of which is conveyed in Wesley's published *Notes*, *Sermons*, and *Minutes*. The exact titles of these were too commonplace to require listing for the assembled preachers.

In the *Minutes* of the Conference held on April 17, 1782, at Ellis' Preaching House, Sussex County, Virginia, two key questions arise and are answered. The first was: "Shall we not erase that question proposed in Deer Creek conference respecting the ordinances?" The answer: "Undoubtedly we must: It can have no place in our minutes while we stand to our agreement signed in Conference; it is therefore disannulled."[13] This is to say that the question of Methodist usage of the sacraments, still in ferment in some areas among some preachers, is out of order, if the constituted charter of our Society, as reaffirmed at the previous Conference of 1781, is to stand. This is to say further, and plainly, that the Methodists are United Societies under Wesley, and not a church. This difference is inherent in the charter that is constitutive of their being as Societies in connection with The Reverend Mr. Wesley. Wesley well understood that this situation was becoming intolerable for the American Societies after the separation of the colonies from England, and from the Church of England. Neither the doctrines nor the discipline of the United Societies was sufficient to perpetuate their continued existence as non-churches in which there were neither ordained ministers nor sacraments. By contrast, the membership of the Societies in Britain could still be referred to the Church of England for the sacramental life of the Spirit.

A second key question from the *Minutes* of the 1781 Conference was this: "Ought not the preachers often to read the *rules* of the Societies, the character of a Methodist, and the plain account if they have got them?" The answer is, "Yes."[14] Almost certainly, the reference is to the *General Rules*; to *The Character of a Methodist* (1742); and, of course, to Wesley's *Plain Account of Christian Perfection* (1766). Plainly we have, once again, the affirmation that these writings of John Wesley contain the express combination of doctrines and discipline which had since 1773 supplied the charter of their being as Societies.

The *Minutes* of the Conference of April 30, 1784 — the Conference at which Jesse Lee was admitted on trial, and the last held before the Christmas Conference — contain this question: "How shall we conduct ourselves toward European Preachers?" The answer is this, obviously speaking of alleged Methodist preachers:

> If they are recommended by Mr. Wesley, will be subject to the American conference, preach the doctrine taught in the four volumes of Sermons and Notes on the New Testament, keep the circuit they are appointed to, follow the directions of the London *and* American minutes, and be subject to Frances Asbury as General Assistant, whilst he stands approved by Mr. Wesley *and* the Conference, we will receive them, but if they walk contrary to the above

directions, no ancient right of appointment shall prevent their being excluded from our connection.[15]

Apart from the familiar reference to Wesley's *Sermons*, *Notes on the New Testament*, and *Minutes*, it is interesting to observe that the disciplinary provisions of the American Annual Conference *Minutes*, accumulated over eleven years since its founding in 1773, now constitute mandatory norms supplementary to Wesley's "London Minutes." This first explicit reference to the developing character of the American Methodist Discipline has had recurrent notice through the years into our own time.[16]

The continuing and unquestioned acceptance by the Conference of its status under the authorization of The Reverend Mr. Wesley is evident. Accordingly, the leadership of Francis Asbury is deemed dependent upon both Wesley and the American Conference in virtue of the continuing concordat established in 1773 and reaffirmed successively in 1780 and 1781, when fermenting schism was finally transcended. It is not too much to say, nor surprising, that by 1782 the American Conference had attained to a paradoxical self-consciousness of independency-in-dependency. The contradiction called for resolution and Wesley responded. But this also provides the explanation for Francis Asbury's insistence — when Thomas Coke arrived in November 1784 — that he could only accept Wesley's proposals for ordination with the consent of a called meeting of Methodist preachers who were at liberty to accept or reject his designated leadership.[17]

PRESENT FINDINGS IN SUMMARY

(1) This review of the matter of "doctrines and discipline" as understood in the record of the American Annual Conferences from 1773 to 1784 makes it utterly plain, as I see it, that the very charter of their existence was the sum of "doctrines and discipline" in certain writings of which John Wesley was the acknowledged author. The United Societies in America, as in Britain, came to be in virtue of voluntary consent to such doctrine and discipline. Without premeditation, Wesley had been the creator of a voluntary religious association *within* the Church of England both in Britain and in America. When the American societies were rendered shelterless after the Revolution, Wesley saw that they must become a church to survive at all.

(2) The sum of doctrine and discipline consented to by the Conference of 1773 was presupposed and conserved, not superceded, by Wesley's plan for constituting a church in 1784. What was added was

a more comprehensive sum of doctrine in the Twenty-Five Articles of Religion (Wesley abridged the Thirty-Nine Articles of the Church of England into Twenty-Four Articles, to which the 1784 Christmas Conference added a twenty-fifth), a liturgy with hymnal (*The Sunday Service*, Wesley's abridgment of The Book of Common Prayer), and an episcopal conception of government.

(3) The place and import of the Twenty-Five Articles was stated by Coke and Asbury in the Preface to the first edition of the *Form of Discipline* and in every succeeding preface of *The Doctrines and Discipline* through 1888. The Twenty-Five Articles were regarded as doctrine which Methodism held in common with Protestant Christianity. In recommending the Discipline, Coke and Asbury noted that "it contains the articles of religion maintained, more or less, in part or in whole, by every reformed church in the world."[18]

But at this point we come upon an historical enigma. The preface which contains the above sentence and which was continued for over one hundred years is followed by an addition that is not preserved after 1798. It reads:

> We would likewise declare our real sentiments on the scripture doctrine of election and reprobation; on the infallible, unconditional perseverance of all who ever believed, or ever shall; and on the doctrine of Christian perfection.[19]

These are not doctrines shared by the generality of reformed churches. Positively stated, the first is the Methodist teaching of universal election to redemption, or universal salvation. The second is justification by grace through faith in the penitent and persevering. The third is at the heart of Wesley's understanding of the fullness of salvation through sanctification. To say that these doctrines disappear from the Preface, however, is not to say that they disappear from *The Doctrines and Discipline*. They in fact find explicit place in it until 1814 when their substance began to be published in a separate volume of *Tracts*, which continued at least until 1856.

(4) Concerning the elimination of the above statement, the reason is probably not obscure. The statement fails to be clear on the doctrine intended except that of "Christian perfection." We are brought, then, to the matter of the content of Wesley's "experimental and practical divinity" whose articles were undoubtedly the substance of Wesley's "Scriptural Christianity" or "The Scripture Way of Salvation."[20]

In this matter of the doctrine which empowered the United Societies, we must recognize that Wesleyan "practical" or "experimental divinity" was prompted fundamentally, not by the *theological* problem, but by the *soteriological* problem: What is the way and the nature of our salvation? This is the same problem that afflicted Luther and pre-cipitated the Reformation. Luther provided one answer to this prob-lem. Calvin's theology of God's "eternal decrees" offered another. To Wesley, the Thirty-Nine Articles were of far less assistance to Wesley than the Homilies of the Church of England. For this reason he found it needful to abridge the former in order to have the Twenty-Four [Twenty-Five] Articles for the American Societies which had been nurutred on his experimental and practical divinity.

It is truly surprising that, of late, one Methodist commentator upon the prohibition by the First Restrictive Rule (unaltered since 1808) of any "additions" contrary to *our present existing and established standards of doctrine*" declares such doctrinal standards mooted and "mysterious." He says he finds no identifiable reference for "estab-lished standards of doctrine" save the Articles of Religion. But in fact, as we shall see, the reference is to none other than the sum of Wesley's "experimental and practical divinity." The latt er is, likewise, Wesley's prescribed cure for a widely prevailing doctrinal anemia in the Church of England. To be specific, the Church had, as Wesley came to see it, all but abandoned the soteriology of the English reformation as voiced in the Homilies and as based on the New Testament. If the commen-tator mentioned above were correct in his claim of a "mysterious" non-entity of the "existing and established standards of doctrine," early American Methodism would have been, I judge, quite shorn of its reason for being from the start.

In Wesley's day, to judge from the available evidence, the Church of England had no place for this "experimental divinity." Accordingly, it declined to heed it, or to publish it, or to practice it. Therefore it had "the form but not the power of Godliness." Wesley had come to discover this in himself in 1737, as the acknowledgment of his *Journal* amply witnesses.[21] The revelation proved to be "a dark night of the soul" preparatory to his discovery and submission to a more scriptural way of salvation than he had hitherto known.

CHAPTER 2

A LITTLE BODY OF EXPERIMENTAL AND PRACTICAL DIVINITY

It is generally agreed by the historians that the later 18th century preachers "in connection with the Rev. Mr. John Wesley" were, by common consent among themselves, devoted and dedicated expositors of the Wesleyan "Scripture way of salvation" which prompted, empowered and advanced the 18th-century Revival both in Britain and America.

Of the nature of this "connection" Wesley spoke with precision in answer to Question 27 of the *Minutes of Several Conversations Between The Rev. Mr. Wesley and Others* (The "Large Minutes"), as early as 1744.[1] Thus it is quite appropriate that John Dickens entitled the minutes of the founding Conference as *Minutes of Some Conversations Between Preachers in Connection With The Rev. Mr. John Wesley*. Likewise, it is not surprising that Jesse Lee, in his account of Methodist societies in the Colonies after 1770, states that

> The Rules by which the societies were then governed, were the same that Mr. Wesley had previously drawn up in England, and have with very little alteration been continued among us ever since. . . .[2]

Jesse Lee probably penned these lines about 1808 and then, to prove his point, quotes from *The Nature, Design, and General Rules of the United Societies* (1743), with added sections from the *Rules of the Band Societies* of both 1738 and 1744.[3]

By Wesley's declaration, as we shall see, the message of the Revival, in sermon, tract, and song, originally and primarily envisioned reform of the nation and the Church of England. As things developed, however, the substantive message of the Revival was soon to become constitutive of the Societies under Wesley and of their character as "united" in virtue of a certain doctrinal focus, stressing *present* salvation and, therefore, present Christian *experience*, together with an innovative order of discipline to advance the ends in view, namely, Christian perfection.

Doctrine and discipline — when properly understood — are hardly to be distinguished from the sum of what, from time to time, John Wesley spoke of as "experimental and practical divinity." This he did in his Preface to *A Collection of Hymns for the Use of the People Called Methodists* (1780).[4] But what precisely this Wesleyan "experimental divinity" was, and how it may be shown to have been constitutive of American Methodism well into the 19th century, has been largely lost from sight by silent dismissal or long standing inattention that has obtained for more than a century.

WESLEYAN EXPERIMENTAL DIVINITY IN OUTLINE

An important clue to the nature of this "experimental and practical divinity" is provided by the "Large Minutes," which were required reading for the early Methodist preachers under Wesley both in Britain and America. Question 3 of the "Large Minutes" reads as follows: "What may we reasonably believe to be God's design in raising up the Preachers called Methodists?"[5]

Wesley here affirms God's special purpose and providential working in his present occupation and that of his assembled colleagues. In the Methodist movement there is not only a divine leading and vocation, but also effectual works by way of God's *presently* active Holy Spirit. The latter is a first principle of Wesley's soteriology. He has personally *experienced* God's working, namely, a revolution of mind and a renovation of life. In the fall of 1738 — following upon May 24 at Aldersgate Street — and while visiting the Moravians under Zinzendorf, he had, he declares in his *Journal*,

> . . . continually met with what I sought for, viz., living proofs of the power of faith: persons "saved from *inward as well as outward* sin," by "the love of God shed abroad in their hearts"; and from all doubt and fear, by the abiding witness of "the Holy Ghost given unto them."[6]

The first principle of Wesley's experimental divinity is, surely, the present and immediate working of the Holy Spirit: "Every good gift is from God, and is given to man by the Holy Ghost. By nature there is in us no good thing. And there can be none, but so far as it is wrought in us by that good Spirit."[7] To the centrality of this emphasis we must turn later.

Consider, now, the answer to Question 3 of the "Large Minutes": "Not to form a new sect; but to reform the nation, particularly the Church; and to spread scriptural holiness over the land."[8] What is the "reform," of the church or of the nation, which is here spoken of? Is the instrumentality of reform scriptural holiness? If so, it may most suitably begin with the church. Does the Spirit of God need to enliven "a valley of dry bones"? Does "the *form* of godliness" need to be replaced by the *power* of it?[9] Is this close to scriptural holiness? It would appear so. If it is, it will also be something experienced and, thus, possibly "experimental" and so reproducible. It may make for "reform," perhaps a reform in several areas of life and of action and, thus, it may be practical also. Herewith we have a second basic principle, even a doctrine of experimental divinity. Wesley prefers "principle" precisely because a "principle" is for activation in human life. We might call it a governing motivation.[10] Charles Wesley said it for all to understand:

> I want a principle within
>   Of watchful godly fear,
> A sensibility of sin,
>   A pain to feel it near
>
> That I from thee no more may part,
>   No more thy goodness grieve.
> The filial awe, the fleshly heart,
>   The tender conscience give.
>
> Quick as the apple of an eye,
>   O God my conscience make;
> Awake my soul when sin is nigh,
>   And keep it still awake.[11]

On its negative side, holiness is a sensibility of and aversion to the unholy. On its positive side it is a cleaving to the Holy. Hence it activates the first Great Commandment. It is, in fact, the acknowledgement and embodiment of this commandment as *a way of life*. This is "experimental divinity" in practice. Such a way of life is unthinkable for the Wesleys, apart from the present working of the Holy Spirit — such is the vitiated human condition as we find it.

A third characteristic of "experimental divinity" is that however correct the creeds of Christendom may be on the point of "original sin," this truth is without consequence until it is owned unequivocally by the "almost" Christian. As Charles Wesley put it in the hymn quoted above, such acknowledgment must take the form of a lively "principle within." John Wesley's *Journal* for the years from 1735 through 1740 is a priceless autobiographical account of the struggle for and final victory of such a principle. It is very much of a piece with chapters 1–8 of St. Augustine's *Confessions*. Both Wesley and Augustine verified *in experience* the truth of the originality of sin. This is the third principle. Victory over it is immemorially celebrated by Charles Wesley in the hymn written upon his conversion, May 21, 1738:

> Where shall my wond'ring soul begin?
>   How shall I all to heaven aspire?
> A slave redeemed from death and sin.
>   A brand plucked from eternal fire.
> How shall I equal triumphs raise,
> Or sing my great Deliverer's praise?
>
> O how shall I the goodness tell,
>   Father, which thou to me hast showed?
> That I, a child of wrath and hell,
>   I should be called a child of God!
> Should know, should feel my sins forgiven,
> Blest with this antepast of heaven!
> . . . .
>
> Come, O my guilty brethren, come,
>   Groaning beneath your load of sin;
> His bleeding heart shall make you room,
>   His open side shall take you in.
> He calls you now, invites you home —
> Come, O my guilty brethren, come.[12]

It follows, then, in the fourth place, that penitence to the point of "self-despair" is the step directly preceding justification and the forgiveness of sins. The theme is recurrent in the hymns of Charles Wesley:

> Lord, I despair myself to heal;
> I see my sin, but cannot feel;
> I cannot, till thy Spirit blow,
> And bid th'obedient waters flow.[13]
>
> At last I own it cannot be
> That I should fit myself for thee;
> Here then to thee I all resign —
> Thine is the work, and only thine.[14]
>
> Yield to me Now — for I am weak;
> But confident in self-despair!
> Speak to my heart, in Blessings speak,
> Be conquer'd by my instant prayer.
> Speak, or Thou never hence shalt move,
> And tell me, if Thy Name is Love.[15]

The same stress upon entire dependency is sounded in the psalmody and hymns of Wesley's *Sunday Service*, the abridgment of the Book of Common Prayer which he sent to the American societies in 1784:

> Out of the depth of self-despair
> To Thee, O Lord, I cry.
> My misery mark, attend my prayer,
> And bring salvation nigh.
>
> . . . .
>
> If thou art rigorously severe,
> Who may the test abide?
> When shall the man of sin appear,
> Or how be justified?
>
> . . . .
>
> But O! forgiveness is with thee,
> That sinners may adore,
> With filial fear thy goodness see,
> And never grieve thee more.
>
> . . . .
>
> His Israel himself shall clear,
> From all their sins redeem;
> The Lord our righteousness is near,
> And we are just in him.[16]

Here are the core themes of "experimental divinity," namely, justification and newness of life. In this same connection Wesley writes of saving faith:

> It is the *free gift* of God, which he bestows not on those who are worthy of his favour . . . but on the ungodly . . . and whose only plea was, 'God, be merciful to me a sinner.' No merit, no goodness in man, precedes the forgiving love of God. His pardoning mercy supposes nothing in us but a sense of mere sin and misery; and to all who see, and feel, and own their wants, and their utter inability to remove them, God freely gives faith. . . .[17]

Wesley's *Journal* for the earliest period of the Revival shows the frequency with which Jesus' parable of "the Pharisee and the Publican" (Luke 18:9–14) figures in Wesley's understanding and preaching: the pre-condition of acceptance with God is never the prayer of the Pharisee, but only and always that of the Publican: "God be merciful to me a sinner!" Nor is the point to be missed that for some time after February, 1738, Wesley was to understand his own pre-Aldersgate Christianity as pharisaical: "Being ignorant of the righteousness of Christ . . . I sought to establish my own righteousness; and so labored in the fire all my days."[18]

But after Aldersgate, and with increasing insistency, the import of Wesley's emerging experimental and practical divinity was that they only are recipients of the grace that justifies, who plead, not their own, but the righteousness of God in Christ (Rom. 3:21–22). At one point in the "Large Minutes," Wesley exhorts his preachers: "O let us herein follow the example of St. Paul!" "Serving the Lord with all humility of mind. . . ." Our doctrine, "Repentance toward God and faith in our Lord Jesus Christ."[19] Later, he enjoins the preachers: ". . . do not mend our Rules, but keep them. . . . You have nothing to do but to save souls. . . . It is not your business to preach so many times, but . . . to bring as many sinners as you can to repentance, and with all your power build them up in that holiness without which they cannot see the Lord."[20]

Thus, the indispensable *praeparatio evangelica* — the threshold that must be crossed, however difficult the passage, as in Wesley's own case it was — that preparation is entire repentance. This involves not just sorrow, but surrender; capitulation to the divine acceptance is mandatory. It is submission to God in Christ Jesus that is already at work in the prevenient solicitations of the Holy Spirit. Of these, none is deprived.[21] Here, once more, Wesley's experimental divinity is concerned primarily with a sinner's *experience* — his own autobiography — wherein the truth of Scripture is immediately "proved" anew.

Having arrived at this vivid understanding, as did Wesley in the momentous early months of 1738, we are also in sight of a fifth doctrine, or better, "principle," of Wesley's experimental divinity. It is the elusive explanation for Wesley's claim to be *homo unius libri*, "a man of one book."[22] He is so because the Pauline gospel, as Wesley discovered, verifies itself precisely in the measure that it becomes ever and again resonant in human experience unto salvation through Jesus Christ. It was on such premises that Wesley could interpret in a way surprisingly plain to him, the words of the Article 6 of the Thirty-Nine Articles, "Of the Sufficiency of the Holy Scriptures for Salvation" — a prime manifesto of the English reformers — viz., "that whatsoever is not read therein, nor may be proved thereby, is not required of any man, that it should be believed as an article of Faith."[23] In other words, proof of Scripture was not provided by reasonable exegesis alone, but rather by way of the renovative experience that characteristically attended all that the Wesleys meant by "living" or "saving faith."

Listen to Hymn 93 of that little body of "experimental divinity":

> How can a sinner know
> His sins on earth forgiven?
> How can my gracious Saviour show
> My name inscribed in heaven?

> What we have felt and seen
> With confidence we tell,
> And publish to the Sons of men
> The signs infallible.
>
> . . . .
>
> We by his Spirit prove
> And know the things of God;
> The things which freely of his love
> He hath on us bestowed. . . .[24]

At the time, not a few clergy of the Church of England judged Charles Wesley to be a bit exuberant in claims like these! The charge was "enthusiasm." But, for the Wesleys, just as justification by grace through faith is experienced in and as the forgiveness of sins, with "the Spirit witnessing with our spirit," so the power of the new life over sin is given its practical and manifest outcome. The proof was in renovated lives. This emerging realization is documented in Wesley's *Journal* for May 24, 1738:

> When I met Peter Böhler again, he readily consented to put the dispute upon the issue which I desired, viz., Scripture and experience. I first consulted the Scripture. But when I set aside the glosses of men, and simply considered the words of God . . . I found they all made against me, and was forced to retreat to my last hold, "that experience would never agree with the *literal interpretation* of those Scriptures. Nor could I therefore allow it to be true, till I found some living experiences of it." He replied, he could show me such at any time; . . . And accordingly the next day he came with three others, all of whom testified of their own personal experience that a true, living faith in Christ is inseparable from a sense of pardon from all past, and freedom from all present sins. They added with one mouth that this faith was the gift, the free gift of God, and that he would surely bestow it upon every soul who earnestly and perseveringly sought it. I was now thoroughly convinced. And, by the grace of God, I resolved to seek it unto the end, (1), by absolutely renouncing all dependence, in whole or in part, upon *my own works* or righteousness; on which I had really grounded my hope of salvation, though I knew it not, from my youth up; (2), by adding to "the constant use of all the" other "means of grace," continual prayer for this very thing, justifying, saving faith, a full reliance on the blood of Christ shed for *me*; a trust in Him, as my Christ, as my sole justification, sanctification and redemption. I continued thus to seek it . . . till Wednesday, May 24.[25]

On that evening Wesley "went very unwillingly to a Society in Aldersgate-Street, where one was reading Luther's preface to the Epistle to the Romans." His testimony to what happened that evening is well-known: "About a quarter before nine, while he was describing the change which God works in the heart through faith in Christ, I felt my heart strangely warmed." Wesley does not stop with the warmed heart. He advances to the point: "I felt I did trust in Christ, Christ alone for salvation, and an assurance was given me, that he had taken away *my* sins, even *mine*, and saved *me* from the law of sin and death."[26]

The final clause — "and saved *me* from the law of sin and death" — is important. It declares that, along with St. Paul, Wesley no longer seeks to "establish his own righteousness" as a Pharisee, viz., the righteousness of the law. Rather, he now receives "the righteousness of Christ" of which, according to his own testimony, he had hitherto been ignorant.[27] Wesley is affirming that justification, by way of "a righteousness of God" in Christ, which he knows Paul teaches in Romans 3, is in fact recapitulated in his own experience at Aldersgate Street. And here, it appears, is the cornerstone of Wesley's "experimental divinity." In a word, the truth of Scripture is "proved" anew in present-day experience; and the Wesleyan Revival to follow generalized this realization for all those who agreed to share it. It was proof of present salvation, and this is the key to understanding the Revival, along with the societies that issued from it.

The italics in the famous lines are Wesley's. Their use is to call up the phraseology of Thomas Cranmer's Homily "Of Salvation," namely, that faith is "a sure trust and confidence which a man hath in God, that through the merits of Christ his sins are forgiven, and he [is] reconciled to the favour of God." Wesley had conceded to Peter Böhler on April 22 that these were the veritable "words of our Church" and, therefore, of the received tradition respecting "the nature of faith."[28] Wesley also conceded the testimony of 1 John 5:20: "He that believeth on the Son of God hath the witness in himself." This meant for the Wesleys that the truth of Scripture, through saving faith, becomes self-evidencing.[29] On these principles rested the sum of experimental divinity.

Our concern here is not with the subject of justification or even with this moment of conversion, but with a point so often ignored, the discrete moment which inaugurated Wesley's experimental divinity. It is, in a word, that the truth of Scripture and of tradition had suddenly become authenticated as the saving word of God for John Wesley, as already it had for Charles.[30] When Wesley's arrival at this moment of truth or of realization is understood as he himself described it in his *Journal*, it is easier to comprehend a matter of moment for all of Wesley's Christian doctrine. The moment of saving faith and its realization in personal experience was, henceforth, to provide Wesley with a criterion for distinguishing between religious "opinions," even those of "orthodoxy," and the saving truths of Scripture. Thus he proved through experience — his own as well as that of others — the authentic Scriptural way of human salvation. In Wesley's *Journal* for May 22–24, 1738, we are supplied the foundation-stone — no longer "the stone of stumbling" — for Wesley's "experimental divinity." The way of salvation by grace through faith plainly includes: entire repentance, surrender, forgiveness of sins, assurance of pardon, and a renovation of life (the new birth), and as Wesley says with St. Paul, "the love of God shed abroad in the heart by the Holy Ghost given unto him."[31]

One may ask whether this foundational principle, that the "Scripture way of salvation" is verified in the experience of "saving faith," is anticipated in the Thirty-Nine Articles. While a reference to "the true and lively faith" appears in Article 12, "Of Good Works," nothing there nor elsewhere understands either the incidence or nature of saving faith as recapitulation of the truth of Scripture in human experience. It is alluded to in Article 17, "Of Predestination and Election"; but here faith is grounded so tightly in the "secret decree" of God whereby the elect enjoy their faith of eternal salvation — pure Calvinism — that Wesley excises it entirely from the Twenty-Four Articles as abhorrent doctrine.[32] Similarly, one may ask whether this foundational principle concerning the "Scripture way of salvation" is anticipated in the Homilies of the Church of England. Hear Charles Wesley again:

> Faith lends its realizing light,
> The clouds disperse, the shadows fly;
> Th'Invisible appears in sight,
> And God is seen by mortal eye.[33]

The answer is a qualified yes, once the concept of "saving faith" (*fides salvifica*) is recognized in the Homilies as distinct from *fides historica*, assent to the sacred history of the Bible. The matter comes up for explicit treatment in the Homily "Of Faith":

> There is a faith, so-called, professed of the mouth that shows itself neither as a way of life or expression in deeds: . . . it consisteth only in believing of the word of God, that it is true. And this is not properly called faith: but, as he that readeth Caesar's Commentaries, believing the same as true . . . even so he that believeth that [what] is spoken of God in the Bible is true, and yet liveth ungodly . . . is not properly said that he believeth in God, or hath faith and trust in God. . . . This dead faith, therefore, is not that sure and substantial faith that saveth sinners.[34]

Saving faith, on the contrary, is that justifying faith whereby sinners are reconciled to God, made acceptable to him and empowered for the newness of life that brings forth good works.[35] So the Homily continues:

> The quick and lively faith . . . is not only the common belief of the Articles of our faith [i.e., orthodoxy], but is also a sure trust and confidence of the mercy of God . . . that he will forgive . . . our offenses for his Son's sake. . . . This is the true, lively . . . and unfeigned faith, and is not in the outward profession only, but it liveth, and stirreth inwardly the heart.[36]

The emphasis here is upon inner experience and life transformation, as in Part III of the Homily "Of Faith," where the words of Jesus in Matthew 12:33 are invoked: "The tree is known by its fruit." Earlier in Part I, "saving faith" is known as Paul declares, "in that it worketh by love" (Gal. 5:6).

> For true faith doth ever bring forth good works. . . . Therefore, as you profess the name of Christ . . . try it by your living . . . mark the increase of love and charity by it toward God and your neighbor; and so shall you perceive it to be a true lively faith.[37]

In the light of the evidence we can say that the Homilies recognize, in principle, an exemplification of saving faith, involving Christian experience, as it is opened and offered by the New Testament. With the Wesleys, in addition to "experience," the word "realization" is used. However stated, doctrine comes to life, and "heart religion," referred to by the early Methodist preachers in America, replaces that "Godlessness of heart" which Melanchthon sought to replace as early as 1521 with *fides salvifica*.[38]

Thus, we have explored the fifth basic principle of experimental and practical divinity. It is the experienced gift of "saving faith" — the faith by which the Christian believes. And since, it is attended by assurance of sins forgiven and acceptance with God the Father, yet another facet of Christian truth is supplied which became the Wesleyan doctrine of assurance — a sixth tenet of experimental divinity.

Furthermore, "experimental religion" entails yet another consequence. Since justification and forgiveness of sins presume, not our own righteousness, but the redemption which is in Christ Jesus (1 Cor. 1:30), Wesley writes of a seventh principle in his *Journal* as follows:

> In my return to England, January, 1738, being in immanent danger of death . . . I was strongly convinced that the gaining a true, living faith was the one thing needful. But still I fixed not this faith on its right object: I meant only faith in God, not faith in and through Christ. . . . I knew not that I was wholly devoid of this faith. . . .[39]

Evidently, justifying or saving faith had suddenly become for Wesley inseparable from a Christology of which he testifies he previously had little or none and which, after May 24, 1738, was to be pivotal. Here the doctrine of the person and work of Christ came to life in his awareness as a fruition of "saving faith" and as a gift of the Spirit, witnessed to his spirit. Had not Paul declared that "it is the Spirit bearing witness with our spirit that we are the children of God . . . fellow heirs of God and fellow heirs with Christ" (Rom. 8:16–17)? The text was to remain at center in Wesley's teaching. And these truths were open to all for experimental realization or verification! Calvinism remained the enemy. But here was reason enough for the Revival, an altogether sufficient reason for the phrase *homo unius libri*, "a man of one book."

Wesley could thus, with ease, refer to Scripture as the "oracles of God," a phrase *au courant* in the theological literature of the age. With Wesley, the phrase carried a particular meaning inseparable from his experimental divinity. In a sense, Scripture testifies of itself and of its own authority for all those who become open to its promises, and, ceasing to rely upon their own sufficiency, submit in penitence of heart to the saving, nurturing and regenerative inflow of God's prevenient grace. Therewith justification by grace through faith becomes for the recipient the "Scripture way of salvation."

Here, then, is another peculiar doctrine of Scripture-truth itself: its substance and content are accessible only by way of the journey through relinquishment of all self-maintenance to a divine sufficiency that grace alone supplies. Wesley's *Journal* for the early months of 1738 shows that he arrives, much to his surprise, at an unexpected finding, that of Paul: "Not that we are sufficient of ourselves to claim anything from ourselves; our sufficiency is from God" (2 Cor. 3:5). "Nor have we anything whereof to boast" (1 Cor. 1:29). The word of Paul's gospel was, for Wesley, verified in his own experience. In this way, Scripture was not, as a totality, necessarily identical with the very Word of God, but does contain the very saving Word of God to humanity. Here was the eighth principle of Wesley's "experimental and practical divinity." On these grounds Wesley knew himself to be, necessarily, *homo unius libri*.

Wesley never numbered his doctrinal principles; but we should add a ninth, namely, the Wesleyan stress upon God's prevenient (or preventing) grace, universal in all and for all, which carries with it his typical affirmation of universal but conditional salvation — conditioned, that is to say, upon repentance, accepting faith, the new birth, and "working out our salvation."[40] The doctrine of prevenient, or preventing, grace makes a solid appearance in Article 10, "Of Free Will," where it is taught that "we have no power to do good work, pleasant and acceptable to God without the grace of God by Christ preventing us [*praeveniente nos*] that we may have a good will, and working with us that we may have that good will."[41]

With Wesley, preventing grace goes before all human response, enabling justifying faith, and therefore, forgiveness of sins. But, likewise, it is preventing grace, for Wesley, that enables the believer to work out his salvation with fear and trembling, as expressed in Philippians 2:12. Moreover, he always concurred with the Homily "Of Good Works" respecting the justified sinner: He is justified by faith only; but, if he does not show forth works suitable to justifying faith and newness of life, he shall "have lost his salvation again." On this proposition Wesley stood firm. It meant that justification implied, indeed required, sanctification, but that both alike presupposed God's preventing grace. The Wesleyan view of the experimental validation of the "Scripture way of salvation" has some precedence in reformed theology, but probably must be referred mainly to the New Testament itself.

We turn next to Question 4 of the "Large Minutes." Here Wesley asks: "What was the rise of Methodism so-called?" The answer supplied is at once autobiographical and doctrinal:

> In 1729, two young men, reading the Bible, saw they could not be saved without holiness, followed after, and incited others to do so. In 1737 they saw holiness comes by faith. They saw likewise, that men are justified before they are sanctified; but still holiness was their point. God then thrust them out, utterly against their will, to raise a holy people.[42]

Whence came this conviction that none are saved without holiness, and what is holiness? Everywhere in Wesley's writings holiness is "faith working by love," even as Paul describes it in Galatians 5:6: "For in Jesus Christ neither circumcision nor uncircumcision is of any avail, but faith working by love." But what is love? Everywhere Wesley's answer is the twofold Great Commandment of Mark 12:29–30. It is entire love of God; secondly, love of neighbor. Of this latter, the same chapter in Galatians says: "The whole law is fulfilled in one word" (Gal. 5:14). Here, then, is holiness or "Christian perfection." It is the whole of life's way unto sanctification — the very "life of God in the soul of man."

Wesley's quite remarkable utterance on the nature of sanctification, or holiness, as early as September 13, 1739, was this:

I believe it to be an inward thing, namely, the life of God in the soul of man; a participation of the divine nature; the mind that was in Christ; or, the renewal of our heart, after the image of Him that created us.[43]

Now, we may ask several questions. Does any of the Thirty-Nine Articles proffer this "condition" of salvation? The plain answer is no. Does Luther or the Augsburg Confession? Again, the answer is no. Is there such teaching in the Homilies of the Church of England? It is possibly implied in the Homily "Of Faith," where Galatians 5:6 is cited — the "faith working by love." This, however, is not identified with "holiness," that is, Wesley's "Christian perfection." Whence, then, is this doctrine of "going on to perfection"? For the Wesleys, it is affirmed in the Gospels, is regnant in Paul's Epistles, and is mandated in John's Gospel and the Epistles.[44]

What measure of righteousness is allowed in the Thirty-Nine Articles? Article 12, "Of Good Works," says that good works "spring necessarily of a true and lively faith"; yet it is not of such quality as to "put away our sins, and endure the severity of God's judgment."[45] The viewpoint is Luther's — "God reigns but sin remains." Regeneration is incomplete for this life. Moreover, Article 9, "Of Original or Birth-Sin," declares that "this infection of our nature doth remain, yea in them that are regenerate."[46] And this imperfection is yet further affirmed in Article 15, "Of Christ Alone Without Sin." With Luther, the justified sinner is taken for righteous or declared righteous. With Calvinism it is "imputed" righteousness. But Wesley declares for Christian perfection. In a word, then, there was virtually no support for holiness, sanctification, certainly not for entire sanctification, in the dominant Reformation traditions (setting aside the Anabaptists). In response, in the Twenty-Four Articles, Wesley reduces Article 7, "Of Original Sin," to the bare remainder acceptable to him, entirely eliminates Article 15, "Of Christ Alone Without Sin," taking his lead from Scripture, Thomas à Kempis, Jeremy Taylor, and Henry Scougal.[47] He holds to Christian perfection as integral to the "Scripture way of Salvation."

For Wesley, two passages from St. Paul are decisive. The first is 1 Corinthians 1:30, "Jesus Christ, who of God is made unto us wisdom, righteousness, sanctification, and redemption." In his *Journal* for June 14, 1739, he declared this "my favorite subject." But he also remarked that while he was preaching on this "favorite subject" at Blackheath, at the invitation of George Whitefield, his "nature recoiled."[48] Thus he conceded that the *natural man* is appalled by the very idea! Long before Reinhold Niebuhr, Wesley was aware of the "impossible possibility" of Christian perfection, but finds it given only and entirely upon the sufficiency of the Holy Spirit.[49] The second decisive passage is Romans 12:1, "that ye present your bodies a living sacrifice, holy, acceptable to God which is your reasonable service."[50]

Thus, with the doctrine of Christian perfection as the second principal pillar of "experimental divinity," Wesley takes his stand with Paul on the cruciform life in the Spirit as the regular Christian vocation; but it is in the Spirit and by its transformative power alone. It is intrinsic to salvation, continuous with justification, and a new way of being in saving relation to God the Father, through our Lord Jesus Christ, and, so, to the neighbor.

In the "Large Minutes," the answer to Question 77 reads, in part, as follows: "With regard to 'working for life'; which our Lord expressly commands us to do. Labor, *ergadzesthe*, means literally *work*. . . . And in fact, every believer, till he comes to glory, works for as well as from life."[51] Such is the paradox, as Wesley understood it, of Philippians 2:12–13. It is because the Spirit of God works in us that we *can* and *must* work, as is definitively argued in Wesley's sermon "On Working Out Our Own Salvation."[52]

A SUMMATION

There is a passage of great importance concerning the relation of justification to Christian holiness in Wesley's *A Farther Appeal to Men of Reason and Religion*. It is perhaps the very core of his thought, as well as a distinctive contribution of Wesley to Protestant theology:

> With regard to the condition of salvation, it may be remembered that I allow, not only faith, but likewise holiness, or universal obedience, to be the ordinary condition of *final* salvation, and that when I say faith alone is the condition of *present* salvation, what I would assert is this: (1), that without faith no man can be saved from his sins, can be either inwardly or outwardly holy; and (2), that at what time soever faith is given, holiness commences in the soul. . . .[53]

On these grounds, Wesley has conjoined the Reformation re-declaration of justification by grace only through faith, that is, Romans 3:22–28, with 2 Corinthians 5:17 and Romans 12:1, and made both forgiveness of sins and the new creation in the likeness of Christ crucified at once the definition of salvation and of "the character of a Methodist." It followed that salvation became a vocation in process called "Christian perfection" and that the rest of life was "working out your own salvation with fear and trembling; for it is God who is at work in you, both to will and to work for his good pleasure" (Phil.

2:12). It did not matter whether one spoke of the *telos*, the end-in-view, as "the living sacrifice" of Romans 12:1 or heeded the exhortation of the Apostle Paul: "Be imitators of me, as I am of Christ" (1 Cor. 11:1).

The core of the Wesleyan teaching concerning "experimental and practical divinity" was an understanding of the "Scripture way of salvation" as *conditional*. On the one hand, there was justification or forgiveness of sins by grace through faith received; on the other hand, the "new birth" carried with it a life vocation, namely Christian perfection, inward and outward holiness as an inescapable obligation. Together, these constitute "the ordinary condition of final salvation." Yet always Wesley teaches this is God's doing by his preventing and saving grace. Wesley is saying: We are not saved without ourselves, as Augustine had long before declared. Such is the constellation of events which, in the Wesleyan view, makes up the eventfulness of the Christian life and Christianity as "experimental religion."

To summarize once more, the grace that justifies, through which there is forgiveness of sins, effects the same change of condition which St. Paul describes as "newness of life" and St. John calls the "new birth." Thus, justifying grace is the presently experienced reality which, *ipso facto*, makes the vocation of "holiness" both a present obligation and, by God's grace, a possibility. This is the case when the Prodigal Son, so to speak, rightly labors to make his "calling and election sure" (2 Pet. 1:10).

This is what came to be discovered by the Wesleys from 1738 through 1744 as the answer to Question 4 of the "Large Minutes," ending in the phrase "to raise a holy people." By 1744 they had wrought into a coherent system the doctrinal themes entailed in the proposition "that men are justified before they are sanctified; but still holiness was their point."[54]

CHAPTER 3

JUSTIFICATION IN EXPERIENCE

> I am glad brother Cromwell and you have undertaken that labour of love, the visiting of Nova Scotia. , , , It will be the wisest way to make all those who desire to join together, thoroughly acquainted with the whole Methodist plan. . . . Let none of them rest in being half Christians. . . . As soon as any of them find peace with God . . . exhort them to go on to perfection.[1]

Thus wrote John Wesley in June, 1785, to the notable Methodist preacher Freeborn Garrettson, after being informed by Thomas Coke that Garrettson and James O. Cromwell were to be on mission to Nova Scotia under the direction of the new Methodist Episcopal Church, formed at Baltimore the previous December. In his admonition to Garrettson we see once more Wesley's express declaration of the binary character of "the Methodist plan" of salvation. The "experimental and practical divinity" of the Wesleys is an ellipse with two foci. The first is justification, wherewith there is "peace with God"; but to stop there is to be "half Christian." The second is "holiness of life and heart"; to go on to perfection is itself fulfillment of salvation.

The 18th-century Wesleyan Revival and the rise of Methodism was surely the consequence of yoking together these two foci with their collateral elements, as identified in the previous chapter. It is now in order to reflect more closely on the nature and import of justification by faith, which precipitated the "mix" called Methodism. After all the years since 1738, it is not clear to many why the "mix" was necessary in the first place. Nor is it clear why it was, and perhaps remains, a catalytic agent for precipitating the Wesleyan "Scripture way of salvation."[2] Our present purpose is to determine whether this "Scripture way of salvation" is not identical with Wesleyan "experimental religion," and whether the founding fathers of American Methodism did not intend to embrace it under the twofold title *The Doctrines and Discipline of the Methodist Episcopal Church.*

WESLEY'S REDISCOVERY OF JUSTIFICATION BY FAITH

As long ago as 1870 Luke Tyerman raised the question: how could it happen that John Wesley "lived so long without a knowledge of one of the greatest, and yet most clearly taught doctrines of the Holy Bible, the doctrine of the sinner's salvation by faith alone?"[3] Tyerman then rehearsed some elements of an explanation, but was far more to the point in asking and, at some length, answering two other questions: first, "what were the doctrines Wesley was taught by Peter Böhler?" and second, "when and how was Wesley converted?"[4] On these matters Tyerman's command and presentation of the evidence remain both instructive and essential, but still incomplete.

Tyerman does not, for example, explore John Wesley's rather surprising conversation with his mother, Susanna Wesley, as recorded in his *Journal* for September 3, 1739. In it she reported that until recently "she had scarce heard such a thing mentioned as having forgiveness of sins now . . . much less did she imagine that this was the common privilege of all true believers."[5] When Wesley asked further whether her father, Dr. Samuel Annesley — the esteemed nonconformist who was rector of St. Giles, Cripplegate, London, until deprived of his parish in 1662 — had either experienced such faith or preached it, her reply was that she believed he had experienced such faith; but "she did not remember to have heard him preach — no, not once — explicitly upon it, whence she supposed he also looked upon it as the peculiar blessing of a few, not as promised to all the people of God."[6]

These candid disclosures by Susanna Wesley in the fall of 1739, following upon the outbreak of the Revival, are worthy of particular attention. Not only was she the incredibly competent school mistress of her children, one of whom could read the Greek New Testament at age seven, but she had, under her father's direction, been so tutored in theology that, judging by her surviving letters, she would have been equal to the best graduate students in theology I have taught in the past forty years.[7]

Accordingly, Susanna Wesley was uncommonly well equipped for discerning commentary upon her father — an Oxford Doctor of Laws, a noted preacher of the day, and an informed and wise nonconforming churchman who stood in the Presbyterian line of Richard Baxter, Richard Allein, and perhaps John Owen and some of the Westminster divines. Annesley had declined subscription to the Act of Uniformity, August 24, 1662. It is of this man that Samuel Palmer's edition of

Calamy's *The Nonconformist's Memorial* concludes a biographical account with these words: "He had uninterrupted peace in his spirit, and the assurance of God's covenant love for the last thirty years of his life. He cheerfully resigned his soul to God, December 31, 1696, aged 77." Behind these words, not hidden from contemporaries, was the sorrow of more than thirty years professional deprivation, eased too late by the Act of Toleration of 1689.[8]

All this is relevant to the question of how the doctrine of justification by grace through faith alone — emphatic in the Homilies of 1547 and prominent still in the Thirty-Nine Articles of 1571 — had fared in the 17th century. More particularly, we need to ask how this doctrine fared after the Elizabethan settlement, either in the "separatist" or the Presbyterian wings of English Calvinism with their varying degrees of nonconformity. However surprising it may seem, the doctrine of justification by faith alone — stated without compromise in the Homilies of the English reformers — became a quite secondary concern to the ascendent Calvinistic ecclesiology of the "gathered" and "covenanted community" or church of the 17th century in England. It is a fact of history that this community, or church, increasingly found its principal comfort and "promise" precisely in "the assurance of God's covenant love" which Calamy's *The Nonconformist's Memorial* attributes to Samuel Annesley. It is "the assurance of God's covenant love" for "the elect." With the Calvinists, all hope of salvation at last rested with the promise of God's "eternal decrees."

Three things tended to follow, all of which are reflected in Susanna Wesley's testimony concerning her father. First, justification by grace through faith was understood as something wholly contingent upon "the eternal predestination of God." Second, justification, or righteousness in God's sight, was something "imputed," not claimed. Third, it implied not a *present* assurance, but a final vindication of the elect only at the last judgment. For such reasons, it might be understandable that Susanna Wesley, in the fall of 1739, should testify to astonishment at her own recent experience of forgiveness of sins while receiving the Holy Communion at the hands of her son-in-law, Westley Hall; that she "had scarce heard of forgiveness of sins now" until of late; and that, respecting her father's views, she judged that his own experience of sins forgiven — perhaps to be presumed — he would probably understand as "the peculiar blessing of a few."[9] So indeed she might suppose, in view of the doctrine, or doctrines, of salvation acquired in her upbringing, including the role and conception of faith prevailing in that tradition. With Calvin himself, faith had not finally advanced beyond assent to truths of Scripture, opened to faith by the

51

testimonium Spiritu Sancti internum, and best taught and believed under the guidance of Geneva and her satellites.[10]

John Wesley's conversation with his mother of September, 1739, has, when examined, some remarkable aspects and overtones. While the conversation itself followed, by more than a year, the spiritual turmoil and crisis through which both John and Charles Wesley were passing in the spring of 1738, it helps to explain why John Wesley initially regarded Peter Böhler's doctrine of salvation, by way of justifying grace through faith, as such a fundamental innovation. In the conversation with his mother, Wesley was still pressing the question of the verity of the Böhler's doctrine of "living" and "saving faith" as open to all people and as attended by two regular fruitions inseparable from it: "dominion over sin, and constant peace from a sense of forgiveness." It was of this faith that he wrote in his *Journal* for May 24, 1738: "I was quite amazed, and looked upon it as a new gospel."[11] He continued:

> If this was so, it was clear I had not faith. But I was not willing to be convinced of this. Therefore I disputed with all my might and laboured to prove that faith might be where these were not, especially where the sense of forgiveness was not. For all the Scriptures relating to this I had been long since taught to construe away, and to call all "Presbyterians" who spoke otherwise. Besides, I well saw, no one could . . . have such a sense of forgiveness, and not *feel* it. But I felt it not.[12]

The issue had become clear: either Böhler's understanding of "saving faith" was in error, or John Wesley was devoid of saving faith and was, evidently, not a Christian. On the one side, Wesley appeared to be without salvation; on the other, he was in error doctrinally and so humiliated. It is not wholly clear which side of the predicament bothered him more in the early spring of 1738. It is important to note, however, that Wesley's last stand was an agreement with Böhler to resolve the dispute — the doctrinal difference between them — by resort to "Scripture and experience."[13]

This is to say Wesley would in 1738 still settle the issue by rational, critical assessment of alleged instances of salvation by grace through faith which conformed to the known New Testament norms or instances. When Wesley had done this, the Scripture consulted conformed so fully with the empirical instances of justifying faith as submitted by Böhler that the evidence was established to Wesley's full persuasion:

> I was now thoroughly convinced. And, by the grace of God, I resolved to seek it unto the end, (1) by absolutely renouncing all dependence, in whole or in part, upon *my own* works or righteous-

ness, on which I had really grounded my hope of salvation, though I knew it not, from my youth up; (2) by adding to "the constant use of all the" other "means of grace," continual prayer for this very thing, justifying, saving faith, a full reliance on the blood of Christ shed for *me*; a trust in him as *my* Christ, as *my* sole justification, sanctification, and redemption.[14]

A full essay would be needed to explore completely the content and consequence of what has been briefly sketched here concerning the *Journal* entry for May 24, 1738. This passage was obviously composed by Wesley in retrospect, after the renovative event of Aldersgate and the inception in his own case of "a new creation." It was given laboratorial dimensions by Wesley's visitation of the Moravians from mid-July through mid-September, 1738. It stands as possibly the most thorough 18th-century study and assessment of Moravian doctrine of "saving faith" as taught by Peter Böhler.

If, however, one desired really to know what John Wesley meant by "practical" or "experimental divinity," the answer is inseparable from Wesley's experience of justification by faith alone and from the tireless, organized, and extensive historico-empirical investigation of the doctrine which followed the experience. Wesley's "practical" or "experimental divinity" is nothing other than "saving faith" as conceived in the language of Peter Böhler, or of the 16th-century Lutheran Reformers, or of the Homilies of the Church of England. By 1739 John Wesley was becoming aware of a united testimony of these sources on the doctrine of justification. His empirical exploration of the doctrinal verities of typical Christian life and experience was, to say the least, unusual; perhaps, it was without precedent.

During his extended visitation to the Moravian communities of Germany, Wesley spent some time in Marienborn. As he recorded in his *Journal* for July 6, 1738,

... here I continually met with what I sought for, viz., living proofs of the power of faith: persons "saved from *inward as well as outward* sin," by "the love of God shed abroad in their hearts"; and from all doubt and fear by the abiding "witness of the Holy Ghost given them."[15]

On the following Wednesday, July 12, 1738, Wesley records Count von Zinzendorf's response, in "a conference for strangers" (visitors), to the question: "Can a man be justified and know it not?" Wesley then lists eight comments by the Count in response to the question, and proceeds to call attention to a deviation from the views of Peter Böhler in six propositions on the subject of justification.[16] Wesley's *Journal* account of these private conversations and group conferences was, in its time, unparalleled, and would have been unsettling to conventional church folk. Nor did all that Wesley found, either of doctrine or discipline, wholly please him.

To explore fully these findings and their import is beyond us. One might be tempted to say that Wesley was venturing upon what would in later times be called the phenomenology of religion. It is closer to the facts, however, to say he was attempting to apprise himself of the recurring features of justifying faith as found in the experience of Christians. He sought reliable grounds in Christian experience for what he came to call "experimental religion." This could be summed up in the other phrase — the "Scripture way of salvation" — if one recognized that the latter signifies an event, a happening, which involves a divine intervention and which elicits a human response.

In a word, the issue confronting Wesley in the spring of 1738 was, in some part, the same as that which confronted Luther two hundred years earlier: what, in fact, is the divinely authorized way of human salvation? Luther's principal quarrel with the church was over this issue. This issue was already in ferment for Wesley on his return from America. Peter Böhler had brought this same issue to his attention emphatically and inescapably. It was a challenge, and Wesley was forced to assess this new doctrinal position thoroughly and carefully. His inquiry and assessment, while it included the sojourn among the Moravians in the summer and fall of 1738, was not consummated until the beginning of his field-preaching career. As he recorded in his *Journal* for Sunday, April 29, 1739:

> I declared the free grace of God to about four thousand people from those words, "He that spared not in his own Son, but delivered him up for us all, how shall he not with him freely give us all things?" At that hour it was that one who had long continued in sin, from a despair of finding mercy, received a full, clear sense of his pardoning love, and power to sin no more.[17]

The *Journal* witnesses that such events were multiplied without number. Here was indeed the "promise" of Scripture — i.e., salvation for all — fulfilled. It was fulfilled now, as a present salvation. Empirical investigation proved it. And in Wesley's studied observation, he found it to include "the sense of forgiveness," assurance, and joy in the Holy Ghost. The inaugural experience issued in "living faith." This was the recognizable "phenomenology" of the onset of a Christian life, whose consummation was in perfecting what had been begun. A revival was imminent because this "Scripture way of salvation" was a transformation of human being as such. This was to become essential Methodism. Its expectancy was Paul's promise that "if any one is in

Christ, he is a new creation, the old is passed away, behold, the new has come" (2 Cor. 5:17). This was indeed a "new Gospel" for the Wesleys! It is evident that John Wesley's grandfather, Samuel Annesley, according to Susanna's testimony, had not so conceived justification by faith, much less taught it.

In answer to the Reverend Henry Stebbing's *Caution against Religious Delusion,* Wesley could reply:

> ... *our* coming to Christ ... must infer a great and mighty change. It must infer not only an *outward change* ... but a thorough *change of heart,* an *inward* renewal in the spirit of our mind. ... Of consequence, the "new man" must imply infinitely more than outward good conversation, even "a good heart, which after God is created in righteousness and true holiness" — a heart full of that faith which, working by love, produces all holiness of conversation. ...
>
> The change from the former of these states to the latter is what I call *The New Birth.*[18]

When compared with his received understanding of justification, this was truly a "new Gospel" for Wesley. Tyerman's observation, as noted earlier, was beside the point — let us say, superficial. Justification had become for the Wesleys thoroughly Pauline in a manner scarcely comprehended in the prevailing tradition whether Reformed or Anglican, i.e., since the Edwardian Reformers. Peter Böhler's doctrine had been the turning of the way, but since the spring of 1739, both of the Wesleys had been advancing beyond the Moravian standpoint. That this is so can, perhaps, best be understood by attending with care the entirety of Wesley's rejoinder to Henry Stebbing in his *Journal* for July 31, 1739. And nowhere is better indicated what was to be meant thereafter, in early Methodism, by "experimental religion."

JUSTIFICATION AND THE KNOWLEDGE OF FAITH

In the matter of experimental religion, or the "Scripture way of salvation," Wesley was aware that, if Peter Böhler's doctrine of the nature and efficacy of justifying faith was, indeed, scriptural, then there must be a positive correlation between the divine promises in Scripture — considered as sacred history or as the divinely ordained way of human salvation — and the recurring event itself as observed and knowable in human experience. It must be recognizable both by the individual subject, who is redeemed, and by others sharing the common experience of praise and thanksgiving. For Böhler, as for the Wesleys, it was the common experience of "saving faith" (i.e. justification) which made common prayer both possible and truly "common."

We may say that the scriptural warrant for this typically Wesleyan principle of positive correlation between the God-given paradigm of our salvation in Scripture and its actualization or fulfillment in our history is classically represented by St. Paul in 1 Corinthians 2:12–13: "Now we have received not the spirit of the world, but the Spirit which is from God, that we might understand the gifts bestowed on us by God . . . interpreting spiritual truths to those who possess the Spirit." This theme runs throughout *A Collection of Hymns for the Use of the People Called Methodists*, that "little body of experimental and practical divinity." It is also prominently stated, if not fully developed, in Wesley's Preface to his *Sermons on Several Occasions*, where he alludes to his principles of scriptural interpretation and teaching. Referring to St. John 7:16–17, he writes:

> Thou hast said, "If any man is willing to do thy will, he shall know." I am willing to do, let me know, thy will. I then search after and consider parallel passages of Scripture, "comparing spiritual things with spiritual". . . . And what I thus learn, that I teach.[19]

That is to say, he preaches or teaches spiritual truth effectually, to those who are enlightened, as well as cleansed and renewed, by God's Spirit. Here is evidence of Wesley's recognition that the understanding of God's will as found in Scripture presumes a conformity of mind and will, or of the human spirit, with God's Spirit. Here is a basic principle of Christian understanding, an epistemology or theory of knowing, according to the Spirit of God in Christ. This basic principle concerning the knowledge of faith is beautifully expressed in one of Charles Wesley's hymns, where he provides a poetic restatement of the "analogy of faith":

> Inspirer of the ancient seers,
>   Who wrote from thee the sacred page,
> The same through all the succeeding years:
>   To us in our degenerate age
> The Spirit of thy Word impart,
> And breathe the life into our heart.
>
> While now thine oracles we read
>   With earnest prayer and strong desire.
> O let thy Spirit from thee proceed
>   Our souls awaken and inspire,
> Our weakness help, our darkness chase,
> And guide us by the light of grace.
>
> . . . .

> The secret lessons of thy grace
> > Transmitted through the Word, repeat,
> And train us up in all thy ways
> > To make us in thy will complete;
> Fulfill thy love's redeeming plan,
> And bring us to a perfect man.[20]

It had become axiomatic with the Wesleys by early 1739 that justification by grace through faith in Christ, the Mediator, is regularly attended by the transforming work of the Holy Spirit as its only sufficient reason:

> Come, Holy Ghost, our hearts inspire:
> > Let us thine influence prove,
> Source of the old prophetic fire,
> > Fountain of life and love.
>
> Come, Holy Ghost, (for moved by thee
> > The prophets wrote and spoke);
> Unlock the truth, thyself the key,
> > Unseal the sacred book.
>
> . . . .
>
> God through himself we then shall know,
> > If thou within us shine;
> And sound with all the saints below,
> > The depths of love divine.[21]

If we translate poetry into prose, we arrive at a doctrine of Christian knowledge in which the work of the Holy Spirit is the *sine qua non* of enablement. Through its working comes conformation between the *promise* and the *way* of salvation in Scripture — the latter conceived as a sacred history, effulgent with the purpose and wisdom of God as it is in Christ (1 Cor. 1:23–25) — and its recapitulation in human lives.[22] These, in St. Paul's words, "are justified by his grace as a gift, through the redemption which is in Christ Jesus, whom God put forward as an expiation of his blood, to be received by faith" (Rom. 3:24–5).

For the Wesleys, this remains the wisdom of God; and, by faith, it is revitalized in successive generations as the everlasting promise of redemption through Christ (1 Cor. 1:30). In short, the doctrine of justification by grace through faith is "proved" by its recurrence, or recapitulation, in that history of which the church is properly the vehicle and the sign. Thus, we may speak of the church as the evangelical succession. It is, however, true that the church is always in need of reformation, because the sign loses its luster and vitality as the church encounters a residually alien and a sinful world inside as well as outside the church.

The "Scripture way of salvation" is the wisdom of God, but it is known as such only to those who, living according to the Spirit, "set their minds on the things of the Spirit" (Rom. 8:6). It is hardly too much to say that, for the Wesleys, these words of St. Paul are determinative both of the true nature of the Christian life and of the power of godliness, as liberated by justification. The latter is the way of forgiveness of sins and pardon, but also the enablement of the new life of faith; in the words of St. Paul, "I appeal to you therefore brethren, by the mercies of God. . . . Do not be conformed to this world, but be transformed by the renewal of your mind, that you may prove what is the will of God, what is good and acceptable and perfect" (Rom. 12:1–2).

It is the mind renewed by the Holy Spirit, according to St. Paul, to which the "wisdom of God" becomes self-evident — "even as the testimony of Christ was confirmed among you" (1 Cor. 1:6). Herein is found the proportionality (*analogia*) between divine wisdom and divinely enlightened human understanding, which also is known by its fruits. Wesley believes with the Apostle that this is so because, through repentance, pardon, and the renewal of the Holy Spirit, the regenerate mind is becoming conformed to the Holy Other. It is becoming restored and recreated in the image of God. This is Wesley's understanding of the Apostle's assurance for the justified sinner: it is "in demonstration of the Spirit and in power, that your faith might not rest in the wisdom of men but in the power of God" (1 Cor. 2:4–5). This doctrine of the knowledge of faith — resting upon the Pauline teaching of the work of the Holy Spirit in and with forgiveness of sins and entailing the transformation of the mind and spirit of the believer — is a fundamental principle of the "Scripture way of salvation" and, therewith, of Wesley's experimental divinity.

We may speak of it, in the language of the Apostle, as "the wisdom of God" given in and with "demonstration (*apodeixis*) of the Spirit and power" (1 Cor. 2:4). For Wesley, faith is not simply final surrender and trust of God through the mercies of Christ. It is that; but it is also cognition, the knowledge of faith, whose verity becomes self-evident in virtue of the work of the Holy Spirit in the transformation of the mind and its conformation to the Holy. For it is also self-manifest in that it shows forth the "newness of life" which both enables and attends it, that is, "faith working by love" (Gal. 5:6). Accordingly, this divinity is also practical, that is, to be practiced, as well as experienced.

FAITH AND EXPERIMENTAL DIVINITY

Perhaps the most comprehensive definition of saving faith in Wesley's works is this:

> Faith, in general, is a divine, supernatural *elenchos* [persuasion; cf. Heb. 11:1] of things not seen, not discoverable by our bodily senses, as being either past, future, or spiritual. Justifying faith implies, not only a divine *elenchos*, that "God was in Christ reconciling the world to himself" [2 Cor. 5:19], but a sure trust and confidence that Christ died for *my* sins, that he "loved *me*, and gave himself for *me*." And the moment the penitent sinner believes this, God pardons and absolves him. . . . This beginning of that vast, inward change is usually termed "the new birth."[23]

Three features of this highly significant summary call for particular consideration. First, the curious phrase which concludes the first sentence is as weighty as it is obscure. In sum, it intends to distinguish sharply between the substantive content of "saving faith" — of which there is "supernatural persuasion" (namely, the work of the Holy Spirit) — and all mere cognition which is grounded in sense-perception and which eventuates in the form of discursive reason (as with John Locke). Such cognition is largely alien to the "knowledge of faith" of which we have been speaking. This cognition may be occupied with present, past, or future data and, theoretically, with "spiritual" things, but only by logical inference from the sensible manifold of natural human experience.

Wesley is concerned here to distinguish between propositions intelligible to "living faith" or experimental religion, on the one hand, and, on the other, three claimants to knowledge of which he is either skeptical or indifferent: metaphysics, "speculative divinity," and "prophecy." For Wesley, justifying or "saving faith" is empowered by "supernatural persuasion" — a concept deriving both from Hebrews, and from St. Paul's doctrine of the Spirit. This alone supplies what we have referred to as "the knowledge of faith."[24] It is this only with which Christians, and Christian experimental divinity, are properly concerned. Such knowledge of faith, so radiant in Scripture, is likewise for Wesley to be found in the Ecumenical Creeds, and in the Homilies and Articles of the Church of England.

The second key feature of Wesley's summary statement about the nature of faith is concerned with the question of identifying the proper subject matter of doctrinal standards for the Wesleys. In the privileged sense, doctrinal standards are found in all three summations of doctrine just noted, and, perhaps, most centrally, in the sum of Wesleyan experimental and practical divinity. This "experimental divinity," as I have been trying to show, may be found in the works of the Wesleys, particularly in John Wesley's *Journal*. We should remember Wesley's own comment from the preface to his *Sermons on Several Occasions*:

> I have . . . set down in the following sermons what I find in the Bible concerning the way to heaven, with a view to distinguish this way of God from those which are the inventions of men. I have endeavoured to describe the true, the scriptural, experimental religion, so as to omit nothing which is a real part thereof, and to add nothing thereto which is not.[25]

It is hardly necessary to recall that Wesley's *Sermons* were being proposed as doctrinal guides and norms for his assistants and lay preachers as early as 1746. They were officially accepted as such by the American Societies, as we have already seen, by 1773. The sermonic literature is, of course, vast, and without question Wesley's "system of doctrine" could easily be identified and exhibited by an arrangement of his sermons so to cover the sum of Christian doctrine. In these essays I have quite abandoned that method with a view to observing his doctrinal formation mainly from his *Journal*, the Wesleyan hymnody, and some of the occasional writings — all quite early and most indicative.

The large role which John and Charles Wesley ascribed to "experimental and practical divinity" comes near to the point of dismissing all philosophical theology. A significant difference of viewpoint on this matter between Samuel and Susanna Wesley is revealed to us by a letter written by his mother to John in February, 1725, as he undertook preparation for Deacon's orders:

> . . . I heartily wish you would now enter upon a serious examination of yourself, that you may know whether you have a reasonable hope of salvation by Jesus Christ, that is, whether you are in a state of faith and repentance or not, which you know are the conditions of the Gospel covenant on our part. . . .
>
> Now I mention this, it calls to mind your letter to your father about taking Orders. I was much pleased with it. . . . But 'tis an unhappiness almost peculiar to our family, that your father and I seldom think alike. I approve the disposition of your mind . . . and think the sooner you are a deacon the better, because it may be an inducement to greater application in the study of practical divinity. . . . Mr. Wesley differs from me, and would engage you, I believe, in critical learning . . . which though accidentally of use, is in no wise preferable to the other. Therefore I earnestly pray God to avert that great evil from you, of engaging in trifling studies to the neglect of such as are absolutely necessary.[26]

John Wesley came to embrace his mother's position on this matter rather than his father's. It would seem that as the twig is bent, so the tree is inclined.

The third significant feature of Wesley's statement about faith is his use of the phrase "a sure trust and confidence." It calls attention to the turning of the way for John Wesley during his conversations with Peter Böhler in the spring of 1738. On April 22, 1738, he met Böhler once more and reported that he now had no objection to Böhler's conception of "the nature of faith." He had found that it did not differ from declared doctrine of the Church of England, that faith is "a sure trust and confidence which a man hath in God, that through the merits of Christ *his* sins are orgiven, and *he* reconciled to the favour of God."[27] Wesley had rediscovered this definition of faith in Part 3 of Thomas Cranmer's Homily "Of Salvation," first published in 1547, during the reign of Edward VI. In this definition Wesley began to find constructive direction for his personal experience of justification by grace through faith and, with it, his "experimental religion." The decisive moment was, no doubt, May 24 following; but it was a process, and one which involved a certain amount of self-disaffection. The beginning of this process was as early as Wesley's careful review of the Articles and Homilies of his church in August and September, 1737, while he was still at Savannah. It continued through his extended visitation of the Moravians in Germany during the summer of 1738, and up to the beginning of his field-preaching around Bristol, on the invitation of George Whitefield, in April, 1739. Therewith, "the great Divide" had been crossed; his declared scruple about "instantaneous" conversion was retired, indeed buried forever.[28]

The general description of the nature of saving faith now under consideration, from *A Farther Appeal to Men of Reason and Religion,* Part I, was published in 1745. This was fairly early, in Wesley's career, but exhibits advanced doctrinal clarity on his part. It embraces at least five aspects:

(1) Faith has a *cognitive aspect.* There is a knowledge characteristic of faith in virtue of the work of the Holy Spirit which induces a "persuasion" of "things not seen or discoverable by our bodily senses."

(2) The *event of faith* is possessed of a *justifying function.* The function presumes a need, namely, liberation "from both the guilt and from the power of sin."

(3) This liberation carries with it a *new status of acceptance with God,* not by any merit of the individual, but through the grace of God enabled by the perfect obedience and righteousness of Christ. The primary content of the knowledge of faith is the transaction of jus-

61

tification itself, which effects the reconciliation of sinful persons to God the Father, always, as with Paul, "through Jesus Christ our Lord." Thus, to the transaction is added both the knowledge of God as Abba, Father, and Jesus as Lord and Christ, as Saviour and Redeemer. A doctrine of God as a God of grace, as well as Sovereign Lord, herewith becomes part of the knowledge of faith.

(4) The knowledge of faith, in consequence, embraces a new *self-understanding* on the part of justified sinners. It is commensurate with the gracious acceptance of the unacceptable, that is, the sinful individual, who in penitence accepts his acceptance in the manner of the Prodigal Son. Here is the place for faith as Wesley found it expressed in the words of the Homily, as "a sure trust and confidence which a man hath in God, that through the merits of Christ *his* sins are forgiven, and *he* reconciled to the favor of God." Now faith finds expression in doxology — praise and thanksgiving.

(5) There is yet another facet of this new self-knowledge or self-understanding. *Justification* — God's acceptance of the sinner, for Christ's sake, in forgiveness of sins — is also *reconciliation*, because it is a reunion which replaces willful self-alienation from God. A new community supervenes upon estrangement. There is an advent of the "Kingdom of God" and membership therein. This, too, is part of the knowledge of faith. St. Paul speaks of being made "heirs" of God with Christ (Rom. 8:17). And Wesley sees this status as a call to holiness in the likeness of Christ. For this the justified believer is now renovated and made a "new creature" after the likeness of Christ (2 Cor. 5:16–17). In short, the work of the Holy Spirit is a "new birth" — a renovation with promise. Hence Wesley was quite serious about these words: "Truly, truly, I say to you, unless one is born of water and the Spirit, he cannot enter the Kingdom of God. That which is born of the flesh is flesh, and that which is born of the Spirit is Spirit" (John 3:5–6).

The nature of "true living faith" which Wesley has in mind, and which he found expressed in the Homilies of the Church of England, when viewed comprehensively with its full range of implications, embraces the whole of Wesley's "experimental religion" and the substance of his "experimental divinity." The latter is the articulate explication of the former. Viewed in another perspective, this experimental divinity can be seen as a doctrine of salvation, as the "Scripture way of salvation." It amounts to a system of Christian doctrine which issues, quite inevitably, from what he calls "experimental religion," that is, "true, living faith" or the faith that justifies.

In his little essay *The Character of a Methodist*, first published in 1742, Wesley provided an example of his understanding of the relationship between doctrine and the life of Christian experience.[29] In the essay, doctrine and life are viewed as inseparable; the one demands the other. Wesley is saying that the character of a Methodist is (or should be) exhibitive of the individual's Christian doctrine; and, conversely, that essential doctrine is (or should be) constitutive of the Christian life.

This message did not cease to inspire and empower early American Methodism until well into the 19th century. This was the message enjoined in Wesley's letter to Freeborn Garrettson, with which this chapter opened. Wesley's letter plainly reiterates his pivotal teaching that "salvation," in addition to forgiveness of sins, entails Christian perfection as a life-long vocation and, thus, the fully disciplined life. For the Wesleys, doctrine was inseparable from the discipline instrumental to its embodiment in the lives of professing Christians.

CHAPTER 4

═══════

CHRISTIAN EXPERIENCE ACCORDING TO WILLIAM WATTERS AND OTHERS

The prevailing doctrinal core of Methodism, well into the 19th century, was the sum of Wesley's experimental and practical divinity as this was comprehended and proclaimed by the early Methodist preachers.[1] That body of divinity was, it appears, the constitutive rationale of all the United Societies under Wesley by the year 1773 in both Britain and America. It continued to be so in America as long as the language of ecclesiastical Methodism reflected the function and aspirations of the earlier societies. These persisted, it seems, into the mid-19th century; with their fading, Wesley's experimental divinity also faded. It was to be replaced by competing emphases such as Christian education at home and the great 19th-century expansion of the Christian mission abroad.

It must be acknowledged that the Wesleyan experimental and practical divinity, which was the primary influence and prevailing message in early American Methodism and which formed the spirit and substance of early Methodist preaching, teaching, exhorting, or catechizing, did not find full-orbed expression in the contemporary official documents, such as the Conference *Minutes* (1773–1798), the *Form of Discipline* (1785–1791), or *The Doctrines and Discipline of the Methodist Episcopal Church* (after 1792). Both of the latter publications do contain, in addition to the Articles of Religion, the *General Rules* and liturgical provisions, substantial amounts of doctrinal declaration in the form of tracts. These tracts were, however, more nearly polemical in intent than confessional in substance. The early *Minutes* contain some record of Conference policy with doctrinal leaning or import, but they provide, on the whole, only the bare bones of the living gospel; the Methodist societies, and persons who rejoiced in the experimental knowledge of saving faith, are hardly perceptible in such literature.

By contrast, the 18th and 19th centuries produced a near flood of religious memoirs. These were predominantly of Quaker, Baptist, or Methodist provenance; but the literature was not without instance in Reformed and Episcopal circles of the period. Biographical or auto-biographical in nature, this literature collectively celebrates the communion of the Divine with the human spirit, often with quite contrasting doctrinal standpoints. Taken as a whole, this literature witnesses to the "varieties of religious experience" which were then current, and exhibits a common disposition to lament and to deplore the form of religion that has, somehow, lost the power of it.

The presence of experimental religion in the teaching of the earliest Methodist preachers is particularly clear in the memoirs of William Watters, whose ministry stretched across the years 1772–1806, and who is customarily recognized as the first native American Methodist preacher. He was the only American attending the 1773 Conference under Thomas Rankin in Philadelphia, slightly over two years following Asbury's arrival in the Colonies. A native of Baltimore County, Maryland, Watters was born in 1751. He was converted under Methodist influences in May, 1771, and following upon his saving experience of grace, had this to say of the Methodists:

> Having never met with or heard of any other people who preached up or professed to know anything of what I now enjoyed — I knew not there were any, and doubt to this day whether there are any (as a sect) who enjoy experimental religion in its native life and power as the Methodists do.[2]

The youthful convert continued:

> I had never been at a class meeting, nor had I intended ever to become a member amongst them; . . . although I had for several months felt a very great attachment to them, believing they were a people devoted to God; but now, having obtained mercy, I felt no hesitation in owning the people that God had owned in my conversion, and I gladly attended one of their meetings the same day. . . .[3]

Watters was a younger son of a large family of nine children. His father, who died early, was apparently a man of of some affluence, and had been a vestryman of the local Church of England parish in Baltimore County. There were two such parishes in the area, and neither, it appears, was preserved from the disadvantages of a decadent ministry. William's elder brother and wife were already Methodists prior to his "awakening" and his conversion. They remained all their lives prominent and useful Methodist laity.

While Watters does not name him, the primary moving influence for Methodism in the area at the very time of Watters' conversion was that of John King, certainly the founder of Baltimore Methodism. King, who was from London, was highly educated and strong-willed, and well known to Wesley, who was double-minded about him.[4] The other influence, almost contemporary, was that of itinerant preacher Robert Williams, probably a Welshman, but sponsored in some measure by the Irish Methodists as early as 1766.[5] He had begun his American ministry in New York, and preached in Wesley Chapel; it was Williams, according to the testimony of Jesse Lee, who introduced Methodism into southern Virginia.

In 1772, as an apprentice, Watters accompanied the veteran preacher Williams to Norfolk and Portsmouth. While Williams pioneered with notable success westward to Petersburg, Watters began a Circuit in the Portsmouth region. In the course of his first extended pilgrimage through the countryside, from village to village, tavern to tavern, Watters observed the prevailing religious practice and devotion of the region and contrasted it with that of the Methodism which he had come to admire:

> The congregations, considering they had but a few hours notice, were tolerably large, and well behaved; but I discovered great ignorance of experimental religion. . . .[6]

Commenting on the three hundred mile trip from Baltimore to Norfolk, he observed:

> Mr. Williams preached several times after this [as at King William's Co. Court House] on our way, and made a point to introduce religious conversation at every convenient opportunity as we rode, sat by the fireside in taverns, and in private houses. But alas! we found very few in the course of these hundred miles who knew, experimentally, anything at all of the Lord Jesus Christ, or the power of his Grace: so that still the prophet's assertion is a lamentable truth: "My people are destroyed for lack of knowledge."[7]

These samples from Watters' memoirs provide ringing and largely representative evidence of the original doctrinal self-understanding of the first Methodist preachers, both British and American, whether "irregulars," such as Strawbridge, King and Williams, or "regulars," as the latter came to be conceived following upon the Philadelphia Conference of July, 1773. Watters attended this Conference together with Williams, both of them going by ship from Portsmouth or Norfolk. This was the conference which, by common consent, regularized both preachers and societies under the direction of Wesleyan doctrine and discipline. Asbury had served as Wesley's delegated representative since 1771. Thomas Rankin was now instituted as Wesley's General Assistant, and presided over the Conference.[8]

Watters came to the 1773 Conference as the first and only native American Methodist preacher. His recognition as such was confirmed by his membership in the assembly. He was, in 1773, but twenty-two years of age. For the year succeeding, 1773–1774, Watters was assigned, with John King, to the New Jersey Circuit. The following year he was assigned to the Trenton Circuit, where he served until the outbreak of the Revolutionary War. Here he had sight of John Hancock and John Adams *en route* to the Continental Congress in Philadelphia.

The doctrines embraced within the orbit of the experimental religion of these early Methodist preachers have been explored in chapters 2 and 3 above. At the center is the pivotal doctrine of justification by grace through faith along with its collateral themes. Certainly these themes echo in the distinctive but unpretentious style of Watters' recollections of his earliest "Christian experience." The account of his attainment of saving faith in the year 1771 is particularly significant: "It was my daily prayer that God would teach me the way of life and salvation, and not suffer me to be deceived."[9] In words reminiscent of Wesley's *Journal* for May 24, 1738, Watters proceeds:

> And though I was a Pharisee all this while, seeking to be justified by the deeds of the Law, by trusting more or less on the performance of these duties. . . .[10]

But he finds that salvation is not by the Law, but by a new birth:

> . . . so I felt in a manner which I have not words fully to express, that I must be born again, born of the Spirit, or never see the face of God in glory.[11]

Repent, therefore, and believe:

> . . . and the Lord again smote my rocky heart, and caused it to gush out with penitential sorrow for . . . many sins against him who has so loved the world that he gave. . . .[12]

He is the reconciliation for our sins:

> . . . and bearing the sins of the whole world in his own body, and dying to make a full atonement for the chief of sinners. . . . Thus was I bowed down . . . to wait at the foot of the Cross, while I was stripped of all dependence upon outward things.[13]

Of resistance to God's grace:

> My God! how little do sinners know what they are doing, while resisting the Holy Spirit, and refusing to have Christ rule over them.[14]

And its cessation:

... he kneeled down with me, and with a low soft voice ... offered up a fervent prayer to God for my present salvation.[15]

A "supernatural persuasion" of things not seen:

A divine light beamed through my inmost soul, which in a few minutes encircled me around, surpassing the brightness of the noon day sun. This divine glory, with the holy glow that I felt in my Soul, I feel still as distinct an idea of, as that I ever saw the light of the natural sun, or any impression of my mind, but know not how fully to express myself, so as to be understood by those who are in a state of nature ... for the natural man receiveth not the things of the Spirit of God, for they are foolishness unto him, for they are spiritually discerned.[16]

This youthful pilgrimage of faith is easily recognized by those who are acquainted with the themes of Wesley's own experimental divinity. It is evident that Watters is confident that the successive moments of this life renewal will be recognized by his preacher colleagues or the laity. The zenith of his conversion has its own distinctive particularity of divine emancipation and illumination. I am not aware of anything quite akin to it in the language of John Wesley. Yet Watters is fully Wesleyan in claiming the declaration of St. Paul, viz., "The unspiritual man does not receive the gifts of the Spirit of God, for they are folly to him, and he is not able to understand them because they are spiritually discerned" (1 Cor. 2:14). And this is indeed Wesleyan also, as the very ground of the knowledge of faith.

In the successive moments of the conversion progression which is, for Watters, entrance upon distinctive "Christian experience," the collateral themes or phases of the comprehensive and somewhat stereotyped process of justification by faith find expression. They are enacted and will be reenacted in some form and measure in the case of all who, in penitence, cease to resist the Divine grace and finally rejoice to accept their acceptance with God through Jesus Christ. These are the marks of "experimental religion," and are the indispensable preconditioning for the holy life.

Herewith, "Christian experience," as William Watters knows it, has its inception and becomes practical. It is practical in the manner and sense in which the matter had long been stated by the Wesleys in the answer to Question 4 of *Minutes of Several Conversations*: "In 1737 they saw holiness comes by faith. They saw likewise, that men are justified before they are sanctified; but still holiness was their point."[17] Therewith, experimental religion became the enabling instrument of the practical, of praxis. The latter was, of course, as with Wesley, "faith working by love," because, already, "God is at work in you, both to will and to work his good pleasure" (Phil. 2:13). This had become commonplace.

The distinctive exaltation attaching to the early American Methodism that William Watters both knows and teaches is that it is a *present* salvation. It is forgiveness of sins *now*, with assurance given by way of the peace of God shed abroad in our hearts by the Holy Spirit. It is the image of God re-formed in the believer; it is the beginning of the "new creation" and the mark of the "new birth." Watters' sentiments recall the words of the Wesleyan hymn:

> O for a heart to praise my God,
>   A heart from sin set free!
> A heart that always feels thy blood,
>   So freely spilt for me!
>
> . . . .
>
> A heart in every thought renewed
>   And full of love divine,
> Perfect, and right, and pure and good —
>   A copy, Lord, of thine![18]

The testimony of William Watters, far from singular, was to be typical and illustrative of "the spirit of Methodism in its primitive form." This very phrase was employed in 1839 to characterize the Christian experience of Thomas Ware, the truly notable itinerant minister and younger contemporary of Watters whose ministry extended from 1784 to 1835. Ware was an intimate of Francis Asbury and John Dickens and a member of the Christmas Conference. The themes of "experimental divinity" find their particular expression in Ware's autobiographical account of his conversion after a stormy period following his discharge, for illness, from the Continental Army. Not only was Ware in revolt from his mother's addiction to the doctrine of "eternal decrees," but through the preaching and personal influence of the early itinerant, Caleb Pedicord, he too came to rejoice in a present salvation. It began in overhearing a hymn sung by a passing horseman:

> Still out of the deepest abyss
> Of trouble I mournfully cry.
> And pine to recover my peace,
> And see my Redeemer and die.
>
> . . . .
>
> I cannot, I cannot forbear
> These passionate longings for home;
> O! when shall my spirit be there?
> O! when will the messenger come?

This song, and its singer, made an indelible impression on young Ware:

> As he walked his horse slowly I heard every word distinctly and was deeply touched not only with the melody of his voice, which was among the best I ever heard, but with words he uttered, and especially the couplet, —
>
> > I cannot, I cannot forbear
> > These passionate longings for home.
>
> After he ceased, I went out and followed him a great distance, hoping he would begin again. He however stopped at a house of a Methodist.[19]

An invitation to hear the traveling preacher was extended by a Methodist acquaintance that very evening. Of the visitation of divine grace which overtook Thomas Ware he wrote:

> Soon I was convinced that all men were redeemed [in Christ] and might be saved — and saved now from the guilt, practice, and love of sin. . . . When the meeting closed, I hastened to my lodgings . . . fell upon my knees before God, and spent much of the night in penitential tears. . . . Mr. Pedicord returned to our village. I hastened to see him. . . . He shed tears over me, and prayed. . . . My soul was filled with unutterable delight. He rejoiced over me as a son — "an heir of God and joint heir with Christ". . . . I was made free. . . . I was now brought to reflect upon the circumstance which had led to this happy change, so sudden, so great, as hardly left a vestige of my former self. By it, all worldly maxims were reversed, and principles quite new, of honour and of shame, were introduced as governing the whole man.[20]

This conforms to Wesley's meaning of "living faith." It scarcely matters where we turn in the rich biographical literature of early 19th-century Methodism. In *A Sketch of the Life of Rev. John Collins, Late of the Ohio Conference*, we may read of a Quaker who unwillingly came under the influence of the preaching of John Collins and, in one sitting, found he was "greatly wanting in that Christian experience which is enjoined in the Bible . . . to all who would be prepared to stand before the judgment seat of Christ. He sought and . . . found that great blessing of justification by faith, and realized peace with God through our Lord Jesus Christ."[21] The *Sketch of Collins*, written by an anonymous author, supplies abundant evidence of the full currency of "experimental religion" as a common expectancy and practice in the "Northwest" of Methodism beginning around 1804.

In 1916 Bishop Francis J. McConnell, writing on *The Essentials of Methodism*, declared: "The first essential which is distinctive of Meth-

odism is the emphasis on conversion. . . . The second Methodist essential is the emphasis on entire sanctification."[22] With these words,
Bishop McConnell recognized the complementary and inseparable
relation affirmed by the Wesleys as between justification as the *means*
and holiness as the *aim* and *consummation* of Christian experience. This
accords with the answer to Question 4 of *Minutes of Several Conversations*, which every Methodist preacher of those days knew by heart.[23]
It is not wholly clear that Bishop McConnell shared Wesley's conception of "the sin that doth so easily beset us," of which justification was
seen by the early Methodist preachers as the cure. Bishop McConnell
was aware, however, that justification and sanctification, or Wesley's
Christian perfection, were the two foci of the ellipse constitutive of
"experimental and practical divinity."

CHAPTER 5

EXPERIMENTAL DIVINITY IN EARLY AMERICAN METHODISM

OF SALVATION: OF JUSTIFICATION AND HOLINESS

According to Jesse Lee, George Whitefield preached his last sermon on September 29, 1770, at Exeter, New Hampshire, "from the top of a hogshead beside the meetinghouse" because it "was too small to contain the congregation." Whitefield's text, according to Lee, was 2 Corinthians 13:5: "Examine yourselves whether ye be in the faith." The next day, September 30, Whitefield died on his knees at the manse in Newburyport, and was buried under the pulpit of "the Presbyterian meetinghouse," where he had loved to preach, and had done so many times.[1]

When we think of the work of the earliest Methodist preachers in the American colonies before the Revolutionary War, it would be serious oversight not to recall that Whitefield was the first, certainly the most spectacular, and possibly the most influential of them all. He had labored, if intermittently, in the seaboard colonies from Georgia to Massachusetts from 1739 to 1770 and was the preeminent preacher of the colonies from the time of the first Great Awakening until his death. Across thirty years he made thirteen trips to the colonies. Together with Benjamin Coleman, Gilbert Tennant, Samuel Davies and Jonathan Edwards, Whitefield belonged to that group of "New Light" or "New Side" preachers of the gospel whose task was, first of all, "awakening."

Jesse Lee reminds us of two things worthy of attention here. The first was Whitfield's approbation of the work of the Methodist preachers:

> In the course of this year, 1770, Mr. George Whitefield passed through Philadelphia, on his way North, and calling on our [Methodist] preachers who were in the city, he expressed to them his great

satisfaction at finding them in this country, where there was such a great call for faithful labourers in the vineyard of their Lord.[2]

The second is the text of Whitefield's sermon — his last — at Exeter: "Examine yourselves, to see whether ye be in the faith." The text continues: "Test yourselves. Do you not realize that Jesus Christ is in you? — unless indeed you fail to meet the test." For such a persistent "Calvinist" as Whitefield is presumed to have been, the admonition is fascinating, because, for a Wesleyan, it would strongly suggest Whitefield to be in self-contradiction regarding the perseverance of the Saints, who cannot fall from grace.

These points remind us of certain things Whitefield shared with the Wesleys. The first is their common commitment to the doctrine of salvation by grace through faith, and faith alone, as a recognizable present actuality, which had little precedent in orthodox Calvinism, English or Continental. The second is their common understanding and insistence that there is a "proof" of faith, which may be known by its fruits prior to the article of death. This also is non-Calvinistic. The lack of proof, as we noted earlier, was that of which Susanna Wesley gave witness in the case of her father, Samuel Annesley. Understandably, John Wesley had no problem in speaking very irenically of Whitefield's life and work in his sermon "On the Death of George Whitefield," while remaining silent on points of doctrinal difference. Wesley acknowledged Whitefield's insistence in "all times and all places" on "the grand scriptural doctrines" and, with the "original Methodists" of Oxford, said Wesley, he shared their "grand principle": "there is no power (by nature) and no merit in man" for justification before God, and that "except a man be . . . born again he cannot see the kingdom of God" or have "in him the mind which was in Christ Jesus," and, further, that early on Whitefield was "led directly to an experimental knowledge of Jesus Christ and him crucified."[3]

Jesse Lee's report that Whitefield conferred with "our preachers who were in the city" of Philadelphia on his passage northward into New England is of considerable interest. Who were "our preachers" to whom Whitefield spoke? According to Lee, Richard Boardman and Joseph Pilmore, sent by Wesley and the English Conference, had arrived in Philadelphia October 24, 1769.[4] The practice of "field preaching" had been begun scarcely a week following their arrival, and Pilmore almost immediately wrote a letter to Wesley dated October 31, 1769:

> We were not a little surprized to find Captain Webb in town, and a society of about a hundred members, who desire to be in close connection with you. . . . I have preached several times, and the

people flock to hear in multitudes . . . out upon the common. . . .
Blessed be God for field preaching! The people, in general, like to
hear the word and seem to have some ideas of salvation by Grace.[5]

The main emphases of early Methodist preaching, beginning with
Whitefield and continued with the preachers and their message under
Wesley, were consistent with the statement of the *Minutes of Several
Conversations*: "In 1737 they saw holiness comes by faith. They saw
likewise, that men are justified before they are sanctified; but still
holiness was their point."[6] The business of preaching was to engender
the recapitulation, or realization, of this doctrine in human lives. The
business of discipline was to facilitate the nurture of such renovated
lives to the end of entire sanctification. The Societies were instruments
of such discipline, to the end of salvation, or of holiness of life; in
Wesley's view, the two were but one.

On such grounds as these, it is not difficult to comprehend the
secondary prohibition of the First Restrictive Rule: ". . . nor establish
any new standards or rules of doctrine contrary to our present existing
and established standards of doctrine."[7] The "present existing and
established standards of doctrine" still meant in 1808, by long-standing general consensus, all that was embraced by the substance of the
answer to Question 4 of the *Minutes of Several Conversations*.[8] The two
foci of the Wesleyan experimental and practical divinity were justification by faith and holiness of life with their corollaries. So understood,
any new standards or rules were either superfluous to the General
Conference of 1808, or diversions from the ends in view. They might
obscure or obstruct the established "Scripture way of salvation." And
this would be the case, with or without the Twenty-Four Articles of
Religion. These, Coke and Asbury had said, are "maintained more or
less, in part or in whole, by every reformed church in the world."[9]

In the first volume of his *History of the Methodist Episcopal Church*,
Nathan Bangs pays tribute to the preachers of the previous generation:

They were men of strong common sense and sound judgment, and
some of them possessed a great . . . natural eloquence . . . [although]
they enjoyed none of those qualifications which arise from . . . classical and scientific study. They were however "mighty in the Scriptures,". . . "full of faith and the Holy Ghost," and "needed not any
to teach them which be the first principles of Christ. . . ." They spoke,
therefore, of the things which they had felt and seen, and God bore
testimony to their word. It was this . . . which gave such success to
their efforts, and inspired the confidence of those who had an
experimental knowledge of divine things.[10]

Concerning the message and the doctrine of these early Methodist preachers, Bangs says this:

> The doctrines too, which they principally insisted upon had a tendency to produce the desired effect upon the heart and life. While they held in common with other orthodox Christians . . . depravity of the human heart, the deity and the atonement of Christ . . . that which they pressed upon their hearers . . . was the necessity of the new birth, the privilege of having a knowledge, by the . . . witness of the Holy Spirit, of the forgiveness of sins, through faith in the blood of Christ, and as naturally flowing from it, provided they persevered in holiness of heart and life. . . . By preaching this doctrine everywhere, to all classes of people, making it prominent in every sermon, and exhibiting it as the common privilege of all penitent sinners to experience, they were blessed of God in their labors and rejoiced over returning prodigals to their Father's house.[11]

EXPERIMENTAL AND PRACTICAL DIVINITY: A SUMMATION

Nathan Bangs openly acknowledges the limited formal education of the early itinerant preachers of first and second generation Methodism, who, nevertheless, "needed not that any should teach them which be the first principles of Christ." Thomas Ware, who was one of their number, was present at the Christmas Conference in December, 1784, where he penned these reflections on his elder brethren there assembled:

> In practical wisdom they appeared to me to excel; and, although few of them affected the scholar, yet they prized learning as a desirable accomplishment. Some of them were acquainted with the learned languages; and most of them were not deficient in general polite literature. But what eminently distinguished them as a body of Christian ministers, was, the happy art of winning souls. In preaching and in debate they were workmen who needed not to be ashamed; and they made wise and useful improvement of the knowledge they possessed. . . . We may, therefore, venture to say, that few men, in any age of the church, knew better how to estimate the sum of good which Heaven kindly wills to man, and few have been so successful in recommending the Bible and Bible religion to their fellow-men.[12]

Ware was a felicitous writer of great perception and pertinency, and his firsthand recollections of Methodism, from its founding, stand a classic among the very modest number of primary sources. For our purpose, the prevailing witness is of the "Bible religion" which is experimentally known and celebrated, and which the early Methodist itinerants aspired to share as the true "Scripture way of salvation" of which they were both examples and the privileged stewards. This "Bible religion," which John Wesley proclaimed in the conclusion of *The Character of a Methodist*, is the sum of the "experimental and practical divinity" discussed in the chapter 2. It was suggested there that this "divinity" was the Wesleyan emendation of the received doctrine of the Church of England as Wesley comprehended that tradition. Insofar as it was altered in emphasis, it was so in order to accommodate the "Scripture way of salvation."

The new accents given to this received doctrine by Wesley included an emphasis upon justification by grace through faith, presuming penitence of heart and mind, and the work of the Holy Spirit. This entailed conviction of and repentance for sin, surrender to God's grace, the forgiveness of sins, assurance of acceptance with God, or reconciliation, and joy and peace "shed abroad in the heart" by the inner witness of the Holy Spirit. Included also was restoration of the lost "image of God" in man or woman, and "newness of life," the "new creation," or the "new birth." Regeneration, in short, was the indispensable new start of authentic Christian life. The language on the last doctrine, the new creation, does not greatly matter, since it is Pauline or Johannine, plain and simple. This Wesleyan emendation is the way of justification, redemption, or regeneration. It fills out or gives content to the statement: "In 1737 they saw holiness comes by faith . . . that men are justified before they are sanctified."[13] This, in Wesley's phrase, amounted to "the plain old Christianity which we teach" and which, he insisted, was the official but unacknowledged doctrine of the Church of England:

> . . . these doctrines [which I teach] are no other than the doctrines of Jesus Christ; that they are evidently contained in the Word of God, by which alone I desire to stand or fall; and that they are fundamentally the same with the doctrines of the Church of England, of which I do, and ever did profess myself a member.[14]

Wesley is responsible for four alterations or innovations of received Anglican doctrine. The first is the "Scripture way of salvation" itself as the experimental method of realization of God's "promises" in Scripture, a "proof" open to experiential verification by all who would ascribe to God's revealed way. Wesley entertained no doubt that this was, however ignored, plainly taught in the Homily "Of Salvation." The second, corresponding to this, is his verification of the truth of Scripture as containing "all things necessary to salvation" and his standard for rejecting what was merely religious "opinion," i.e., either "controversial" or "speculative divinity." The third is his attribution of such verification in experience, following Scripture, to the working of the Holy Spirit — the Third Person of the Trinity — for the work of whom there was virtually no provision in the 18th-century Anglican theology. Fourth is the pattern of the "living sacrifice," the cruciform life of faith, or "Christian perfection" (Rom. 12:1), conceived as the norm and goal of "saving faith" and, to the extent of "entire sanctification," attainable in this life, at least in principle.

In all, perhaps, we may number nine integrally related doctrines which comprise the sum of Wesleyan "experimental and practical divinity," depending on the manner of listing. This summation was most surely presupposed by Thomas Coke and Francis Asbury in the first edition of *A Form of Discipline For Ministers, Preachers, and Members, Now Comprehended in the Principles and Doctrines of the Methodist Episcopal Church in America and Approved At a Conference Held In Baltimore, in the State of Maryland, on Monday, the 27th of December, 1784, In which Thomas Coke and Francis Asbury Presided.*[15] If, in fact, Coke and Asbury invoked this title as indicative of the event, the burden of proof lies heavily upon any who affirm that "the principles and doctrines" mentioned were not understood by them as including the sum of Wesley's experimental and practical divinity, as the founders understood and preached it in 1784.[16]

FAITH IN TWO COMPLEMENTARY FORMS

Living faith, as I have argued in chapter 1 above, passes from doxology, through *homologia* or personal witness-in-agreement, to declaration in prayer, hymn, testimony, or preaching, and finally, to communal expression in a group consensus. That consensus regularly issues in a working rule of faith, an intra-mural verbal consent of the common mind to the common faith. The rule of faith in early Methodism embraces the common mind of the group as its agreed upon self-understanding of the way of salvation as normally experienced. The measure in which, with the early Methodist preachers, doctrine is verified in experience and, conversely, experience confirms doctrine, is remarkable in the literature of the 18th and early 19th centuries. A particularly striking instance is found in the example of Benjamin Abbott of New Jersey, a preacher of signal power who was converted in 1774. When supplied a copy of Bellamy's *New Divinity* by his local Presbyterian minister, Abbott threw it aside saying he would read it no more "as my own experience clearly proved to me that the doctrines it contained were false."[17]

The rule of faith is, so to speak, a corporate "Amen." In early Lutheran doctrine, it was often spoken of as *fides qua creditur*, viz., the faith *by which* what is affirmed is a convinced personal testimony and witness. In St. Paul's letters, this is the faith which saves (Rom. 10:10). As such, it is not the creed but that which begets the creed. Or, in other words, it is acknowledgment of life-conferring realities experienced *as* life-conferring, or justifying, or redeeming (1 Cor. 1:30). In Wesley's view, following closely upon St. Paul, such acknowledgment, with both mind and heart, is always dependant upon the inward working of the Holy Spirit.[18] It is, thus, a gift; it is regarded as divinely empowered. Accordingly, "living faith" is for Wesley a supernatural *elenchos* or persuasion of things not seen and only spiritually discerned (Heb. 11:1; 1 Cor. 2:10–14). This understanding of saving faith, or *fides qua creditur*, has, for Wesley, two main sources: the letters of St. Paul and the Homilies of the Church of England. The latter have, in turn, an affinity with the earliest Lutheran reformers, in particular, Philip Melanchthon's historic *Loci Communes*.

The complementary but contrasting kind of faith, which properly presupposes the former, is *fides quae creditur*, the faith or consent to that which is believed. Here, the *what* of faith is described, namely, the content of creed or confession — the propositions or articles confessed. In these two complementary forms or modes of faith, we encounter a quite subtle twofold conception of the nature of faith which is regularly ignored or obscured in the history of Christian doctrine and only from time to time recovered.

For Wesley, the faith that saves is, of course, justifying faith. As earnestly as Melanchthon, Wesley is concerned to distinguish *fides salvifica*, "saving faith," from *fides historica*, faith conceived as assent to propositions propounded by the church, as in the late Middle Ages. Justification by grace through faith is not simply assent to propositions, however edifying they may be; it is experimental appropriation of God's grace by individual persons through the immediate inspiration of the Holy Spirit.[19] Until one has grappled seriously with both of Wesley's sermons on "The Witness of the Spirit," he is not likely to comprehend this matter in Wesleyan perspective. Accordingly, the faith that saves, or justifying faith, points out or discloses all doctrine essential or necessary for salvation, beginning with repentance, forgiveness of sins, assurance of pardon, awareness of reconciliation, newness of life, ensuing love of God and humanity, etc. These are the collateral themes of Christian doctrine of which justification by grace through faith is the engendering first principle. Herewith are described the life-conferring or redeeming realities which are personally experienced in the process of such justification. These realities are properly and primarily the content of creed, the *fides quae creditur*. According to Wesley, this *credo* is not "controversial" or "speculative" but "experimental and practical divinity." This is so because it is, in the Wesleyan view, verified in experience and mediated by the Holy Spirit:

> By salvation I mean, not barely, according to the vulgar notion, deliverance from hell, or going to heaven; but a present deliverance from sin, a restoration of the soul to its primitive health; . . . a recovery of the divine nature; the renewal of our souls after the image of God, in righteousness and true holiness, justice, mercy, and truth.[20]

What the early Methodist preachers and people supposed about faith, following Wesley, was that without such transformation of existence as Wesley describes, pious truths might be affirmed and implied, but no regeneration or new birth or actual reconciliation to God occurred. Right belief does not save, according to Wesley, but only forgiveness of sins and restoration to newness of life, which results in going on to perfection in the environment of a divine-human association.

For such reasons Wesley declared that "the distinguishing marks of a Methodist are not his opinions of any sort."[21] Likewise he says, repeatedly, that "true Christian faith is, not only to believe the Holy Scriptures and the Articles of our faith are true," but also to have "a sure trust and confidence to be saved from everlasting damnation by Christ, whereof doth follow a loving heart to obey his commandments."[22] By this faith only are we justified.

Wesley does not mean to denigrate the creeds, i.e., the *fides quae creditur* or the substance of that which is believed. His point is rather that such belief does not amount to saving faith, or reconciliation, or regeneration. The faith that saves is "experimental" in several senses, but primarily because it is a "supernatural *elenchos*" consequent upon the work of the Holy Spirit.[23] As emphatically as the Homilies of the Church of England, Wesley insists that the faith that saves is not a work of men but of God. This is "the first principle of Christ," referred to by Nathan Bangs; for knowledge of it, the early Methodist preachers need look to none since, in experience, they are taught of the Holy Ghost.

Respectfully but emphatically, Charles and John Wesley discount doctrinal and socially approved communal orthodoxy of whatever kind as phony substitutes for "saving faith." Assent to Holy Church, Pope, Council, or Creed, cannot make a Christian. Nor, among Protestants, will assent to the Bible as creed, the "paper Pope," serve as saving faith. The Wesleyans are always insisting that the truth of Scripture avails nothing till it becomes, by grace through faith, the ruling inward principle of human life itself. For the Wesleys, presumptive orthodoxy — the sum of presumed right opinion — is of itself vanity, empty of God's saving grace. To any declarative absolutism of creed John Wesley will not succumb.[24]

Wesley will not succumb because he will not confound saving faith, i.e., the *fides qua creditur*, with the *fides quae creditur*, that which is believed, the Creed. To do so would neatly evade the first commandment of the Pauline gospel — the "Scripture way of salvation," the "faith whereby we are justified":

> . . . therefore St. Paul requires nothing on the part of man, but only a true and living faith. Yet this faith does not shut out repentance, hope and love, which are joined with faith in every man that is justified. But it shuts them out of the office of justifying.[25]

But it should be observed, Wesley cautions, "what that faith is whereby we are justified":

> With regard to the *condition* of salvation, it may be remembered that I allow not only faith, but likewise holiness or universal obedience, to be the ordinary condition of *final* salvation. And that when I say faith alone is the condition of *present* salvation, what I would assert is this: (1), that without faith no man can be saved from his sins, can be either inwardly or outwardly holy; and (2), that at what time soever faith is given, holiness commences in the soul. . . .[26]

Accordingly, the *rule of faith* which was acknowledged by the early American Methodists can be recognized as the "Scripture way of salvation." It is present more precisely in the twofold condition of salvation. The condition entails both justification and holiness, each implying the other. These are the two foci of the ellipse of early Methodist doctrines.

OF CONTROVERSIAL DIVINITY

This "Scripture way of salvation" and its summation in what we have called "experimental divinity" is contrasted with another kind of divinity which is largely ignored in our time by old line Protestantism. "Controversial divinity," or so-called "fundamentalism," was scarcely conceived and certainly unnamed in the 18th century. It acquired its modern conceptualization in *The Fundamentals*, which was published and found currency in American Protestantism following the 1905 Niagara Conference.[27]

How does this look from the perspective of Wesley's experimental divinity? This question has received little attention in this century. Wesley does indeed declare "Scripture to be of God," and the treasury of God's revealed way of salvation; but, so far as I have observed, there is nowhere evidence in Wesley's writings of an appeal to Scripture as infallible.[28] To the contrary, in the preface to *The Sunday Service of the Methodists*, Wesley notes that "Many Psalms are left out, and many parts of others, as being highly improper for the mouths of a Christian congregation."[29] This is a statement inevitably incompatible with a doctrine of "plenary inspiration" of the Scriptures.

It is clear in retrospect that for John Wesley — and, quite possibly, for 19th-century American Methodists — a "fundamentalist" (defined, let us say, as "one for whom faith is fundamentally belief in the infallible text of Scripture-history") has, on such grounds alone, no assurance of salvation. For Wesley such belief, in and of itself, does not and could not possibly qualify as "saving faith." Faith that justifies is a gift of the Holy Spirit, effectual for conversion, regeneration, or the new birth. It is understood as an experienced change of life which brings forth appropriate fruits.[30] If the fruits are not holiness of life, the faith is refuted.

It appears that for Wesley and for those who, as participants, understood the nature of "experimental religion," belief in the so-called "fundamentals" of the early 20th-century Protestant evangelicals would hardly differ from judgments of fact or of value, however precious and ardently affirmed. They would not belong to the utterances of "saving faith" or the doctrines of experimental divinity. They would not rate as a rule of faith. An opinion, for example, concerning history, even biblical history, and acceptable to a given religious community, was, by Wesleyan Methodists, not regarded as thereby qualified as testimonials of "saving faith," or of Wesley's "living faith." Recurrently, Wesley insists that "experimental religion" does not rest upon true opinions or upon deliberations of theoretical intelligence as such: "Whosoever . . . imagines that a Methodist is a man of such and such an opinion, is grossly ignorant of the whole affair; he mistakes the truth totally."[31]

A nearly identical view on this was shared by Philip Melanchthon, Thomas Cranmer, and John Wesley. However separated in time, they stood in a succession of those who agreed concerning the proper credentials of a sinner before God. For each, right belief, or mere "orthodoxy," supplied the sinner no better credentials for acceptance with God than those of "demons" — the *daimonia* of James 2:19. This they accented as corrective to long-prevailing sentiment, each in his time: Melanchthon in his *Loci Communes Theologici* (1521), Cranmer in the Homilies of the Church of England (1547), and Wesley, with those Homilies fully in mind, in his confession to Peter Böhler in April, 1738, and in his manifesto sermon on "Salvation by Faith" at St. Mary's, Oxford, in June, 1738.

For these reformers alike, *fides historica,* as it was called by the tradition, i.e., faith or belief in the verity of the narratives of biblical history, was not of itself saving faith at all. "The devils believe only the history," declares Melanchthon, based on James 2:19; "they do not believe that the Son of God has come to them for good."[32] That is, they do not respond fittingly, namely, with conviction of sin and repentance unto salvation. He quotes Bernard of Clairvaux with approbation: "Bernard rightly says that we must not only believe that God will forgive the sins of others, but that he will graciously forgive us, each of us, our sins."[33] "Through faith we are justified," says Melanchthon; "the promise is to be received in faith, . . . [and] whoever does not receive the promise does not believe all of God's word. . . . 'I believe in the forgiveness of sins'. . . means my sins are forgiven me. Not to believe this is to believe only the external history."[34] "The devils believe only the history. . . . As far as heaven and hell . . . so far are we to separate true faith from the knowledge that the devil and godless men possess."[35] Such was Melanchthon's understanding of the important distinction between, on the one hand, God's promise of our salvation through the merits of Christ accepted by faith as moved by the Holy Spirit, and on the other hand, belief (*Glaube*), however theoretically cogent or however ardent, in the *fides historica,* the external history of the Bible narrative.

This view reappears and is reaffirmed in Homilies of the Church of England, the First Book of which, containing twelve sermons, was published in 1547, early in the reign of Edward VI. It had been in preparation under the auspices of Archbishop Thomas Cranmer and colleagues since its authorization by the ecclesiastical Convocation of 1542 but was not approved by Henry VIII.[36] Cranmer had been a representative of the King to the Imperial Court of Charles V in 1532, and his ambassadorship included a visit to Wittenberg and personal acquaintance with the leaders around Luther; he secretly married the niece of the German reformer, Andreas Osiander, while on the continent in 1552.

The important distinction between *fides historica,* or belief, and *fides salvifica,* or saving faith, is expressed in three of the first four sermons of the Book of Homilies. These it was that were composed, it is judged, by Cranmer himself; and it was the distinction between mere belief, assent, or "dead faith," and "the true, lively, and un-feigned faith" that "worketh by love" and "without which no good works can be done," which caught John Wesley's attention and helped to bring him to painful awareness of evident indictment in his own case.[37] He had not himself made this all-important distinction until it was forced upon him by Peter Böhler.[38]

Here, in the Homilies "Of Faith" and "Of Salvation," Wesley was reminded of "the faith of devils which believe God" but not unto repentance and conversion of life. This belief was contrasted with "unfeigned faith, not in the mouth and outward profession only, but which liveth, and stirreth inwardly in the heart . . . a faith not without hope and trust in God, nor without the love of God and our neighbors, . . . and to follow the same . . . in doing gladly all good works."[39] Here also Wesley was informed that "the quick and lively faith . . . is not only the common belief of the Articles of our faith, but it is also a sure trust and confidence in the mercy of God through our Lord Jesus Christ, . . . and if we return again unto him by true repentance, that he, God will forgive and forget our offences for his Son's sake. . . ."[40]

By his own assessment, this "quick and lively faith," taught by the Homilies of his Church, Wesley found anemic if not quite absent in his own case. Nor can it much be doubted that about this period Wesley was ready to concede what appears in his *Journal*, on meeting with Peter Böhler at Oxford on March 5, 1738:

> I found my brother at Oxford, recovering from his plurisy; and with him Peter Böhler. By whom (in the hand of the great God) I was on Sunday the 5th clearly convinced of unbelief, of want of "that faith whereby alone we are saved," with the full, Christian salvation.[41]

It may further be noted that the Homily "Of Faith" also gave notice to Wesley that a faith which consisted "only in believing the word of God, i.e., the Bible that it is true . . . is not properly called faith":

> . . . but, as he that readeth Caesar's *Commentaries*, believing the same to be true, hath thereby a knowledge of Caesar's life and notable acts, because he believeth the history of Caesar, yet is not properly said to believe in Caesar, . . . even so he that believeth and all that is spoken of God in the Bible is true, and yet liveth ungodly . . . is not properly said to believe in God, or hath such faith and trust . . . that he may surely look for grace and mercy. . . .[42]

Many 20th-century "fundamentalists" — not wholly unlike John Wesley in the late spring of 1738 — would suffer surprise to know that the Homilies of the Church of England do not, on such grounds alone, hold them to be Christians, that is, subjects of "saving faith." The latter is something other than belief, or even conviction, that the biblical history is true, or the text of Scripture infallible. For Wesley and his contemporaries, the matter at issue did not include a dogma of the infallible text as the test of Christian fidelity. Such belief was not saving, for it was not a present experience of justification, with assurance of sin's forgiven, and the onset of a regenerate nature committed to life in the likeness of Christ in response to the redemptive influence of the Holy Spirit.

Wesley got his clarification on the nature of *fides salvifica*, the faith that saves, from the Homily "Of Salvation" of which also Thomas Cranmer was author. In Savannah in the early fall of 1737, Wesley had instructed his congregation on the Creeds, the Thirty-Nine Articles, the Book of Common Prayer and the Homilies of his Church.[43] When, therefore, he encountered in Peter Böhler an interpretation of the gospel, and the nature of saving faith, that challenged the sufficiency of his own, it is understandable that he should resort to those doctrinal standards, including the Homilies, which quite recently he had reexamined for the purpose of pastoral instruction of his people.

What Wesley recovered from the Homily "Of Salvation" can best be stated in his own words. His *Journal* records that on April 22, 1738, he met again with Böhler:

> I had now no objection to what he said of the nature of faith, viz., that it is (to use the words of our Church), "A sure trust and confidence which a man hath in God, that through the merits of Christ *his* sins are forgiven, and *he* reconciled to the favour of God." Neither could I deny either the happiness or holiness which he described as fruits of this living faith. "The Spirit beareth witness with our spirit that we are the children of God. . . ."[44]

Faith is here described as "sure trust on confidence which a man hath," the basic theme which reappears several times in the Homily "Of Salvation." While John Wesley could on April 22 declare no objection to Böhler's view of "saving faith" as expressed in the words of the Homily of his Church, he did not yet affirm it as his own and thus, in the words of Böhler, obtain from Christ "his promises to poor sinners." Wesley did, subsequently, own such benefits, namely, "a full reliance on the blood of Christ shed for *me*; a trust in him as *my Christ, as my* sole justification, sanctification, and redemption."[45] His *Journal* makes it abundantly clear that this confession, or *homologia*, was owned by Wesley as his personal experience only with and after Aldersgate, May 24, 1738. Till then, that confession remained but a general proposition, as both Melanchthon and Cranmer had understood, but not yet personally claimed by John Wesley.

As late as April 22, he "could not understand how this faith should be given in a moment: How a man could at once be thus turned from darkness to light, from sin and misery to joy in the Holy Ghost."[46] This "instantaneous work" was not of his own doing, as he saw in retrospect. It was done by way of an overruling intervention of the Holy Spirit. It became an instant happening: "I felt I did trust in Christ, Christ alone for salvation, and an assurance was given me that he had taken away *my* sins, even *mine*, and saved *me* from the law of sin and death."[47]

In a moment, the general truth about saving faith as taught by Melanchthon and by Cranmer found firsthand personal realization in the experience of John Wesley. Both John and Charles Wesley received in their own lives the promises of God through Christ, or the "Scripture way of salvation," within a few days of one another. This was the beginning of a new way of being in relation to God and man, in virtue of the preventing grace of God through the Holy Spirit. The platform now availed for the advance of the 18th-century Revival under the Wesleys; and the great insurgence of experimental religion in the western world and in the American colonies was to advance and continue for at least a century. It took the form of "living faith" attended by a vital manifestation of "inward" and "outward righteousness," and appears to have been a reforming power in American society throughout the 19th century.

CHAPTER 6

ORTHODOXY, PARADOX, AND EXPERIMENTAL DIVINITY

> The distinguishing marks of a Methodist are not his opinions of any sort. His assenting to this or that scheme of religion, his embracing any particular set of notions. . . .
>
> — *The Character of a Methodist*[1]

> The points we chiefly insisted on were: First, that orthodoxy, or right opinions, is, at best, a very slender part of religion, if it can be allowed to be a part of it at all.
>
> — *A Plain Account of the People Called Methodists*[2]

> But what is faith? Not an opinion, no more than it is a form of words, not any number of opinions put together, be they ever so true.
>
> — "A Letter to the Lord Bishop of Gloucester"[3]

TRUE OPINIONS IN RELIGION

If true opinions and, therefore, orthodoxy, according to Wesley, have scarcely a place or role in religion, at least in its Methodist expression, then what place or need may there be for doctrinal standards? The statements quoted above are far from exceptional in Wesley's published writings and seem, on the face of it, inhospitable to the very notion of standards of doctrine and their historic use and function in the Christian churches.

Such words as "the distinguishing marks of a Methodist are not his opinions of any sort" have from time to time suggested to some — both Methodists and others — that doctrinal standards have little right of place in Methodism. Some even suspect that the often-alleged latitudinarianism of Methodism in the 20th century, or its current so-called doctrinal "pluralism," has, in fact, a long pedigree that goes back to no less authorities than the Wesleys themselves.

Sometimes judgments of this sort have been prompted by Wesley's well-known but poorly understood "password" from 2 Kings 10:15: "Is thine heart right, as my heart is with thy heart? If it be give me thy hand. . . . No difference between us (if thou art a child of God) can be so considerable as is our agreement."[4] Those suspicious of easy ecumenicity regularly overlook the point that the unanimity of the heart which Wesley applauds actually invokes Paul's definition of saving faith: "For man believes with his heart and so is justified, and he confesses with his lips and so is saved" (Rom. 10:10). In Wesley's view, such a person is already the subject of saving faith and so may be presumed to have crossed the only threshold to the Christian life. Moreover, those who find in this camaraderie of "heart-religion" a want of doctrinal sobriety easily miss the import of the rightness of heart that invites community.

The relationship captured in the phrase, "right, as my heart is with thy heart," is, for Wesley, fulfillment of the second great commandment. And that is impossible without fulfillment of the first, the love of God, as in Mark 12:29–30. The two together signify one who is "going on to perfection." Thus, rightly understood, this almost proverbial Wesleyan invitation to Christian fellowship may be seen, however surprising, as doctrinally cogent by Wesley's standards. In it there is affirmation of an indissoluble complementarity and union of those two pillars of Wesley's "experimental divinity," that is, justification by grace through faith and sanctification, i.e., Christian life going on to perfection. This, for the Wesleys, was the only promising ground of human community.

Any suspicion of doctrinal indifference on Wesley's part, however, is quickly retired on four grounds. First, there was Wesley's verification of Peter Böhler's innovative (for Wesley) doctrine of justifying faith by finding its manifest affirmation and exposition in the Homilies of the Church of England.[5] The second is Wesley's occasional indictment, especially in the earlier years of the Revival, of contemporary churchmen of rank for both open and silent departures from the doctrine of the church.[6] To "a serious clergyman of the Church of England" who inquired of Wesley on what points he differed from other clergy of the church, Wesley answered:

> [I differ] in none from that part of the Clergy who adhere to the doctrines of the Church; but from that part of the Clergy who dissent from the Church, (though they own it not) I differ in the points following. . . .[7]

The list includes four or five basic doctrines declared in both the Homilies and the Articles of Religion. To be noted especially in this regard is *A Farther Appeal to Men of Reason and Religion*, together with Wesley's letters, private and public; these are exemplary sources for such critique in which the norms for Wesley are repeatedly asserted to be the Homilies and Articles of Religion of the Church of England. Yet, as we have already seen, such creedal declarations are not, in and of themselves, enough to certify "living" and "saving faith."

But, third, there is no way to attribute doctrinal indifference to John Wesley and to acknowledge, at the same time, his formidable provision for normative doctrine in the United Societies onward from the *General Rules* of 1743, the *Minutes of Several Conversations* of 1744–1789, the *Model Deed* prescribing Wesley's *Sermons* and *Notes on the New Testament* as standards for preachers assigned to Wesleyan chapels in Britain, and those constituting Conferences of American Methodism beginning in 1773 and 1784. These norms were linked with the doctrinal substance — including the liturgy and sacraments — of the *Sunday Service* which Thomas Coke delivered to the Christmas Conference along with the Twenty-Four Articles of Religion, abridged by Wesley from the Thirty-Nine Articles of the Church of England. It is obvious that Wesley's *Standard Sermons* were to represent doctrinal norms for at least a century following the Christmas Conference in American Methodism, and in British Methodism following the *Deed of Declaration* of 1784. Nor have the *Sermons*, as a compendium of Wesleyan doctrine, ever been officially disallowed or superseded as "doctrinal standards" in British or in American Methodism. They have been, however, first neglected, and then quite forgotten.

In the fourth place, and finally, we have already directed attention to the measure in which the *Collection of Hymns for the People Called Methodists* (1780) was rather conspiciously declared by Wesley in the preface to be "a little body of experimental and practical divinity." The same may be said of most of the published hymnals of the Wesleys from 1739 onwards, as the prefaces declare. This is especially true of the poorly known *Hymns on the Lord's Supper* of 1745, long recognized as a body of sacramental divinity.

Never has the leadership of an emerging branch of Protestant Christianity more truly relied upon its hymnal in ecclesial expression, to teach doctrine and so to inculcate its salient doctrinal norms. The Wesleys, as reformers, supplied their followers, in an unprecedented measure, with the means to *sing* the Creed. Moreover, it was the continuing usage of that hymnody and the liturgy of Methodism, deriving from the 18th century, that supplied and preserved what does in fact survive of the "experimental and practical divinity" of the originative era, along with its doctrinal impulse. It is now our business to identify the differences between that doctrinal impulse and understanding and the ever-recurrent "orthodoxy," or "true opinion" in religion. Orthodoxy, as we have seen, Wesley viewed as all but superfluous.

On the evidence presented here, which consists only of fragments of the whole story, it plainly cannot be doctrinal standards as such that Wesley discounts as insignificant. Rather, one should look for some basic difference of *nature* as between what the Wesleys understand by *normative doctrine* and something else named "opinions" in religion, or that claims the name and parades as "orthodoxy" on surreptitious grounds, in the view of the Wesleys. Also, if we are alert, we may surmise that the Wesleys have in mind a profound difference between "living faith" on the one hand, and "belief," i.e. espoused or inherited beliefs that are not rooted in immediate personal experience, on the other. For the Wesleys, authentic doctrinal standards are possessed of a grounding and status which espoused "opinions" in religion, however fervently entertained or adamantly defended, do not have.

From much observation, but also from buffeting and even bitter personal experience, the Wesleys — and both of them by much the same route — had come to understand that orthodoxy, ever protesting its verity, may exist, not for *intrinsic*, but only for *extrinsic* reasons. They actually came to perceive that piety, even their own, may be mixed, and that in progressing from the mere *form* of religion to the *power* of it, i.e. to holiness of life, no substitute for the gifting grace of God in justification by faith avails for salvation. By 1738 the Wesleys had come to acknowledge no other cogent foundation for Christian doctrine. Here is the crux of the matter.

"The distinguishing marks of a Methodist are not his opinions of any sort." That is the shocking sentence. The rest of *The Character of a Methodist* states and describes the truly distinguishing marks. In most respects, the essay is a sum of Wesleyan doctrine in the uncommon form of a portrait of the Christian life, not fully attained, but "on the way to perfection." Although the above sentence does not commend doctrinal indifference for the Methodist, it nevertheless does say with near-unparalleled emphasis on the part of the most scholarly, popular evangelist Christianity has known, that "true opinions" in religion (by which Wesley regularly means the Christian religion) *are not primarily constitutive* of it, and, if in any degree, only secondarily.

Yet, all of his professional life, Wesley was as much or more a defender of the Articles, the Homilies, and the Book of Common Prayer of the Church of England, as any clergyman of the 18th century. Such defense was a near-constant presupposition of his endeavor.

And the paradox grows tighter in that there is no question that Wesley himself became such a Christian that he could scarcely evade being "orthodox" — unless "orthodoxy" is the wrong way either to describe or to understand the living faith of a real Christian. Let us move on to that consideration, for there is no way to ease the paradox without the help of "experimental divinity" as Wesley knew it.

DOCTRINAL FOUNDATIONS: THROUGH EXPERIENCE ONLY

For the Wesleys, authentic doctrinal standards are so understood because they possess a *grounding* and, therefore, an *authority* that "orthodoxy," or "true opinion" in religion, has failed to acquire. With orthodoxy the *import* or *meaning* of true opinions has not become *truth for me* as a believer. Its truth remains second-hand. In short, what is deficient in every orthodoxy is the personal experience of justifying faith and "working out our own salvation with fear and trembling." And Wesley's quarrel with the Church of England was not so much with its long-authorized doctrine as with its defect of discipline for implementation or nurture of Christian life. The church was without discipline capable or disposed to nurture and induce appropriation of living and saving faith in believers, as Cranmer's Homilies understood such faith.

The Wesleyan dissent from "orthodoxy," while even more emphatic, is continuous with the Reformation dissent, particularly that of the Lutheran wing. It is dissent, that is, from the predominant conception of faith in late medieval Catholicism. To a large extent, faith had become merely assent to what was taught by Holy Church and required of individuals to believe for their salvation. Salvation and submission to ecclesial authority, climaxed in the Papacy, were virtually indistinguishable.[8] The Lutheran reformers, in promulgating the doctrine of justification by grace through faith, were obliged, therefore, to redefine and restate the meaning of faith. Nowhere in the early Reformation under Luther was this more ably and earnestly done than by Philip Melanchton in his *Loci Communes Theologici* (1521). The core of his treatment is entitled "Justification and Faith," and there Melanchthon has this to say:

> You will see that the gospel is sprinkled throughout the whole of Scripture in a remarkable way; and the gospel is simply the preaching of grace or the forgiveness of sins through Christ. . . . He who hears the threats [of damnation] and acknowledges the history [of redemption through Christ], does not yet believe every Word of

God; but he does who . . . in addition to the history believes the [gracious] promises. It [salvation] is not a matter of *believing the history about* Christ; that is what the godless do. What matters is to believe *why* he took on flesh, *why* he was crucified, . . . that he might justify as many as would believe on him. If *you* believe that these things have been done for *your good* and for the sake of saving *you*, you have a *blessed belief.* Aside from faith of this kind, whatever they [the Papists] call 'faith' is deceit, lying, and false madness.[9]

What, therefore, is faith according to Melanchthon?

. . . *this cannot take place unless the Spirit of God renews and illuminates our hearts.* . . . Accordingly, faith is nothing else than trust in the divine mercy promised in Christ.[10]

Salvation for Melanchthon is "not a matter of believing the history about Christ; this the godless do." Rather, it is trust in Christ as my saviour. This is just what Wesley found reiterated in the Third Part of the Homily "Of Salvation":

For the right and true Christian faith is, not only to believe that holy Scripture, and all the foresaid articles of our faith are true; but also to have a sure trust and confidence in God's merciful promises, . . . whereof doth follow a loving heart to obey his commandments.[11]

Then, as with Melanchthon, it is allowed:

And this true Christian faith neither any devil hath, not yet any man, which in the outward profession of his mouth, and in his outward receiving of the Sacraments, in coming to church, and in all other outward appearances, seemeth to be a Christian man, and yet in his living and deeds showeth the contrary.[12]

The reference to the devil as "believer" takes its scriptural source for both Melanchthon and Thomas Cranmer — author of this and other Homilies — from the Epistle of James (2:19). The reference underscores for both reformers the qualitative difference between *saving faith* that relies upon God's forgiveness of a truly penitent heart through Christ, on the one hand, and a "godless" man, or devil, on the other, who assents to a divine event but declines for himself both its relevance or its benefit by way of penitence for sin, or proves faithless by not failing to bring forth the fruits of faith — "for by their fruits ye shall know them" (Matt. 7:16).

Not to be missed in both Melanchthon and Cranmer is the effort to redefine *faith*, or to define *the faith that saves*, in differentiation from *belief.* The latter simply consents to matters of fact (e.g. in the case of Satan) or alleged fact (e.g., as with persons who assent to what the church declares to be the true). As Melanchthon states the case, godless belief is merely "a matter of believing the history about Christ." It is not acknowledging Christ as my personal redeemer. It is indifferent to this meaning of Jesus Christ *for me*, and thus is, however paradoxically, *faithless* "belief." So widespread was this distinction in 16th-century Protestantism that it is not at all surprising to find that Richard Hooker, father of Anglican theology, should declare:

> Therefore the first thing required of him which standeth for admission to Christ's family is belief. Which belief consisteth not so much in knowledge as in acknowledgment of all things that heavenly wisdom revealeth; the affection of faith is above her reach, her love to Godward above the comprehension which she hath of God.[13]

With these testimonies in hand, what do we find on turning to John Wesley? Let us quote from *An Earnest Appeal to Men of Reason and Religion*. Of the famous Council of Trent, on the nature of saving faith, Wesley observes that "they have decreed: 'If any man hold *fiduciaum* (trust, confidence, or assurance of pardon) to be essential to faith, let him be accursed.'" He continues:

> Thus does that Council [of Trent] anathematize the Church of England. For she is convicted hereof by her own confession. The very words in the Homily on Salvation are: ". . . Even the devils . . . believe that Christ was born of a virgin; . . . that he wrought all kind of miracles, . . . that for our sakes he suffered . . . to redeem us from death everlasting. . . . These articles of our faith the devils believe; and so they believe all that is written in the Old and New Testament. And yet, for all this faith, they be but devils, . . . *lacking the very true Christian faith*."[14]

Plainly, then, Wesley's view accords with that of the Reformers, that there is, under Roman auspices, a "faith" which is *not* "saving faith" and which the Council of Trent justifies as orthodoxy. It is merely a judgment of fact on the part either of a "devil" or a "believer," and so a true *doxa* or opinion. As such, it is not saving, according to Wesley, for, as with devils, the fact inspires further rebellion. In the case of Catholic believers, there is assent to a saving history, but not penitence unto acceptance of God's acceptance in Christ, or justifying faith. But, to clinch the point of the anathema of Trent upon the Church of England, Wesley further quotes the Homily "Of Salvation" regarding the faith that saves:

> "The right and true Christian faith is not only to believe the Holy Scriptures and the articles of our faith are true; but also to have a sure *trust* and *confidence* . . . to be saved from everlasting damnation through Christ." Or (as it is expressed a little after), "*a sure trust and confidence which a man hath in God, that by the merits of Christ his sins are forgiven, and he reconciled to the favour of God*."[15]

The words in italics, here quoted by Wesley, had been often recurrent in his written and spoken word, since (according to his *Journal* for April 22, 1738) Wesley met with Peter Böhler once more and could freely report:

> I had now no objection to what he said of the nature of faith, viz., that it is (to use the words of our Church), "A sure trust and confidence which a man hath in God, that through the merits of Christ *his* sins are forgiven, and *he* reconciled to the favour of God." Neither could I deny either the happiness or holiness which he described as fruits of this living faith.[16]

Here are the two pivotal doctrines of Wesley's experimental and practical divinity — justification by faith and, consequentially, holiness of life or sanctification, and in that order only. Furthermore, it is the nature of "right and true Christian faith" in believers to be possessed of this happy and holy assurance. It is a gracious gift of God's Holy Spirit and attended by transformation of mind and life. It is this experience which differentiates "saving faith" from "true opinions" or "orthodoxy"; for the latter without the former have, perhaps, foundation with humans, but are not known to be of God. Wesley's concurrence with Böhler on this understanding of the nature of faith — a nature he had hitherto quite overlooked — he had found corroborated by the Homily "Of Salvation." On this foundation stone he was to build all other doctrinal standards henceforth. And its corollary in doctrine Wesley expounds thus:

> Hear St. Paul is clearly describing the nature of *his* faith: "The life I now live I live by faith in the Son of God, who loved *me* and gave himself for *me*" [cf. Gal. 2:20].[17]

Such faith issues in a transformation of life by way of "new birth," a new creation that is going on to perfection.

Wesley's disallowance of "opinions" as substitutes for "saving faith" derives, first, from his complete sympathy with the 16th-century Reformers. They rejected a view of "faith" which reduces it to obedient assent to doctrinal affirmations on the authority of a church, which has salvation or damnation (without appeal) at its disposal. This breeds "orthodoxy" for extrinsic, not intrinsic reasons. The intrinsic reason for a "right and true Christian faith" is God's gift of justifying grace through faith, as St. Paul had discovered.

But the second reason for Wesley's dismissal of orthodoxy, while fully related to the first, is profoundly autobiographical. By his own admission, saving faith for Wesley had, through a long ordeal of pharisaism,[18] come to mean that which was the crux of Protestant dissent for Melanchthon and Cranmer. It was that saving faith conformed to God's way of redemption through the grace of the Redeemer in justification by grace through faith.

Of justification, we have Wesley's personal testimony to saving grace in his *Journal*, and particularly, the climax of his momentous exchange with Peter Böhler in May of 1738. Wesley reported that since he remained under the "law still, and not grace," he must needs abandon his search "to establish his own righteousness." Moreover, his faith still had God for its object and was, he now admitted, "not faith *in* and *through* Christ." Forgiveness of sins, as a present assurance, he knew not, nor had he known it hitherto, as an option of "saving faith." Thus Wesley relates that he was driven to renounce "all dependence upon my own works" and to resort "to the constant use of all other means of grace, continual prayer for this very thing, viz., justifying faith." This Böhler emphatically witnessed, and Wesley found confirmed in the Homilies, as "justifying, saving faith, a full reliance on the blood of Christ shed for *me*; a trust in him, as *my* Christ, as *my* sole justification, sanctification and redemption."[19]

At this juncture it is fitting to compare the *Journal* for Saturday, April 22, 1738, with the consummation in Wesley's account of his experience on May 24, at Aldersgate Street, where "one was reading Luther's preface to the Epistle to the Romans." What happened in the *experience* of John Wesley at "about a quarter before nine" was, it appears, very much a recapitulation in his own experience of the lines on saving faith and forgiveness of sins in Part III of the Homily "Of Salvation," "a sure trust and confidence in God, that by the merits of Christ his sins be forgiven, and he reconciled to the favour of God."[20] I judge that if there is one foundation stone of the Wesleyan "experimental and practical divinity," it has its manifest instance in this recapitulation of precisely that doctrinal statement from the Book of Homilies of the Church of England, which was all but forgotten in the Church of Wesley's day and earlier.

With John Wesley it came to life in firsthand immediate experience; the same thing had overtaken Charles a little before. It was understood by them as "a blessed work of the Holy Spirit."[21] On the matter of this justifying faith, let us attend Wesley, once again, in his *Letter to The Rev. Dr. Conyers Middleton Occasioned by His Late "Free Inquiry"* (1749).[22] With a massive use of the early church fathers, Wesley "took apart" Middleton's *Inquiry* — a volume of three hundred and seventy-three quarto pages — with such devastating logic (in the space of twenty days to publication) as few Deists among the English clergy of the Age of Reason would have cared to earn as public demolition and disclosure. Moreover, Wesley did so without resort to charges, however warranted, either of deceit or heresy, while at the end, in Part VI, he earnestly invited his adversary to reconsideration of the saving truth of the Christian religion. This he did in a series of propositions with commentary that may come close to being the most helpful insight Wesley has left us into his theological method and the relation between "experimental religion" and doctrinal standards.

We are reminded here by Wesley that "genuine Christianity" is "a principle in the soul" and that, as such, it manifests itself in the kind of "character" Wesley had earlier described. This "character" was already known from Wesley's somewhat perplexing but important essay, *The Character of a Methodist* (1742). This "character" is sketched, says Wesley, in the Old Testament and fully manifested in the New Testament. In the latter, the norms described in Christ's Sermon on the Mount are also commandments. But they are commandments-with-promise, though only through the agency of the Holy Spirit.[23] It is, moreover, a "promise," the enablement of which is supplied only by way of justifying faith and as God's gift. Of this point we have learned not to be surprised, however out-of-mind the work of the Holy Spirit had become in the prevailing Caroline Divinity. Such had been the case for over a century, and was still the case in the mid-18th century.

But what is the nature of this faith, by which the commandments-with-promise may find fulfillment? Says Wesley:

> But what is faith? Not an opinion, no more than it is a form of words; not any number of opinions put together, be they ever so true.[24]

Then with allusions to a well-known appurtenance of Catholic piety, Wesley continues:

> A string of opinions is no more Christian faith, than a string of beads is Christian holiness.
>
> It is not an assent to any opinion, or any number of opinions. A man may assent to three, or three-and-twenty creeds: He may assent to all the Old and New Testament, (at least, as far as he understands them,) and yet have no Christian faith at all.[25]

The paradox is here, again, being stated by Wesley with shocking clarity! But now he articulates the root difference between orthodoxy — true opinions in any number — and saving Christian faith:

> The faith by which the promise is attained is represented by Christianity, as a power wrought by the Almighty in an immortal spirit, inhabiting a house of clay, to see through that veil into the world of spirits, into things invisible and eternal; a power to discern those

things which, with eyes of flesh and blood, no man hath seen or can see; . . . . This is Christian faith in the general notion of it.[26]

On such a premise, it is not hard to understand why Wesley, in *An Earnest Appeal* (which was addressed mainly to rationalism in the Church of England and its clergy), should press the question at issue: "Do we leave [i.e., abandon] the *fundamental doctrine* of the Church, namely, salvation by faith?"[27] Having confronted the detractors among the clergy with the plain evidence of the Homilies, the Articles, and the liturgy of the Church, Wesley confronts the unbelievers:

> Let every reasonable man now judge for himself, what is the sense of our Church as to the *nature* of *saving faith*. Does it not abundantly appear that the Church of England supposes every particular believer to have a sure confidence that *his* sins are forgiven, and *he himself* reconciled to God?[28]

Nor is there the slightest question that, in his appeal to the Homilies, Articles, and the Book of Common Prayer, Wesley in *A Farther Appeal to Men of Reason and Religion* all but silenced the censures of churchmen who, in attacking the Wesleys, were proved either in ignorance of or departure from the doctrine of the Church of England.

Be these things as they may, the matter for our most strict attention is fivefold. First, the experience of justification by grace through faith is, by the standard of both Scripture and doctrine of the Church, inaugural for every Christian life that claims the name. Second, this is attended by assurance of sins forgiven and acceptance by or "reconciliation" with God, through Jesus Christ as Lord. Third, precisely this is new life or transformation of human existence after the manner of Christ and thus is vocation. Fourth, this status in its entirety is the meaning of "saving faith," that is, *fides qua creditur*, the faith by which we, in fact, believe what is held to be Christian doctrine. Fifth, in the absence of this foundation, "true opinions" ("orthodoxy" in religion) are, though perhaps better than nothing, not saving faith and often are deterrent substitutes for it, even excuses for its avoidance. On such grounds nothing can be plainer as to the foundation of what was understood by the Wesleys and early Methodism as "experimental and practical divinity." Wesley can thus address contemporaries of the clergy:

> Do some of you ask, "But dost thou acknowledge *the inward principle?*" I do, my friends: And I would to God every one of you acknowledged it as much. I say, all religion is either *empty show*, or *perfection by inspiration*; . . . Dost thou experience this principle in thyself? What saith thy heart? . . . Art thou acquainted with the "leading of his Spirit," not by notion only, but by living experience?[29]

ORTHODOXY DISMISSED: FINDINGS IN SUMMARY

We conclude that when Wesley holds rigorously that true opinions, or assent even to true Christian doctrine, does *not* make a Christian, he is far from discounting Christian truth or doctrines as such. On the contrary, Wesley is saying several things all related to one another.

(1) He is saying that orthodoxy, so-called, is defective in the measure that the truth of "Christian doctrine" has not come to life as a new way of being in relation first to God and, then, to one's fellows.

(2) He is saying that the only God-given way in which Christian truth may and does come to life in this fashion is through justifying faith, as St. Paul taught. This entails a work of the Holy Spirit, forgiveness of sins, the "new birth" or renovation of life, and "renewal of our souls after the image of God."[30]

(3) He is saying that just as justification is the unexceptionable gateway to human salvation, so also its "condition" is holiness of life. Of the latter he teaches "that at what time soever faith is given, holiness commences in the soul."[31] This is the vocation of "Christian perfection" incumbent upon all real Christians. It will show forth its fruits in "the character of a Methodist" or of a "true Christian" — its equivalent of whatever denomination.

(4) He is saying that "saving faith," as indicated, represents a change of life, not merely of mind or opinion from untrue, or defective, to true judgments. In this, as already noted, he follows a line of emphasis found in Melanchthon's *Loci Communes* and in Cranmer's Homilies "Of Salvation" and "Of Faith." The same stress is found in the writings of Richard Hooker, usually regarded as the father of Anglican theology, who speaks thus:

> Devils know the same things which we believe, and the minds of the most ungodly may be fully persuaded of the truth; which knowledge in the one [devils] and persuasion in the other [the ungodly], is sometimes called faith, but equivocally, being indeed no such faith as that whereby a Christian man is justified.[32]

What is the difference, then, between these judgments of demons, or of the ungodly, and what is rightly called faith? Hooker's answer concerning justifying or saving faith, however quaintly stated, is consistent with Wesley's, two centuries later:

> It is the spirit of adoption that worketh faith in us, in them not; the things which we believe, are by us apprehended, not only as true, but also as good, and that to us: as good, they are not by them apprehended; as true, they are.[33]

Wesley is in entire agreement with the two points of difference between saving *faith* and true *opinions*, or "orthodoxy," here noted by Hooker. Wesley concurs that it is "the spirit of adoption" which works faith in the Christian believer: "And therefore every man [or woman], in order to believe unto salvation, must receive the Holy Ghost."[34] Since "opinions" are the outcome of the natural exercise of discursive reason alone, neither Hooker nor Wesley finds such judgments to be authorized by the Spirit of God; therefore they are *not* declarations of saving faith:

> As the light of nature doth cause the mind to apprehend those truths which are merely rational; so that saving truth, which is far above the reach of human reason, cannot otherwise, than by the Spirit of the Almighty, be conceived.[35]

So speaks Hooker. Wesley takes an identical stand, with greater specificity respecting content of saving faith:

> Faith, in general, is a divine, supernatural *elenchos* of things not seen, not discoverable by our bodily sense, . . . Justifying faith implies, not only a divine *elenchos* [i.e. persuasion], that "God was in Christ reconciling the world unto himself," but a sure trust and confidence that Christ died for *my* sins, that he loved *me*, and gave himself for *me*. And the moment a penitent sinner believes this, God pardons and absolves him.[36]

So we may ask: is not this viewpoint which Wesley shares so fully with Richard Hooker an adequate indication of the grounds upon which he distinguishes radically between "true opinions" in religion and saving faith? The former, quite on its own, is persuaded of the truth of judgments; the latter, "saving faith," presupposes the moving, renovative, and efficacious work of the Holy Spirit. For Wesley, in the 18th century, the absence of efficacious working of the Spirit shows itself pervasively among nominal Christians in the "*form* without the *power* of godliness" — in short, in religious pretense, indeed, even in Wesley's own acknowledged pharisaism.[37] Such pretense may go on affirming the creeds, but has no grounding in a transformed life. It has not begun at the only divinely authorized beginning of "living faith," namely, justification by grace through faith, "the *fundamental doctrine* of the Church."[38]

REASONS THE MIND KNOWS NOT OF: "HEART-RELIGION"

Finally, we ought not to miss Hooker's second effort at stating the difference between the "equivocal" conforming judgments of the ungodly and those of justifying faith. For the latter, things cognized are apprehended he says, "not only as *true*, but also as *good*." By the ungodly, to the contrary, they are not apprehended as "good," but only as true. Justifying faith apprehends God's work of redemption in Christ so as not only to concede the alleged fact, but also to affirm its renewing grace unto our salvation. Thus Hooker teaches that Christian faith is not mere "belief" but whole-souled "acknowledgment" of sins forgiven.[39]

Such faith entails profound thanksgiving. Regularly, it appears as doxology. It is, as with Wesley, rooted in the Pauline norm: "For a man believes with his heart and so is justified and he confesses with his lips and so is saved" (Rom. 10:10)[40] For Wesley, "heart religion" versus valid judgments of fact, i.e., true opinions, amount to the whole difference between, on the one hand, justification and newness of life (salvation in process) and, at best, on the other, conventional Christianity, or, at worst, pretense behind which to hide in pharisaic pride sufficient to evade the work of the Holy Spirit.

As a reformer, Wesley understood that the most formidable obstacles to "living" or "saving faith" are pretentious counterfeits. For such reasons he wrote, rather early in the Revival, *An Earnest Appeal to Men of Reason and Religion* and then the three parts of *A Farther Appeal to Men of Reason and Religion*. These contain a resiliant hope addressed to all: "Sometimes you find, in spite of your principles, a sense of guilt, an awakened conscience." Wesley invites such persons to reconsideration:

> Now cannot *you* join in all this? Is it not the very language of your heart? O when will you take knowledge that *our* whole concern, our constant labour, is to bring all the world . . . to solid, inward, vital religion! What power is it then keeps us asunder? —Is thine heart right, as my heart is with thy heart? . . ."[41]

For many if not for most of those to whom Wesley penned his *Appeals,* the response to the above solicitation was often negative. That which Wesley spoke of as "solid, inward, vital religion" he believed he had found authorized in the Pauline witness to the Corinthians: You are "our letter of recommendation, written on your heart, to be known and read of all men; . . . written not with ink but with the Spirit of the living God, not on tablets of stone but on tablets of human hearts" (2 Cor. 3:2–3).

For the Wesleys, it is the working of the Holy Spirit in the formation and maturation of "living faith" which supercedes the common role and rule of "true opinion" as an exercise in religion, mainly, of the discursive reason. Mere orthodoxy in religious matters, being a poor substitute for saving faith, lacks the indispensable grounding in experimental "heart religion." "Experimental religion" always meant for the Wesleys, and once meant for the early Methodists, a present effectual working of the Holy Spirit. In the *Letter to Conyers Middleton*, the matter is summed up thus:

> [Christian faith] is a divine evidence or conviction wrought in the heart, that God is reconciled to me through his Son. . . .
>
> To believe (in the Christian sense) is, then, to walk in the light of eternity; and to have a clear sight of, and confidence in the most High, reconciled to me through the Son of his love.[42]

Accordingly, it is manifest to the Wesleys that the long-standing but forgotten view of "the nature of saving faith" entertained by the Homilies of the Church of England has two facets which, therefore, they possess authorization to reaffirm. The one is that, invariably, saving faith is the effectual working of the Holy Spirit; the other, that it "supposes every particular believer to have a sure confidence that *his* sins are forgiven and *he himself* reconciled to God."[43] This again is justification by grace through faith. Unknown to the Wesleys till 1738, they now find it to be "the *fundamental doctrine* of the Church,"[44] the "Scripture way of salvation," and, along with sanctification, the core doctrine of "experimental and practical divinity."

What, finally, is to be said of the Wesleyan paradox, viz., that "the distinguishing marks of a Methodist are not his opinions of any sort," or that "right opinions" have, if any at all, but a "slender" role in religion? Nothing is plainer than that there are, for the Wesleys, fundamental doctrines of the church to which they presume others, along with themselves, subscribe as a badge of belonging, or of membership in the church. When, however, church people settle for the badge, or assent to the symbol, without living participation in what it signifies, then orthodoxy, or "secondhand" Christianity, supervenes, and the *form* of religion prevails without the *power* of it.

CHAPTER 7

EMISSARIES OF THE GREAT SALVATION

Take heed to thyself and to thy doctrine. 1 Timothy 4:16

THE TASK AND THE SOURCES

In his characteristically succinct account of the General Conference which met in Baltimore, May 6, 1808, Jesse Lee reports that on May 18, at the "ordination" of William M'Kendree — the first native bishop of American Methodism — Bishop Asbury "preached an ordination sermon" on the text from 1 Timothy: "Take heed to thyself, and to thy doctrine."[1] Whether the text reflected current discussion in conference leading to the "First Restrictive Rule," or prompted it, is not known. It does point to principal matters which shall occupy us for the remainder of these studies.

The question now to be addressed is whether, and in what measure, the substance of John Wesley's "experimental and practical divinity" had currency in early American Methodism, in both theory and practice. If it is found to be present in theory, it will be spoken of as *doctrine.* If it is current in practice, it would be, in Wesleyan understanding, nurtured and enforced by *discipline,* that is to say, by the *General Rules of the United Societies* and the *Minutes of Several Conversations,* 1744–1789.

What, then, is the evidence and whence comes it? The answer, of course, is that it derives from a proper comprehension of the doctrinal import of early Methodist history in America. That history has had recurring investigation, beginning with the first thirty-page summation by Thomas Coke and Henry Moore in their *Life of the Reverend John Wesley* (1793).[2] It had its first comprehensive synopsis, in narrative and monographic form, with Jesse Lee's publication in the year 1810 of his then somewhat underrated *Short History of the Methodists.* Methodist history, however, had no further advancement until Nathan

Bangs published the first volume of his comprehensive four-volume *History of the Methodist Episcopal Church* with the Methodist Book Concern of New York in 1839. By 1857 that volume was in its tenth edition, yet its initial publication came more than half a century following the establishment of the Methodist Episcopal Church at the Christmas Conference of 1784 at Baltimore.

It is probable, from the *Minutes*, that a negative report of the Committee of Review of the 1808 General Conference resulted in a decision of that body to decline publication by the Methodist Book Concern of a manuscript before them entitled *A History of the Methodists in the United States of America*.[3] It was one of four manuscripts under consideration by the publishing house. According to existing procedure, it was referred by the Editor of the Methodist Book Concern to the Committee of Review of the General Conference for either favorable or unfavorable recommendation to the Conference for action.[4] The Editor of the Book Concern was at that time the very able Ezekiel Cooper, a prominent member of the General Conference with nine years of spectacular success as publisher and promoter.[5]

The report of the Committee of Review respecting the manuscript *History of the Methodists* proved to be unfavorable to publication. Thus, to the General Conference in session, its recommendation was non-approval. It included, moreover, the critical observation "that they have taken a cursory view" of the manuscript, "but as the work appears, in their view, more like a simple and crude narrative of the proceedings of the Methodists than a history, they think it would be improper to publish it."[6] They meant, of course, to publish it as explicitly approved by the Church and, thus, as something of an official account of the history in question.

So far as I am aware, we have no evidence of any synoptic narrative of American Methodism submitted for publication to the Methodist Book Concern prior to this one of 1808, save the thirty pages of Book 3 of the Coke and Moore *Life of Wesley*, published in America by the Book Concern in 1793. Nor, as time would tell, was any alternate in fact to appear until 1839.

Meanwhile, the Committee of Review proposed to restrict the "travelling preachers" of the Methodist Episcopal Church to publication of religious literature relating to the Church only through the offices of the Book Concern. This policy had a history that went back to the founding Conference of American Methodism at Philadelphia in 1773, under Thomas Rankin. That Conference had directed: "None of the preachers in America to reprint any of the Mr. Wesley's books, without his authority . . . and the consent of their brethren."[7] It had also interdicted Robert Williams' publication and distribution of Wesley literature as a part of his traveling ministry under Boardman and Pilmore in the years 1769–1773. Now, in 1808, the Committee of the General Conference moved that all publication by traveling Methodist preachers "shall come through the channel of our general Book Concern."[8] There were many good reasons for this, and some otherwise that need not here be reviewed.

The report of the Committee, being presented and moved for adoption, was tabled by a substitute motion, pending prior Conference decisions respecting time, place, and constituency of the succeeding General Conference, then at center of extended discussion. On May 25 the recommendations of the Committee of Review in reference to the four pending manuscripts for publication were, one by one, summarily approved and thus all four were rejected for publication. This meant that, among other things, the manuscript *History of the Methodists* was not approved for publication by the Book Concern.[9] The unnamed author, if a "travelling" Methodist preacher, was however free to proceed with publication otherwise if he so chose, since foreclosure upon such publication was *not* adopted by the Conference.[10]

Failing approval by the the General Conference of the four manuscripts under review, Nelson Reed, leader of the Baltimore Conference delegation, moved during the final session of the Conference, on May 26, "that a history of the Methodists in America be published; that such preachers, as have it in their power, be requested to furnish materials for the same, and that some person or persons be appointed to prepare it for the press." The motion was seconded by John Pitts, also of the Baltimore Conference, but it was lost.[11] Twenty-three months thereafter a volume entitled *A Short History of the Methodists in the United States of America*, written by Jesse Lee, appeared. It was published, not by the Book Concern in New York, but by McGill and Cline of Baltimore. No denominational approval had been necessary.

Nathan Bangs, who was a voting member of the 1808 General Conference and a younger member of the New York Conference, along with Ezekiel Cooper, and some years later as Book Editor (1820–1828) a successor to Cooper, commented on this matter in the preface to Volume I of his important *History*, which treated the years 1766–1792.[12] He observed that although there were ample materials for a history of Methodism following the year 1800, sources for the period from 1766 to 1792 were "comparatively barren, as but few of those who were instrumental in planting Methodism in this country have left particular records of their labors and sufferings, with which the page of history might be enriched."[13] Bangs then referred to the primary sources for his *History*:

> In speaking of the authorities on which I have relied for information in the compilation of this history, I feel it an act of justice to refer particularly to Lee's *History of the Methodists*, and to Bishop Asbury's *Journal*, principally because they have not been appreciated according to their worth.[14]

He describes briefly the historical resources of Asbury's *Journal* and acknowledges that he has "made Bishop Asbury the principal hero of the narrative, borrowing freely from his *Journal*." Of Jesse Lee he says further:

> As to Lee's *History*, though it might have been more amplified in some particulars, and less minute in others, yet I consider it the most important narrative we have of early Methodism, in these United States, and the most valuable text-book for the future historian.[15]

Bangs further observed that, next to Asbury, Lee traveled most extensively through the country, including New England, and had "an important part in the various transactions of the church, both in the Annual and General Conferences," and adds that

> . . . what enabled him to state the facts which he has recorded with the greatest accuracy, he also kept a daily record of his travels, and marked with the eye of a keen and attentive observer whatever came within the circle of his observation.[16]

In this early and authoritative observation of Nathan Bangs we have some of the essentials for comprehending the limitations for access to the history of primitive American Methodism in comprehensive and coherent narrative form. It might have been richer, we may suppose, if the motion of Nelson Reed at the final session of the 1808 General Conference had been approved. It might have facilitated the gathering of much, however fragmentary, materials and memoirs from a host of older retired or "local preachers," of which there were, at the turn of the century, a considerable number. The plain fact is that most of the particularities of earliest Methodist corporate life and experience remain to us in the few autobiographical remainders, and mainly in the form of memoirs, which survive. It is to a few of these, most of which are now found mainly in rare book rooms, that I propose to turn for answer to the question, whether and to what extent Wesley's "experimental and practical divinity" had currency in first generation American Methodism. As we shall see, the answer to our question is not cloudy.

WESLEY'S FIRST MESSENGERS: A DOCTRINAL CONSENSUS

However obvious it may be that institutional Methodism had its discernible beginnings with the preaching of Philip Embury in New York in 1766 and, somewhat earlier, with the redoubtable preaching and class formation of Robert Strawbridge at the log meetinghouse at Sam's Creek, Frederick County, Maryland, the early working doctrinal consensus of American Methodists hardly begins here. Plainly, this doctrinal consensus was imported along with the rich experience of the British evangelical Revival under the Wesleys and was grounded directly upon key documents, including hymnody, published by John and Charles Wesley. These are commonplaces of the history.

But there is an added dimension, for as American Methodists entered the field in the later 18th century, they also entered upon a widespread, if variegated, evangelical climate that had its emergence in the work of leaders of the Great Awakening (1740–1743), such as Jonathan Edwards, Gilbert and William Tennant, Benjamin Coleman, and especially George Whitefield — the most commanding preacher to the masses in Europe or the colonies from 1740 to 1770.[17] This evangelical state of affairs in the American colonies, though not un-challenged, was early known to Wesley through several avenues of contact, but the first notice of this intelligence is preserved to us in Wesley's *Journal* for October 9, 1738, only eleven months after his departure from Savannah:

> On Monday, [October] 9, I set out for Oxford. In walking, I read the truly surprising narrative of the conversions lately wrought in and about the town of Northampton, in New England. Surely, this is the Lord's doing, and it is marvelous in our eyes.[18]

When, therefore, we explore the vitality of "experimental religion," we are also to bear in mind its presence in varying forms and intensities in the American scene for more than thirty years prior to the mission of Richard Boardman and Joseph Pilmore, who arrived in Philadelphia October 24, 1769, with the authorization of Wesley and the English Conference.

Joseph Pilmore — Wesleyan Assistant, 1769–1774

John Wesley summed up the "fundamental doctrines" on which Whitefield "everywhere insisted," namely, "the *new birth* and *justification by faith*."[19] It was thus quite in keeping for Joseph Pilmore to report the following in his *Journal* for October 27, 1769 — shortly after his arrival for duty, at Wesley's direction, in Philadelphia:

> I spent an hour in the morning very comfortably with Mr. Edward Evans, an old disciple of Jesus, and one who has stood fast in the faith for near thirty years. He is a man of *good understanding*, and *sound experience* in the things of God. . . .[20]

Edward Evans was already known to Captain Thomas Webb two years before the arrival of Boardman and Pilmore from England in October 1769. He had been converted in the early 1740s under the preaching of Whitefield in the first wave of the Great Awakening. He was for a time associated with the Moravians, but fell away and was for some years an independent "New Light" preacher in New Jersey. Under Pilmore he became leader of a class at old St. George's in Philadelphia.[21]

Pilmore's language in his approbation for Edward Evans is highly charged with theological connotations. What he speaks of as "good understanding" denotes a positive judgment of Evans' doctrinal integrity. By the phrase "sound experience," Pilmore expresses the view that Evans was at home with experimental religion, and doubtless implies that he personally knew himself as justified by faith and, thus, regenerate as a recipient of justifying grace.

May we not judge that a similar appraisal was made by John Wesley respecting George Whitefield in his sermon on the death of Whitefield in November, 1770? There, in commending Whitefield's early "course of studies," namely, "such books as entered into the heart of religion and led directly to an *experiential* knowledge of Jesus Christ and him crucified,"[22] Wesley was plainly acknowledging "experimental religion" the fruits of which he shared with George Whitefield. So far at least, this had made them fellows in the Gospel message. Just so, Pilmore recognized Evans, as one influenced by Whitefield, also to be an apostle of experimental religion and thus of "good understanding" and "sound experience."

Wesley's third note of esteem in the 1770 memorial sermon was the observation that, in his youth, Whitefield had, by God's grace, experienced release from "the spirit of bondage," and through "living faith" — a highly charged concept for John Wesley — was enabled to abide under "the spirit of adoption" wherewith, according to Romans 8:15, we all may become children of God and "joint heirs" with Christ.[23] Somewhat later in the sermon, Wesley was emphatic in asserting that "justification by faith" and "the new birth" were "the fundamental doctrines" on which Whitefield "everywhere insisted," with which emphasis and accent, of course, Wesley was in complete accord.[24]

For Wesley "an experimental knowledge of Jesus Christ and him crucified," which he shares with Whitefield, is the glad assurance of the contrite sinner that his sins are forgiven in the mercy of God and that through the grace of Jesus Christ our Lord, he or she is an adopted child and made a "joint-heir" of the Kingdom. And so they are to walk, not according to the flesh, but according to "the law of the Spirit of life in Christ Jesus" (Rom. 8:2). Therefore this faith is here, manifestly, a consciousness of a *present* salvation. It is the person's apperception of and witness to the prime doctrine of justification by God's grace in Christ through faith. The stress upon this realization of present salvation in the "new birth" was, from the beginning, a distinguishing feature of Wesleyan doctrine as proclaimed by the Methodist preachers in America.

Joseph Pilmore's *Journal* for the years 1769–1774 is among the few, and the best, historical witnesses of the gospel message of the earliest Methodist preachers. In it the centrality of Christian experience is plain enough. Such experience is a work of grace through the immediate activity of the Holy Spirit on occasion of effectual repentance, or, conversely, in the liberation attending forgiveness of sins and "newness of life." These are, in Pilmore's view, marks of "vital religion."[25] They denote also "the Gospel way of salvation."[26] Moreover, Pilmore speaks of this justification by faith, with victory over the power of sin, as "spiritual religion."[27] He names it "the way of salvation"[28] or, more frequently, "the plan of Gospel salvation."[29] Pilmore's *Journal* for December 16, 1772, reports the following event during the course of his first preaching tour from Norfolk, Virginia, to the Carolinas:

> The next day [at Indian Town], I preached to a vast number of *Predestinarians* [Calvinists], but I resolved not to grieve them about *opinions*, so I preached *experimental religion* from that fine passage in Psalm 89. "Blessed are the people that know the joyful sound. . . ."[30]

In departing Portsmouth and Norfolk, following eight months of ministry and establishment of Methodist "classes" in both cities, and two in neighboring country centers, Joseph Pilmore writes of his final meeting with the Norfolk people, April 15, 1773:

> I found a fine congregation and preached with particular . . . freedom of heart. Afterwards I met the Society I had formed before I went to the South, took in a new member, and was comforted in speaking with them about *experimental religion* and the life of God in the soul.[31]

Pilmore's last words recall *The Life of God in the Soul of Man*, the book by Henry Scougal, the Scottish theologian of the mid-17th century, which profoundly assisted Wesley in understanding regeneration "as a change from inward wickedness to inward goodness; an entire change of our inmost nature from the image of the devil . . . to the image of God."[32] Without question, Joseph Pilmore understood well that Wesley took this change to be the onset of "Christian perfection" or sanctification, and that he so taught. Justification, therefore, was for Pilmore, as for the Wesleys, irrevocably paired with sanctification and the "new creation." Here, again, were the two pillars of the system of Wesleyan experimental divinity. Nor is there any doubt that Robert Williams, who recurrently accompanied, preached and ministered with Joseph Pilmore in Virginia in 1772–1773, taught an identical gospel that both of them had brought from England and the English Methodists at the direction of John Wesley.

Francis Asbury — Disciplinarian in the Way of Salvation

Francis Asbury and Richard Wright were commissioned by John Wesley and the English Conference and arrived in Philadelphia on October 27, 1771. They were warmly and kindly received by Francis Harris, a prominent Philadelphia Methodist, by the congregation, and by Joseph Pilmore, the latter in residence and exercising the leadership assigned by Wesley to him and his associate, Richard Boardman, in 1769.[33] Pilmore had seen to the provision of a meeting house, Old St. George's Church in which, probably to his surprise, Asbury was to preach his first sermon in America.[34] The Society had been formed by Captain Thomas Webb as early as 1767.[35] Asbury's first American declaration of both faith and mission came in the sermon he preached before his departure for New York on November 6. The text was Romans 8:32: "He that spared not his own Son, but delivered him up for us all, how shall he not with him freely give us all things?" As Asbury certainly recalled, Wesley had used the same text in his early field-preaching at Newgate, near Bristol, Sunday, April 29, 1739, as was reported in the famous lines of Wesley's *Journal*:

> At that hour it was, that one who had long continued in sin, from a dispair of finding mercy, received a full, clear sense of his pardoning love, and power to sin no more.[36]

Of whom Wesley spoke in this account, only he knew; but it was not a stranger! In these words Wesley affirmed against Calvinism the message of "salvation for all" under the agency of the Holy Spirit.

Francis Asbury would do likewise and to these ends he began his mission in the colonies.

Having remained but nine days with the brethren in Philadelphia, Asbury set out for New York, preaching on the way in both Burlington, New Jersey, and Staten Island, at homes of Methodist sympathizers who had been made known to him. He arrived in New York City — called York in that day — and was welcomed by Wesley's designated Assistant, Richard Boardman, who was presently not well.[37] After sharing the services and preaching at Wesley Chapel, Asbury, "being fixed," as he said, "to the Methodist plan," soon journeyed northward for visitation of outlying towns east of the Hudson River, including Westchester, West Farms, Bartow, New Rochelle, and Rye. His message aimed to show "the nature and necessity of repentance" and "the nature and necessity of faith." These two related themes are in some respects the burden of the second and third published extracts of Wesley's *Journal*, covering the period from February 1, 1737, to November 1, 1739, and also of *An Earnest Appeal* and *A Farther Appeal*, which Asbury had brought with him to America.[38]

A second visit to Westchester took Asbury to the home of Ebenezer White and his wife, both of whom had deep religious interest. White was a practicing physician. Preaching was house-preaching in that neighborhood. Here, Asbury stressed "the willingness of Christ to save *now*."[39] Evidently, Asbury had long since concurred with the proposition at issue for Wesley on April 22, 1738: "Whosoever believeth *is born of God*." Along with Wesley, he had come to accept, if not to understand, that justification by faith is "an instantaneous work," since also the New Testament disclosed few instances which were not instantaneous.[40]

At New Rochelle, somewhat farther north, Asbury preached at the house of Frederick Deveau, a French Protestant who had already opened his home to both Joseph Pilmore and Robert Williams. A few days thereafter, at New Rochelle, he took his text from Romans 3:23: "All have sinned and come short of the glory of God."[41] Thus, for Asbury, in the Wesleyan line, the originality of sin was a first premise, indeed, the presupposition of the "Scripture way of salvation."[42]

In January, Asbury found the people at Rye, still farther up country, either "insensible" to his message or sympathetic to the quite sufficient orthodoxy of the Episcopal order. He noted also that "the meeting house," of the Presbyterians was in ruins.[43] Returning toward New York, Asbury accepted an appointment at New City, now the Bronx, on January 16, and preached to an assembled congregation. "I spoke to them," wrote Asbury, "with some liberty, and they wished me to come again." He adds:

> A wise old Calvinist said, he might *experience* all I mentioned, and go to hell. I said, Satan *experienced* more than I mentioned, and yet has gone to hell.[44]

From this truly subtle exchange, we have the clear indication that Asbury was preaching the Wesleyan doctrine of "justification by faith alone" and also that the faith which truly saves is open to all who will receive it. This was in Presbyterian country, and Asbury's preaching plainly contradicted the Calvinist doctrine of "eternal decrees." The latter was still resilient Presbyterian orthodoxy, if contested in those years with intra-party challenge in Jonathan Dickenson and Samuel Davies. Nor was "Calvinism" quite without representation in varying degrees in other denominations, including the Episcopalians.

The response of the "old Calvinist" to Asbury's sermon carried a number of implications: (1) that to presently experience the joy of salvation with the alleged forgiveness of sins and acceptance with God would not revoke the eternal decree to salvation, but simply confirm it; (2) that the experience of a present salvation was superfluous if the one experiencing acceptance with God was already elect, in any case, from all eternity; (3) that, by the eternal decree, it was evident that some would be free to believe savingly, while those who did not believe were, evidently, predestined to reprobation; (4) that all this stress upon a present experienced redemption through saving faith in the universal mercies of God was, therefore, applicable only to the elect, leaving the reprobate reprobated still; and (5) that such preaching as Asbury's, if not futile, was evidently superfluous!

Whatever else one may think of it, this Calvinist critique of *present salvation* through justifying faith is valid enough, if its hypothesis of "eternal decrees" is conceded. If Asbury, on the occasion, supplied no on-the-spot refutation, such response as he made, nevertheless, suggests his acquaintance with the issues in contest and with some ways in which Wesley handled such an assault on "free grace," both in his *Farther Appeal* and especially in his *Principles of a Methodist*. Asbury was on target in replying as he did, that "Satan experienced *more* than I mentioned, and yet is gone to hell." What he meant, more precisely, was that Satan experienced more freedom than Asbury had claimed for penitent sinners in the forgiveness of sins, and their reconciliation to, and acceptance with, God.

In addition, Asbury is alluding to a defiant insubordination of Satan to the sovereign Creator. But this insubordination must presuppose the power of free choice to resist God, contrary to Calvinism. The condition *sine qua non* of the fall, then, was God's very gift of freedom! This, by comparison with the "bondage of sin" in the case of human beings, is the "more" which Satan "experienced," in Asbury's claim, "and yet is gone to hell." This freedom to resist God's Spirit Asbury understood to be an axiom of Wesley's experimental divinity.

We can take but one more leaf out of Francis Asbury's *Journal*, for we must pass on to other witnesses. On Monday, December 21, 1772, he writes:

> I set out for Bohemia Manor; and though my body was much fatigued with my ride, . . . yet in the evening I enforced these words: "Be diligent that ye may be found of him in peace, without spot, and blameless"; and endeavoured to show them, that, in *justification*, we have peace, in *sanctification* we are without spot, and in *perfect love* we are blameless; and then proceeded to show them wherein we must be diligent.[45]

In this commentary on 2 Peter 3:14, Asbury manages to embrace the two main pillars of Wesley's experimental divinity: justification is affirmed together with the second great work of God's grace through Christ Jesus, namely, sanctification "working by love," or Christian perfection. Sanctification, as we have constantly seen, presupposes justification with forgiveness of sins and the "new birth." Asbury is fully aware that, for Wesley, sanctification "implied a continued course of good works, springing from holiness of heart." In the *Farther Appeal*, Wesley writes that

> By salvation I mean . . . a restoration of the soul to its primitive health, . . . a recovery of the divine nature; the renewal of our souls after the image of God, in righteousness and true holiness. . . .[46]

For Asbury, this plainly commands the "diligence" of 2 Peter 3:14, or the *disciplined life*; and, in a notable way, Asbury was, among his fellows, an unfailing monitor or disciplinarian. History was to prove that Francis Asbury possessed those qualities for leadership in the colonies for which Thomas Taylor had pleaded with John Wesley in 1768: "If possible, we must have a man of wisdom, of sound faith, and a good disciplinarian."[47] Perhaps better than most, Asbury understood that the nature and design of the *General Rules of The United Societies*, drawn up by the Wesleys in 1743, were aids for justified sinners to "work out their salvation with fear and trembling," and that this was indistinguishable from Christian perfection as life-vocation.

It was at the Methodist Conference in London in 1770, that, with his lay preachers and others, Wesley again faced openly the standing Antinomian error which he apparently saw at work in the ranks. It proceeded by making the key doctrine of justification by faith, when claimed, an excuse for indifference to or disregard of "man's faithfulness" in his own salvation. It was the ancient error that Paul identified: sinners who, as it were, presumed "to sin that grace might abound" (Rom. 6:1).

Wesley perceived this Antinomian evasion, or self-deceit, as a deadly foe to "the renewal of the work of God."[48] It was the very problem cited in the *Minutes of Several Conversations*: When "God thrust them forth to raise up a holy people . . . Satan threw Calvinism in the way; . . . and then Antinomianism which strikes at the root."[49] To this, the declaration of the 1770 London *Minutes* reasserted as needful for salvation: (1) man's faithfulness, (2) working for life, and (3) works as a *condition* of salvation — as the Homilies had, for Wesley, made abundantly clear.

Among Calvinist friends of the Revival in England, a storm was aroused over the 1770 Conference *Minutes*. They were presumed to be a bald abandonment by Wesley of "salvation by grace alone." John Fletcher was to rise to defend Wesley's *Minutes* in his *Checks To Antinomianism*. Francis Asbury, who was for the year 1770 assigned to South Wiltshire, was doubtless to be readied for his epochal mission at the following Conference in Bristol of 1771 with an aroused and lively awareness of the inescapable responsibility of justified sinners for their "faithfulness" in their call to holiness; for the latter was nothing less than their very salvation.

The importance of the emphasis of the *Minutes* of 1770 seems never to have diminished in the life and work of Asbury, and perhaps contributed to his role as indefatigable disciplinarian. And for the purposes of these studies, the *Minutes* of the 1770 London Conference are to be seen as explicit illustration of a pervasive and inherent feature of "experimental and practical divinity." The *Minutes* illustrate clearly how doctrine cannot be separated from that personal and communal discipline by which its truth becomes radiant and incarnate in a human life, or indeed in what Wesley described as "the character of a Methodist."

CHAPTER 8

NATIVE AMERICAN PROFESSORS OF
EXPERIMENTAL RELIGION

His *experience* of the grace of God: This was evidently deep and
genuine. At the time he first made *a profession of experimental religion,*
the number of *experienced Christians* was small . . . but he built upon
Christ; he experienced justification by faith in the merits of his death
. . . and persevered in the *exercise* of this faith in good works, in all
holy conversation and godliness, until the end of his life.[1]

DOCTRINES EMBODIED IN DISCIPLINED LIVES

The author of the lead quotation was a younger contemporary and
colleague of Jesse Lee, who wrote at the close of the first quarter of
the 19th century. Faithfully and without flourish he supplies us with a
balanced summation of "a profession of experimental religion" in
word and life, which, while it speaks of but one, is in fact, illustrated
in the careers of four early Methodist itinerants, slightly older contemporaries of Lee of whom we have surviving memoirs. All are alike in
possessing, in their time, "a profession of experimental religion," that
is, they personally profess it, in life as well as word, and are "exercised"
in its fulfillment.[2]

And this, it is clear from Wesley's writings — especially *The Principles of a Methodist* and *The Character of a Methodist* — was the program
inherent in the "living faith" of a justified sinner, who pressed on to
"work out" his salvation. Christian "faithfulness" was to be an *illustration* of "the sum of Christian doctrine" by embodiment of its two
principal articles. These are *justification by grace through faith,* wherein
a Christian life begins with forgiveness of sins and, secondly, *holiness of
heart and life,* which has its start in regeneration, according to Wesley.[3]
This holiness in the likeness of Christ advances onwards to perfection
through sanctifying grace — but not without the "faithfulness" of the

newborn person.[4] Wesley adopts the idea of the "working out" of one's salvation from Philippians 2:12, and teaches it with complete realism. It is this that in the lead quotation is referred to as *perseverance* "in the *exercise* of this faith."

The word "exercise" is recurrent in the memoirs of the early Methodists. It is used technically, in a way quite foreign to modern usage. For them it was the entire endeavor of unfaltering faithfulness to the cruciform way — the *imitatio Christi*. This, they learned from John Wesley, is the way of "final justification." As the Wesleys stated: "They saw . . . that men are justified before they are sanctified; but still holiness was their point."[5] This platform or, better, this plan of salvation, was given emphatic declaration at the London Annual Conference of August 7, 1770. Following established practice, it was published in the *Minutes* of the Conference:

> . . . as the meritorious cause of justification is . . . Christ, so the condition of it is faith, faith alone.
> . . . both inward and outward holiness are consequent on this faith, and are the ordinary, stated condition of final justification.[6]

This statement shortly became a matter of controversy, provoking public criticism and attacks upon John Wesley by the Calvinistic wing of the evangelical Revival. To what extent, if any, the declaration of the 1770 *Minutes* departed from long-standing Wesleyan doctrine we may consider by recalling this statement from Part I of Wesley's *A Farther Appeal to Men of Reason and Religion* (1745):

> With regard to the *condition* of salvation, it may be remembered that I allow not only faith, but likewise holiness or universal obedience, to be the ordinary condition of *final* salvation. And when I say that faith alone is the condition of *present* salvation, what I would assert is this: (1) that without faith no man can be saved from his sins, can be either inwardly or outwardly holy; and (2) that at what time soever faith is given, holiness commences in the soul. . . .[7]

The "inward and outward holiness" spoken of in the 1770 *Minutes*, while they are also a regenerate person's "faithfulness" as enabled by the Holy Spirit, were together in 1745 declared to be "the ordinary condition of *final* salvation." Thus, long before 1770, Wesley had excluded the Antinomian from salvation by the latter's own failure to meet the "ordinary condition" of it. When Francis Asbury accepted the appointment for his mission to America at the Conference in Bristol, August 6, 1771, there can scarcely be doubt that this reaffirmation of the place and role of discipline in the consummation of the Christian's vocation was understood by him as a central mandate of "living and saving faith." The 1770 *Minutes* stated that (1) human "faithfulness" is required, and in the likeness of Christ; (2) that "every believer, till he comes to glory, works *for* as well as *from* life" (i.e., *for* sanctification as well as *from* justification); and (3) that "salvation is not by the merit of works, but by works as a *condition*."[8]

Nothing, then, was so plain as that the "Scripture way of salvation" also entailed the Cross, that is, the strenuous way of St. Paul's "living sacrifice" (Romans 12:1). We might say that it entailed, on Wesley's showing, "the character of a Methodist." To a remarkable degree it is just this that we may observe among the early Methodist itinerant preachers: they not only *preached* the gospel, they *experienced* it, and in their several measures they sought to be, as it were, its *illustration*.

Although it may be fearful to mention, awesome, and possibly disturbing, we are here quite close to what St. Paul spoke of as "saints." These, I judge, have in this century scarcely had the status either of *desiderata* or of likelihood among church people. Yet it is without doubt the case that early American Methodists received and aspired to Christian perfection, not only as a *desideratum*, but actually as a "condition" of "final justification" before God. This was their standard of doctrine and discipline, although it is surely not found among the Articles of Religion.

AUTOBIOGRAPHY AS CHRISTIAN WITNESS

Among the early native Methodist preachers there are, to my present knowledge, but seven who have left substantive autobiographical memoirs of their life of Christian witness in the first generation, i.e., in the years 1773 through 1794. This period is documented by *The Minutes of the Methodist Conferences, 1773-1794*, edited and published by John Dickens in 1795. Our studies have necessarily referred to these *Minutes* as a foremost primary source of American Methodist history. In this respect, they are to be classed with Lee's *Short History of the Methodists*, Asbury's *Journal and Letters*, the *Journal* of Joseph Pilmore and the *Journals of the General Conference*, 1792–1836.

John Dickens was not only the first Book Editor of the infant Methodist Book Concern, but was judged to be its creator by Bishop Holland N. McTyeire in his own *History of Methodism* (1884). Dickens was among the earliest Methodist preachers recruited to the cause. According to the *Minutes* we are considering, he was "received on trial" at the crucial Annual Conference at Deer Creek, Harford County, Maryland, in 1777. It was crucial because it was the last attended by Wesley's General Assistant, Thomas Rankin, who, being (like Wesley) loyal to the King, experienced severe tensions incident to the Revolution. Dickens was that year received "on trial" with thirteen other young men, most of whom were to "win their spurs" for the Lord with high honors. Yet we know this not because any of the group left memoirs, not even Dickens, but because a few others kept ministerial records and journals which survived.

John Dickens was the representative who received Thomas Coke on his arrival at New York in November, 1784, and accompanied him to Delaware for his meeting with Francis Asbury. It was he who at the Christmas Conference, December 15, 1784, proposed for adoption the name of the new church — The Methodist Episcopal Church. We should not know these particulars save for the witness of the younger preacher, Thomas Ware — later himself to serve as Book Editor — who was present and recorded them in his *Sketches of the Life and Travels of Thomas Ware*, published long afterward in 1832.[9]

The premature death of John Dickens in 1798 deprived us, we may suppose, of memoirs which, because of his early acquaintance with the movement in its beginnings, would have contained much which has been forever lost. Nathan Bangs, who came into full connection only in 1802, recognized the paucity of contemporary records of the first generation in the preface to his *History of the Methodist Episcopal Church*. The measure of this deprivation is clear: Of the 379 young men received into "full connection" in the Methodist Conference between 1773 and 1795, so far as I know, there are at our disposal but seven autobiographical witnesses of native origin, apart from Asbury's *Journal* for the period.[10] The place at which this impoverishment is most telling is not, I judge, in the sphere of persons, dates, events and eventualities, but in the province of personal religious witness and exposition of the doctrinal foci and spiritual tone and temper of the societies, which were, finally, the moving power of early Methodism. Hence there are some grounds for suspicion that, from quite early in its history, American Methodism was losing, or being deprived of, direct relationship to its originative and formative doctrinal sentiments. An oral tradition survived, to be sure, but the bulk of personal records and journals vanished. Those that came to publication were few, indeed, and thus all the more important.

There was, it seems, a certain diffidence and reluctance on the part of the early Methodist preachers to be committed to print. William Watters, for example, says this in his preface to his *Short Account of the Christian Experience and Ministerial Labors of William Watters*:

> I can tell you that until some time past, I never intended during my life, that the world should be troubled with anything of the kind [his memoirs]. Although I have been particular in keeping an account of

my *experience* and *religious exercises*, yet, until a few months past, no one ever saw it.[11]

Yet Watters had been undaunted and tireless in preaching for years the "Scripture way of salvation" which, plainly, had been advanced through his own affirmed religious *experience* and *exercises*. These were indeed the means of confirming to him the saving power of the gospel that he felt impelled to share. It was the pressure of certain associates that prevailed upon Watters to publish his journals.

It is precisely this understanding of the awakening role and converting function of autobiographical and biographical literature in the proclamation of the Christian message and, in particular, of "experimental religion," which is so strikingly prominent in the awareness and provision of John Wesley. Almost no one has given adequate attention to the fact that, in the course of his career as author and publisher, Wesley — according to Richard Green's *Bibliography* — published some forty separately printed autobiographical or biographical accounts of saving faith — excluding both the *Christian Library* and the *Arminian Magazine*. Some of these memoirs went into many editions, and not a few, such as Wesley's extract of Jonathan Edwards' *Life of the Late Rev. Mr. David Brainerd* (1768), ran to nearly three hundred pages. There were others of similar magnitude and some of but a dozen pages. The London *Minutes* of August 1768 include this mandate among other answers to Question 23, "What can be done to revive and enlarge the work of God?": "Let every preacher read carefully over the *Life of Mr. Brainerd*. Let us be followers of him, as he was of Christ."[12] Here Wesley enjoins imitation of Christ as exemplified in the life of Brainerd.

We have, then, sufficient explanation for the notice by Freeborn Garrettson in the preface to his *The Experiences and Travels of Freeborn Garrettson*, which came to publication under John Dickens at Philadelphia in 1791. Garrettson acknowledged that he was "some time ago solicited by John Wesley to send him an account of my experiences and travels." He was, as he put it, "at a loss to know what was best to be done . . . but after some consideration" notified Wesley of his compliance. When, however, he began to write, he was overtaken with "some scruples." These he communicated to Wesley who, he said, "intreated me to lay aside my scruples and comply." He reported that at length having "prepared the piece" and sent it off, it was lost by ship-wreck, and that shortly after Wesley persisted in his request, saying that "if it did not arrive soon it would not be in time for him to see it." Garrettson observed that this "was in fact the case; for whilst I was sitting in my room in Albany [on the Hudson], finishing a letter to be enclosed, a friend came in, and presented me with a newspaper, in which I read the account of the death of that eminent servant of God."[13]

The truth is that, in letters extending over the years 1785–1789, Wesley had on four separate occasions repeated this earnest request, beginning with a letter which Garrettson received in Halifax, Nova Scotia, where he had been stationed as preacher by the Methodist Conference. From Dublin, Ireland, on June 26, 1785, Wesley had written that

> . . . though I have not seen you, I am not a stranger to your character. By all means send, when you have opportunity a more particular account of your *experience* and travels. . . . It is a very desirable *thing that the children of God should communicate their experience to each other.*[14]

It is, then, to the experiences of these early Methodist preachers — those of justifying and of sanctifying grace — that we must turn for additional and vital witness of the "Scripture way of salvation."

WITNESSES TO DOCTRINE WITH DISCIPLINE

One may wonder whether the whole-souled preoccupation of the early Methodist preachers with proclaiming the gospel of a present salvation indisposed them to harvest in a literary form the unfolding of their days in a ledger of assets and liabilities. So Garrettson, to justify committing his message and mission to print, concludes his preface admonishing his readers thus:

> I earnestly advise all those into whose hands this short diary may fall, to read it with earnest prayer; then peradventure, it will have its desired effect on their hearts. In this account, I did by no means intend to gratify curiosity, but to be instrumental in bringing precious souls to the Lord Jesus Christ.[15]

Garrettson goes yet further in the preface and lists five steps that may lead to justification, or forgiveness of sins, as restoration to new life under God.

Surely the controlling motivation of this preface was one uniformly shared by the first generation of Methodist preachers: love of neighbor expressed in a commanding aspiration to share with others their own joyous liberation from the guilt and from the power of sin. Inseparable from this freedom, and equally motivating, was a sense of reconciliation to God the Father through God's own grace in Jesus Christ, and participation in the Kingdom without end as joint-heirs with Christ.

In regard to this quite vibrant and astonishing philanthropy of the Spirit it is timely to recall both William Watters himself and his high esteem for his veteran contemporary in work of the gospel, Richard Owen. Passing through Leesburg, Virginia, in the Spring of 1786, Watters found Owen "dangerously ill." Subsequently he wrote what otherwise would not have been known:

> He [Owen] was the first American Methodist preacher . . . awakened under Robert Strawbridge. He was a man of respectable family, of good natural parts, and considerable utterance. Though encumbered with a family, he often left wife and children . . . and went into many distant parts, before there were any traveling preachers . . . and, without fee or reward, freely published the Gospel to others, which he had found to be the power of God unto his own salvation.[16]

Minton Thrift, editor of Jesse Lee's *Memoirs*, made a similar comment on Lee's ministerial motivation:

> To turn sinners from darkness to light, and from the power of Satan to God, is the grand design of the Christian ministry . . . We do not mean to depreciate learning, but in regard to the Christian ministry, it holds a secondary place to *experimental and practical religion*. Those who are inwardly moved by the Holy Ghost, whether learned or unlearned, will give evidence of divine mission . . . by success in bringing sinners to the knowledge of the truth as it is in Jesus.[17]

The motivation that was attributed to Jesse Lee by an admiring younger associate plainly was also the commanding motivation of each of the early Methodist itinerants. Moreover, there was a corollary: these early American Methodist itinerants did not understand their calling and authority as being concerned with an ecclesiastical certification of orthodoxy or a theological system of true "opinions." They spoke "not with plausible words of wisdom," but, as Paul claimed of his message, "in demonstration of the Spirit and power" (1 Cor. 2:4). This, indeed, was the claim of Thomas Ware regarding them.[18]

The following is a record of the names of those Methodist preachers whose journals or memoirs have survived, insofar as known to this writer, together with place of birth and the date of full Conference membership: William Watters, Baltimore Co., Maryland, 1773; Philip Gatch, Baltimore Co., Maryland, 1774; William Glendinning, Moffatt, Scotland, 1776; Freeborn Garrettson, Baltimore Co., Maryland, 1777; Jesse Lee, Prince George Co., Virginia, 1785; Thomas Ware, Salem, New Jersey, 1786; Benjamin Abbott, probably Salem, New Jersey, 1790. In the remainder of this chapter it is my intention to allow the authors of these memoirs to speak, and as much as possible in their own language.

EARLY PRACTITIONERS OF EXPERIMENTAL DIVINITY

William Watters (1751–1833)

There are two things that mate in William Watters' account of his conversion: his own deliverance from the bondage of sin and his keen awareness of the plight of those who have not yet been released:

> My burden was gone . . . my soul and all that was within me rejoiced in the hope of the glory of God: while I beheld such willingness . . . in the Lord Jesus, and my soul so rested in him, that now, for the first time, I could call Jesus, Lord 'by the Holy Ghost given me.' The hymn being concluded, . . . my prayers were all turned to praises.[19]

Then, reflecting upon "those who are unexperienced in the things of God," Watters quotes 1 Cor. 2:14 — the classical passage for those who understood the *analogy of faith*:

> The unspiritual man does not receive the gifts of the Spirit of God, for they are folly to him, and he is not able to understand them because they are spiritually discerned.[20]

Thus "living faith," as Wesley first learned and later taught it, is recapitulated in the experience of this first traveling preacher and Conference member of American Methodism. Moreover his message and ministry — based upon this new spiritual discernment — is acknowledged as an obligation to be fulfilled by sharing it with others.

When Godfrey Watters, a man of English stock, died, leaving his wife, Sarah Adams, and seven sons, he had become an affluent farmer and was a vestryman of the local parish of the Church of England. This was, probably, around 1767, when the colony of Maryland was still under the governance of the English Crown and Parliament. Of his seven sons, William Watters seems to have been among the younger. William says that his father "left us not rich but in comfortable circumstances, and I believe in faith and solemn prayer he committed us to God."[21]

The family lived and held property at Deer Creek, in the Susquehannah Hundred, a subdivision of Harford County, not far from Baltimore. William Watters begins his account of his religious experience with July, 1770. At that time his elder [probably oldest] brother Henry, with his wife, Mary — already convinced Methodists — welcomed Joseph Presbury, an exhorter who had been converted and trained under Robert Strawbridge, to their house for preaching.

They also invited friends and kin, and William was present, evidently with one or two other brothers.

While William, who was but nineteen, could not, he says, well understand Presbury's teaching on the "need to be born again," he did begin to see the "heinousness of sin" and "his want of Christ as a present Saviour." The meetings were continued and William, along with his brothers Nicholas and John, was a participant. One of these brothers, whom William does not name, was a witness of William's conversion. Of that brother, probably Nicholas, William Watters some years later wrote: "He was cut to the heart and humbled to the dust, while all his objections to experimental religion fled as smoke before the wind." Then, of his own experience of grace, William rejoices to declare: "This memorable change took place in May 1771, in the twentieth year of my age; in the same house . . . where I was born as a child of wrath, I was also born a child of grace."[22] He then continues with these remarkably Wesleyan observations:

> We had no regular preaching in those days, nor had there ever been but three preachers in Maryland, Williams, Strawbridge, and King, so that we were frequently for months with very little preaching . . . but in one sense we were all preachers; the visible change that sinners could not but see, and many openly acknowledged, was a means of bringing them to seek the Lord.[23]

In the fall of 1771 William Watters' second elder brother [John?], who had, he says, been a father to him and was "a moral man and a strict Churchman, and one of the vestry of the Episcopal Church," also "was blessed powerfully with a sense of his sins forgiven, and the love of God shed abroad in his heart by the Holy Ghost given unto him."[24] It is evident that Watters and his brothers became acquainted with the lay preacher Robert Williams, when, in 1770, he came south from New York and Philadelphia under the authorization of Boardman and Pilmore. In the fall of 1772 William Watters was persuaded of a call to preach. He had previously been but an "exhorter." He accepted invitation of Robert Williams to accompany him as an understudy on a preaching mission into Virginia. On their journey through central Virginia, Watters found that the people were utter "strangers to heart religion" and that there were "very few who knew, experimentally, anything of the Lord Jesus Christ, or the power of his grace. . . ."[25]

It was on this extended stay in the area of Norfolk and Portsmouth that young Watters became acquainted with Wesley's assistant, Joseph Pilmore. Perhaps at the direction of Pilmore, Watters, with indifferent success, sought to begin a circuit in the area during the summer and fall of 1773. Meanwhile Robert Williams carried the "Scripture way of salvation" south and west to Petersburg and to the borders of North Carolina. Watters reports that Williams "returned from Petersburg and adjacent country, where he had been preaching for several months with great success, and was the first Methodist preacher who had ever been in those parts," and adds that "Mr. Devereux Jarrett and Mr. McRoberts both received him with open arms and bid him a hearty welcome to their parishes."[26]

Here is a near eyewitness account of a fascinating and heartening episode in the early history of American Methodism, namely, the warm collaboration with the Reverend Devereux Jarrett, rector of the Bath Parish of the colonial Church of England in Dinwiddie County — the notable reforming parson of the "established church of Virginia." Save for one other, namely the Reverend Archibald McRoberts, Jarrett stood alone in the cause of reform and the "experimental religion" he had somewhat strangely acquired, not by way of his own communion, but from the dissident Presbyterians of Hanover County. The collaboration continued for years and surely reached one of its peaks in 1775 and 1776 when George Shadford tended the southern circuits of Virginia before departing for England in 1778.

Watters was appointed to the Brunswick Circuit in 1777, with Freeborn Garrettson and John Tunnell. Thus he himself made personal acquaintance with the other Anglican reformer, Rev. Mr. Archibald McRoberts, of Powhaton County parish:

> On the way, I had the pleasure of hearing Mr. McRoberts preach Christ and him crucified to a listening multitude. He was the first Minister of the Church of England that I ever heard preach Christian experience.[27]

From Powhaton County, Watters proceeded south to the Brunswick Circuit, the area of his responsibility, which embraced Dinwiddie County and, thus, the Bath Parish of Devereux Jarrett. Watters says that "his barn, well fitted up with seats and a pulpit, was one of our preaching places, and I found him very friendly and attentive to me while I stayed in those parts."[28] By 1777, with the rising tensions precipitated by dissension over the Revolution and the exodus of the majority of English clergy, the question of the sacraments had become more and more difficult for Methodist people, especially in Maryland and Virginia. Watters observed that "our present situation of having but few ministers [i.e. ordained ministers of the Church of England] left in many of our Parishes to administer the ordinances of Baptism and the Lord's Supper" had became a severe problem:

For as yet we had not the ordinances amongst us, but were dependent on other denominations for them. Some received them . . . from the Presbyterians, but the greater number with the Church of England, it being before our separation, and our becoming a regularly formed Church.[29]

This problem and issue, which in 1778–1780 brought the Methodist movement very close to division and, perhaps, dissolution, was mercifully transcended by the grace of God and the irenic mediation especially of William Watters attended also by Freeborn Garrettson.

Philip Gatch, 1751–1834

Both William Watters and Philip Gatch, although considered Conference members well into the 19th century, ceased the life of travelling preachers before the founding of the Methodist Episcopal Church in 1784. Watters temporarily "located" in 1783, and Gatch in 1779, when he married Elizabeth Smith of Powhaton County, Virginia. Watters and Gatch were received into full membership in the Conference that met in Philadelphia in 1774. They were both born in 1751 and reared in Baltimore County, Maryland. Both were baptized and, with their families, were confirmed and practicing members of the Church of England. Later in life, Gatch had occasion, as a Methodist, to be grateful that in his youth he had learned his Catechism and knew the Book of Common Prayer, as he says in one place, "by heart." Both Watters and Gatch "experienced" the "new birth" under an exhorter trained by Robert Strawbridge: Watters under Joseph Presbury, and Philip Gatch under Nathan Perigau, who was, according to Gatch, "the first to introduce Methodist preaching in the neighborhood where I lived."[30]

At the first, his father opposed strenuously Philip's association with the Methodists, and pointed Philip to his older brother, as one who knew better. Writes Philip Gatch:

That brother was present when I received the blessing, and became powerfully converted. My father inquired of him the next morning what had taken place at the meeting; he gave the particulars, and wound up saying, if they did not all experience the same change, they would go to hell.[31]

Shortly after, Gatch reports, "My parents and most of their children, a brother-in-law and two sisters, in about five weeks had joined the church." Plainly he meant "classes," two of which had been formed by Nathan Perigau.[32] Gatch had stated early in his memoirs that his parents "belonged to the Episcopal Church; and that though *destitute of experimental religion*, they paid attention to its restraints and forms, which was a benefit to me."[33] He had read widely in religious literature — including *The Whole Duty of Man* and Russell's *Seven Sermons*, the latter then popular and influential as a publication of "New Light" Presbyterianism of the Great Awakening.[34]

Aware on the one side of an urge to speak and to exhort, Gatch was cowed by a sense of weakness on the other. He was assisted by the first chapter of Jeremiah, and learned what Acts implied "in tarrying in Jerusalem till endued by the power from on high." From reading Wesley's sermon on "Salvation by Faith" he inquired in mind, spirit and in prayer: Why not *now*? He experienced forgiveness of sins but not sanctification. His experience of the divine empowerment was to come when, as he says,

> The instruction of the Divine truth was sealed in my soul by the Holy Ghost. My joy was full. I related to others what God had done for me. This was in July, a little more than three months after I had received the Spirit of justification.[35]

Gatch received a formidable assignment by Thomas Rankin in 1774 to the uncultivated New Jersey circuit, accompanied only briefly by John King. Later he was sent to the Kent circuit on the eastern shore of Delaware, where he was obliged to restore the confidence of the Methodists in the area after a shameful failure of an itinerant predecessor, Abraham Whitworth, who had been dismissed. There, and later in Virginia, Gatch encountered fierce and, finally brutal persecution which forced him to "locate" for a time but not to cease his ministry, which he carried on as a local preacher while he lived in Virginia, that is, until 1798, when he married Elizabeth Smith of Powhaton County, Virginia. He served responsibly in a controversy between north and south over the administration of the Sacraments, which for many in Virginia and Maryland seemed forced upon them in the years 1778–1780. In his *Memoirs*, Gatch says this of his wife's family:

> The family, previous to the reformation in Virginia, belonged to the Established Church, and lived in Parson [Archibald] McRobert's parish, who was friendly to the Methodist preachers, who first visited the south. Mr. Watters makes honorable mention of him. He said in his journal, "On my way I had the privilege of hearing Mr. Mc-Roberts preach Christ and him crucified to a listening multitude. He was the first minister of the Church of England I ever heard preach Christian experience."[36]

Here we find Philip Gatch, who joined the Conference in "full connection" with his youthful colleague, William Watters, in 1774, quoting Watters' report because he agrees with Watters' assessment across the span of more than thirty years. Experimental religion, which the early Methodist preachers knew that they shared both with McRoberts and Devereux Jarrett, as with John Wesley, was intended to be, and had been in fact, a reforming power in the Church of England, both in the colonies and in the British Isles. Gatch could so testify from ample experience.

Freeborn Garrettson (1752–1827)

For Freeborn Garrettson, who was admitted into "full connection" at the Conference at Deer Creek, Harford County, Maryland, May 20, 1777, the Wesleyan "Scripture way of salvation" was most certainly experienced.[37] It became for Garrettson the sum of the Christian doctrine of salvation. That such was the case was utterly clear to Francis Asbury, who relied upon Garrettson greatly in the stressful and (for Asbury) confining time of the Revolutionary War, particularly in the years 1778–1781. A letter written to Garrettson by John Wesley in June, 1785, and preserved by Nathan Bangs in his biography of Garrettson, makes plain Wesley's knowledge of Garrettson's mind and character.[38] Bangs published *The Life of the Reverend Freeborn Garrettson; Compiled from His Journals* in 1832; this is some indication of the measure of Garrettson's stature in the eyes of an able younger contemporary. It is very important to note the prominance of the word "experience" — that is, both justification and sanctification — in the titles of the personal memoirs of both Watters and Garrettson.

Garrettson was born August 15, 1752. His parents were well-to-do members of the Church of England. His mother, he says, had been enlightened under the ministrations of George Whitefield. He was also aware of those "blessed men of God, the Tennants," who preached much in those parts. Garrettson, like Philip Gatch, had also read Russell's *Seven Sermons* prior to his conversion under Daniel Ruff. The latter was raised spiritually under the tutelage of Robert Strawbridge. The process of Garrettson's conversion was inaugurated by a near-fatal fall from a horse. He first heard Francis Asbury at Deer Creek, Maryland, at the house of Robert Watters, eldest brother of William, in 1772. But it was not until he encountered the preaching of Daniel Ruff in 1775 that he came under the overwhelming conviction of the sin of resistence and capitulated. He heard these words from Ruff: "I have come once more to offer you life and salvation, and it is the last time: choose or refuse." The effect of these words on Garrettson was dramatic:

> I was instantly surrounded with a divine power: heaven and hell were disclosed to my view, and life and death were set before me. . . . Man hath power to choose or refuse in religious matters; otherwise God would have no reasonable service from his creatures.[39]

At the conclusion of this account of his conversion, Garrettson added, doubtless as later commentary: "The enmity of my heart was slain — *the plan of salvation* was opened to me. . . ." The phrase, as Garrettson was to learn, came from Wesley.[40]

Following the Conference of 1777, Garrettson journeyed with Watters and Tunnell to circuits in southern Virginia. Thereafter, he went west to Roanoke and on into North Carolina.[41] He had freed his own slaves, following upon his conversion, and was moved to inculcate "the doctrine of freedom in a private way."[42] Moreover, he set apart times to preach alone to the blacks. He believed such a thing as Christian perfection was attainable in this life, and preached it, while he held firmly to Christ his Redeemer in "the witness of my justification."[43] In Garrettson we constantly perceive a stress upon the theme of Gal. 2:20, "it is no longer I that live, but Christ who lives in me." William Watters, in that period on the Brunswick circuit, reported coming upon persons he believed "further advanced in the Divine life than any he had conversed with" and aspired to experience for himself what he called, "the great salvation."[44] This was also the case with Garrettson. In the same period, he testified that "for more than a week an earnest struggle continued in my heart for all the mind which was in Christ."[45]

Thus we have in the case of early American Methodists an evident comprehension of Wesley's "Scripture way of salvation," namely, that it is only inaugurated by the grace of justification and must be consummated by the grace of sanctification, which is regularly to be manifested in Christian perfection. This was communicated to Garrettson as he pursued his mission among the Methodists in Nova Scotia in 1785 by a letter from Wesley, which is important because of its doctrinal norms and disciplinary regulations in combination, supportive of a methodology of salvation:

> It will be the wisest way to make all those who desire to join together, thoroughly acquainted with the whole Methodist plan, and to accustom them from the beginning, to accurate observation of our rules. Let none of them rest in being half Christians [i.e., justification without sanctification] . . . as soon as they make peace with God, to exhort them to go on to perfection.[46]

Here Wesley expresses a direct admonition to Garrettson that was recurrent in the *Minutes* of the British Conference, namely, the stress upon the inseparability of doctrine and discipline. Question 23 of the *Minutes* of the Conference of 1768 had stated it this way:

> Be conscientiously exact on the whole Methodist Discipline. And that you may understand it, read over carefully, the *Plain Account of the People Called Methodists*, and the several *Minutes of the Conferences.*[47]

It is of first importance to note that to this emphasis on Wesley's part, Garrettson responds with the words: "Close doctrine and discipline I dearly love."[48]

Jesse Lee (1758–1816)

Jesse Lee was the second son of Nathaniel and Elizabeth Lee. Nathaniel was a substantial plantation farmer in Prince George's County, Virginia, some fifteen miles south of Petersburg. The eldest son was Peter; the youngest son, John, was born on March 12, 1770. Of the early Methodist itinerant preachers we have attended, or, of those for whom we have surviving memoirs, Lee is the only one whose father's conversion preceeded his own. He reports that his father, Nathaniel, was "brought under serious concern for the salvation of his soul" in 1772; he "came under conviction," and experienced liberation, "the Lord visiting his soul with pardon and peace; he then knew that God, for Christ's sake, had taken away all his sins."[49] The impression made upon Jesse Lee by this transformation in the life of his father was deepened shortly after by his mother's being "brought under conviction." Lee writes that she "did not rest until she obtained forgiveness of her sins."[50]

Lee informs us that his family ancestry, on both sides, went back to the early English settlement of the colony. At the time of his brother John's birth in 1770, there was, in his words, "no religion in his father's family: but his parents were moral people, and constant attendants on the established Church of England." Further, he reports that "they generally took their children with them to church, when they were old enough to receive instruction."[51] Although these words were written in the preface to the tragic *A Short Account of the Life and Death of the Rev. John Lee* — published in 1805, many years after the state of affairs described and in Jesse Lee's doctrinal maturity — their simple notice of the absence of "religion" in the "established" Church was but a matter-of-fact, low-key, statement about a Church with "the form but without the power of Godliness."

This commonplace Wesleyan critique was, however, fully learned by Jesse Lee before he ever left Prince George's County, for it was also taught by the neighboring parson, Rev. Devereux Jarrett of the Bath parish.[52] In his important *The Life and Times of the Rev. Jesse Lee*, Leroy Lee assures us that "among those savingly converted to God under the ministry of Mr. Jarrett" was Nathanial Lee, Jesse's father.[53]

Following his reference to his mother's experience of justifying grace, Lee himself says that "I was awakened when I was about 15 years old, by my father's private conversation, and was converted in the beginning of the following Spring, which was in the year 1773."[54] That was also the year of the first Methodist Conference, which met in Philadelphia under John Wesley's General Assistant, Thomas Rankin, accompanied by George Shadford. Lee was to have some acquaintance with Shadford through the latter's powerful preaching in the nearby Brunswick Circuit, where an extraordinary revival outburst took place in the years 1775–1776.[55] In this Devereux Jarrett was a collegial figure, a fully supporting spirit, and a practical collaborator in the administration of the Sacraments and in several other ways. But another important and influential person enters the arena as a contributor to the vitalizing of the religious life of Jesse Lee's community:

> About that time [1773], Robert Williams, an Englishman, who was a Methodist preacher, came into Virginia, and preached near where we lived. He was the first Methodist preacher that ever came to Virginia. We attended on his ministry whenever we had an opportunity, for twelve months before he began to form societies; and when the first Methodist societies were united together, before any circuit was formed in Virginia, my father and mother, my eldest brother and myself, all joined in society with the Methodists.[56]

Such is the oldest extant eyewitness account of the establishment of Methodism in southern Virginia. It was an event coincidental with the similar work of Joseph Pilmore in Norfolk and Portsmouth for many months in the same year, in which William Watters was a youthful apprentice.

The *Memoirs* that preserve fragments of Lee's *Journal*, through quotation of selected passages, preserve also his commentary following upon the conversion of his parents. Here he observes that "while he frequently heard them talk about their conversion and being born again . . . nothing I heard . . . took hold of my mind for some time." Then follows a paragraph of great significance:

> One of my mother's relations came to my father's and stayed all night; the topic of conversation was *experimental religion*. While engaged on this interesting subject, my father observed, "that if a man's

sins are forgiven, he would know it." That sentence, "if a man's sins were forgiven him, he would know it," took hold of my mind and I pondered it in my heart.[57]

Following this event, Lee reports that "my distress of soul, at that time, was very great, and never wore off till my sins were forgiven."[58] Shortly after, he says that "the Lord came to my relief, and delivered my soul from the burden and guilt of sin."[59] This, according to the surviving text supplied by Minton Thrift, is related to the coming of Robert Williams, the first of the Wesleyan preachers, to Lee's neighborhood. Thrift observes that "the doctrines of this minister of Christ were just suited to his [Lee's] state of mind . . . and built up in him faith and love."[60]

In the case of Jesse Lee, the assurance of saving faith — that normal expectation of the Church of England, according to Wesley, that "every particular believer [will] have a sure confidence that *his* sins are forgiven, and *he himself* reconciled to God" — is in some measure again fulfilled.[61] And is not this what is meant in part by "reformation" in the church? It is that part called justification; and this it was that Jesse's father claimed a man would know if his sins were forgiven. The remaining part of Wesley's plan of salvation was advancement in "inner and outward holiness." As Thrift put it,

> It pleased God about this time, to show him [Lee] the necessity of a deeper work of grace beyond that he had experienced in justification, or sins forgiven. And this he found to be holiness of heart and life, and a will entirely quiescent to the will of God.[62]

THE EARLY METHODIST MISSION

Today, one may travel north and south from Georgia to Maine on ample highways, or east and west from the Eastern Shore of Maryland to Charleston, West Virginia, over bridged rivers and mountain passes with no delays. It should be remembered that the early Methodist itinerants, such as Jesse Lee, managed these vast distances on horseback with but a single purpose: to bring the gospel to "precious souls." A telling summation of this mission is found a letter to John Wesley from Freeborn Garrettson. The letter is dated April 20, 1785, and was written from Halifax on Garrettson's appointment to Nova Scotia, five months following the founding of the Methodist Episcopal Church at Lovely Lane Chapel, Baltimore:

> Rev. and Dear Sir, — Known to me, yet unknown, I have many things to write, but am afraid of burdening you, or of taking up your precious time, which I believe you are redeeming moment by mo-

ment. I bless God that I ever heard of your name, or read your numerous works. *Close doctrine and discipline I dearly love.* This spring is fourteen years since I was powerfully convinced without the use of human means. The doctrine of the first Methodist preacher I ever heard was as precious ointment to my wounded soul. I was sure he was a servant of the living God. I have been travelling in your connection nine years, during which time (I desire to write it with humility) God has granted me health, so that I have seldom missed preaching the whole of that time. My lot has mostly been cast in new places, to form circuits, which much exposed me to persecution. Once I was imprisoned; twice beaten; left on the highway speechless and senseless; (I must have gone into a world of spirits, had not God in mercy sent a good Samaritan that bled, and took me to a friend's house;) once shot at; guns and pistols presented at my breast; once delivered from an armed mob, in the dead time of night, on the high way, by a surprising slash of lightning; surrounded frequently by mobs; stoned frequently: I have had to escape for my life at dead time of night. O! shall I ever forget the Divine hand which has supported me. O that I could love my God more, and serve him with a more perfect heart.

It was three years from my conviction, before I was brought through the pangs of the new birth. Eight months elapsed after I was called to preach, before I was willing to leave my all and go out. I wanted to live in retirement, and had almost got my own consent to sell what I had in the world, and retire to a cell. God withdrew himself from me. I was very near desperation, for I was travelling, as it were, alone. I betook myself to my room, except when I was wandering through the woods and fields, till I was worn away to a skeleton; and all this time I was kept from unbosoming myself to the lovers of Jesus. Strong impressions I had to go forth in Jehovah's name to preach the Gospel. When I thought of it, I was pained to the very heart: it seemed like death, so great was the sense I had of my weakness and ignorance. By day I was drawn out in the study of the Holy Scriptures, and in the night season, when fast asleep, preaching aloud, till I have been as wet with sweat, as if dipped in a river. O! what a precious time I had when I gave up my own, to the will of God. I saw there was no other way for me to be saved. I was determined, if required, to go to the ends of the earth; yea, I promised the Lord if he would stand by me, and required it, I would go to the very mouth of hell. Blessed be God, he has been very kind and good to me ever since.

The second year I travelled, I was powerfully convinced of the necessity of holiness. For a considerable time I waded through deep, but sweet distress. I had a discovery of the purity of the law, and the impurity of my own heart: being conscious it was my privilege to become pure in heart, I determined not to stop short of it. Sensible I was it came by faith. I was under deep exercises to preach no more, till I received that blessing. There was a time when I had a greater nearness to God, but I did not receive the witness till a twelve-month afterward. F. Garrettson.[63]

This letter, which without further explanation Nathan Bangs entitles "An Unfinished Letter to Mr. Wesley," is here quoted in full, not only because it sketches the entire dedication and fidelity of Garrettson's itinerancy under persecution, mob violence, and imprisonment, but because this autobiographical account supplies us with what is not easily found elsewhere. It amounts to a summation of the common doctrine of the early Methodist preachers, precisely related as personal experience, or autobiography. It is salvation-doctrine come to life! Embracing both pillars of Wesley's "experimental and practical divinity" — justification and holiness of heart and life — it moves from awakening and conviction of sin, to acceptance of God's acceptance through the mercy of Christ (saving faith and justification), to forgiveness of sins, "the witness of God's Spirit with our spirit that we are children of God," reconciliation, and the call to faithful service "to the ends of the earth;" and, finally, the press onward to Christian perfection, or working out one's "final salvation" with fear and trembling. Here is both the *order* and the *way* of salvation. And it is a way in which doctrine and discipline are mated for a single purpose. That purpose is the recapitulation of saving faith, described in Scripture, but now realized in present experience.

To be noted closely is both the centrality and the source of "the doctrine of the first Methodist preacher" (Daniel Ruff) that was "precious ointment" to his soul, in the testimony of Garrettson. That decisive source was John Wesley, as Garrettson declares: "I bless God that I ever heard your name, or read your numerous works. Close doctrine and discipline I dearly love." According to Bangs' account, this letter marked the beginning of a correspondence between Wesley and Garrettson that continued until 1789. It should be apparent that the saving doctrine described by Garrettson in this first letter is no other than Wesley's "experimental and practical divinity."

CHAPTER 9

EXPERIMENTAL RELIGION IN LOW PROFILE

Almighty God, who hast given us thy only begotten Son to take our nature upon him and at this time to be born of a pure virgin: Grant that we, being regenerate and made thy children by adoption and grace, may daily be renewed by thy Holy Spirit; through the same our Lord Jesus Christ, who liveth and reigneth with thee and the same Spirit ever, one God, world without end. Amen.

— The Collect for Christmas, in The Book of Common Prayer.

AN EXTENDED TRADITION

In the concluding chapters of this study, it will be appropriate to bear steadily in mind the following words from *The Imitation of Christ* by Thomas à Kempis, with which John Wesley was intimately acquainted from his college years at Oxford:

What availeth it a man to reason high secret mysteries of the Trinity, if he lack meekness, whereby he displeaseth the Trinity? Truly nothing. For high curious reasons make not a man holy nor rightwise, but a good life maketh him beloved with God. I had rather feel compunction of the heart for my sins, than only to know the definition of compunction.[1]

That this sentiment was among the seeds of what the Wesleys came eventually to recognize as "experimental religion," "heart-religion" or "practical divinity" is scarcely to be doubted; in putting "compunction of the heart" above the "definition" of it (in the head), à Kempis announced a great part of the rationale of John Wesley's "experimental and practical divinity." Thus it may be the case that the viewpoint of the *Devotio Moderna* of the late Middle Ages was to find its ripest expression, after Thomas à Kempis and his Brethren of the Common Life of the 15th century, in the distinctively Wesleyan proclamation of the gospel of the 18th century, first in Britain and then in

America. From this perspective, the chief shortcoming of much so-called modern Protestant theology, and the corresponding preaching of the recent past, has been its obsessive preoccupation with proper *definitions* of Christianity instead of its espousal as a right *way* of being in relation to both God and neighbor.

As we have seen in previous chapters, such were the grounds of John Wesley's persistent, but in our time poorly comprehended, denial that the Christian religion is, or can be, comprised of "true opinions," that is, of "orthodoxy" of whatever species. Yet, it is hardly to be doubted that much so-called "evangelical" Protestantism in America today is scarcely more than a conglomerate mix of opinions, often inherited, sometimes acquired, and ardently propagated.

From the Wesleyan perspective, such Protestantism in its several varieties to an alarming extent promotes — for reasons of special interest, often of a secular and even nationalistic nature — various dogmatisms. These never derive from "experimental religion" in the Wesleyan sense, or from justification by grace through faith in the Pauline sense. Yet the latter, rediscovered by Luther, engendered the Reformation of the 16th century. At Smalcald, in 1537, Luther declared "justification by faith alone as the article of the standing or falling of the Church."[2] Wesley would agree, but add to it "holiness of heart and life," by grace enabled and by faith received. According to both Luther and the Wesleys, therefore, we do not have *bona fide* Christian evangelicalism until we begin at the point of acknowledged divine judgment upon our common sinful humanity.[3] In this, both Luther and Wesley agree with St. Paul: "Wretched man that I am! Who shall deliver me from the body of this death?" (Rom. 7:24). The Wesleys had learned by 1738 that without explicit consent to this as the starting point, the New Testament witness to the way of salvation in Christ is not heard in a way that saves.

From Thomas à Kempis onward, then, any evangelical Christianity may be suspected as phony unless it begins with the radical *compunction* of which St. Paul speaks, and has shared it. Thus, for à Kempis, Luther, and the Wesleys, only as the divine judgment upon sin is owned, rather than evaded, may saving renovation be followed with thanksgiving: "Thanks be to God, through Jesus Christ our Lord!" (Rom. 7:25). These views were integral to the original early Methodist witness, together with the "newness of life" that made for the "living faith" which, committed to "inward and outward holiness," works out a "final salvation" with "fear and trembling."

The sudden and astonishing, if belated, discovery by John and Charles Wesley in the Spring of 1738 that, indeed, just *this* is the case, was the beginning of Methodism as a religious movement of reformation in the English-speaking world. Its terse summation in the "Large Minutes," which we have previously stressed, deserves constant recall:

> In 1729, two young men, reading the Bible, saw they could not be saved without holiness, followed after it, and incited others to do so. In 1737 they saw holiness comes by faith. They saw likewise that men are justified before they are sanctified; but still holiness was their point.[4]

As we look, therefore, for original doctrinal standards in early Methodism in America, it seems in order to remember that these words were in fact the *first premise* of that "catechism" of the early Methodist preachers, namely, *The Minutes of Several Conversations Between Mr. Wesley and Others,* and this well into the early 19th century. Indeed, upon this document and *The Nature, Design, and General Rules of the United Societies* were based the several topics of the *Form of Discipline* and, after 1792, *The Doctrines and Discipline of the Methodist Episcopal Church.* On this basis primarily rests, from the start, the inseparability of doctrine and discipline in American Methodism. In the *Minutes* and the *General Rules,* discipline is explicitly formulated as the indispensable *instrumentality* for the formation of "inward and outward holiness" of life. The latter is defined by the doctrine as the *telos* or end-in-view. But the doctrine here referred to as the end-in-view is indistinguishable from Wesley's soteriology. So fully does the discipline advance the doctrine that it is, literally, presupposed by the latter.

Thus, we may properly claim that the message of early Wesleyan Methodism — its *doctrine* — in tandem with its instrumentality — its *discipline* — was the Wesleyan answer to the question of Romans 7:24: "Who [or what] will deliver me from this body of death?" Methodism was, in truth, a methodology with an end-in-view. It was a message of God's salvation through Christ, open to all without exceptions. It was, thus, set against traditional Calvinism from the first, as the "Large Minutes" openly declared: "When Satan could not otherwise hinder this, he threw Calvinism in the way."[5] This was to define Methodism eventually as anti-Calvinistic, or Arminian, in its doctrine of salvation by grace through faith. The testimony of Nathan Bangs on this point is as pertinent as it is authoritative:

> The doctrines, too, which they principally insisted upon, had a direct tendency to produce the desired effect upon the heart and life. . . . That which they pressed upon their hearers with the greatest earnestness was, the necessity of the new birth, and the privilege of a knowledge, by the witness of the Holy Spirit, of the forgiveness of

sins, through faith in the blood of Christ; and as a necessary consequence of this, and as naturally flowing from it, provided they persevered, holiness of heart and life. On this topic they dwelt with an emphasis and an earnestness peculiar to themselves.[6]

Here, plainly, are not only the two foci of the Wesleyan doctrinal ellipse — justification and Christian perfection — but also some of the coordinate themes we have identified as belonging to Wesley's experimental and practical divinity.

EXPERIMENTAL DIVINITY IN LOW PROFILE

It is to be hoped that this study has thrown enough light upon the substance and function of Wesley's experimental divinity to make more clear its central place in any serious discussion of original Methodist doctrinal standards. It is, however, somewhat remarkable how low a profile this "system of doctrine" has in the contemporary official documents of early American Methodism, such as the Conference *Minutes* (1773–1794), the *Form of Discipline* (1785–1789), or the *Doctrines and Discipline* (after 1792). That such a "system of doctrine" was functional and uniformly presupposed is the testimony of all remaining memoirs and biographies of the early period which we have attended. Of this we have seen intimate glimpses in the surviving witness of such worthies as William Watters, Freeborn Garrettson, Jesse Lee, Thomas Ware, and others.

In the introduction to his *History of the Methodist Episcopal Church*, first published in 1839, Nathan Bangs (whom all would concede to have been doctrinally a most knowledgeable Methodist leader of the earlier 19th century) refers no less than five times to the "system of doctrine" in the usage of the American Methodists as "experimental and practical religion."[7] In his introduction, Bangs aims to recount when, where, and how the Wesleyan "experimental and practical religion" supplemented, corrected, or enriched the state of Christian life and teaching in the colonies and, subsequently, after 1784, in the United States of America under the aegis of the Methodist Episcopal Church.

Regarding the fruits of such doctrinal preaching, exhortation, and teaching, the encomium of Thomas Ware for John Lambert — a man less than thirty years of age, whose death was reported at the Conference of 1787 — is illustrative:

> We had the record of the death of two young men who had fallen in the itinerant ranks, John Lambert and James Thomas. The former was a native of New Jersey, taken from the common walks of life. He

had in four years [since the Methodist Episcopal Church was organized] without . . . classical learning, or any regular theological training, actually attained an eminence in the pulpit which no ordinary man could reach by . . . any human means whatever. He was most emphatically a primitive Methodist preacher, preaching out of the pulpit as well as in it. The graces with which he was eminently adorned were: intelligence, innocence, and love.[8]

Here we are plainly in touch with the fruitions of "experimental religion" along with its practice. The same story is repeated in the case of Joseph Mitchell, who in 1798 began such a revival in the Vergennes Circuit of western Vermont that, two years later, Vermont had six circuits. During this revival, Elijah Hedding — who was to become, some thought, second to Asbury in the shaping of American Methodism in the early 19th century — was converted.[9] Such were facts that can be multiplied times without number in the message and work of the early American Methodist itinerant preachers. At the same time, the doctrine and message of these apostolic travelers of "the wilderness," had but modest, or only incidental, expression in the offical documents of the Church. Hence at mid-century David Holmes, editor of *The Methodist Preacher*, an important symposium of Methodist doctrine, could say in his preface:

> The theology of Wesley, and of those who have rallied under the standard that he raised . . . has ever been distinguished by its pure Scriptural character. . . . Their doctrine and motives are directly from the Scriptures. Their theme is the Gospel, plainly stated in its facts, doctrines, provisions, and results. They find no liberty to dilute the truth, or soften its severity, to render it more acceptable.[10]

That the "system of doctrine" of the Methodists had long been wanting formal and comprehensive statement, however, Holmes quite plainly understood. He supplied a partial explanation, and something of an apology. The sermons he published were by notable earlier and contemporary Methodist preachers, and are sufficiently representative of some topics of Christian doctrine to approximate a "system." But, while attention is given to both Christology and ecclesiology, the predominant doctrinal interest and discussion is the way of salvation. As a modest compendium of Methodist doctrine, the volume was probably without precedent on its publication in 1854. A year earlier, in 1853, the *Works* of Stephen Olin, the then late president of Wesleyan University, and, earlier, of Randolph Macon College, were published. Accounted a Methodist theological thinker of exceptional power in his time, Olin left discourses and sermons which do not resemble a "system," but in which he lauded "the great truths of revealed, experimental religion."[11]

SALIENT METHODIST DOCTRINE: THE PLAN OF SALVATION

If it is indeed the case, as David Holmes declared, that his Methodist forebears "rallied under the" doctrinal "standard" raised by Wesley, and that "their theme is the Gospel," then our special attention is required. It is very significant that the first sermon in Holmes' *The Methodist Preacher* is by Wilbur Fisk, late president of Wesleyan University. In "The Properties of the Law and the Gospel Distinguished," Fisk declares that "the term Gospel . . . is a proper name of this system of Grace," that is, "of salvation by Jesus Christ."[12] Fisk is saying here that the gospel long preached by Methodists, as he understands it, is identical with those doctrinal standards raised by Wesley and subsequently published abroad by Methodist preachers. Further, he is plainly implying that this Methodist gospel is not other than that portion of the theological encyclopedia known as soteriology, or doctrine of salvation.

Fisk's competence for this judgment is incontestable. Entering upon his ministry in 1818 and esteemed as a leading educator and theologian by his contemporaries, his representation of the meaning of the word "gospel" in prevailing Methodist usage must be credited. His discussion attributes a long-standing status to this usage, and this we have found verified in the surviving ministerial memoirs which we have examined from 1773 until the death of Francis Asbury and Jesse Lee in 1816. It is further to be noted that Fisk identifies himself with the "system" of Methodist doctrine he describes as primarily a soteriology, and at the same time represents its currency among his Methodist brethren as prevailing and unchallenged. It is significant that David Holmes takes no exception to this viewpoint in the preface to *The Methodist Preacher* in 1852, written thirteen years following the premature death of Wilbur Fisk in 1839. In these matters, one is reminded of Wesley's counsel to Freeborn Garrettson in 1785:

> It will be the wisest way to make all those who desire to join together, thoroughly acquainted with the whole Methodist plan. . . . Let none of them rest in being half Christians . . . as soon as any . . . find peace with God, to exhort them to go on to perfection.[13]

This is what Joseph Pilmore spoke of as "the plan of salvation" in his *Journal*, and William Watters called "the great salvation," by which he meant, "Christian perfection," as we have seen previously. When we put these findings together with the witness of Nathan Bangs, there seems to be a manifest consensus respecting the "gospel" preached by these early Methodists: quite evidently it was restatement of Wesley's "Scripture way of salvation." From the days of Pilmore, Watters, Robert Wiliams, and Jesse Lee, it was denominated "experimental religion."[14]

In the mid-19th century, according to such authors as Nathan Bangs, Wilbur Fisk, David Holmes, and Leroy Lee, there was still an identifiable consensus on Methodist doctrinal standards which are, collectively considered, mainly a soteriology. It was understood as a Methodist "system of doctrine," however, which was deemed complete in three respects: first, it was entirely biblical; second, it was a complete plan of salvation; and third, it had been verified as true in the experience of thousands and for them, therefore, was self-authenticating. Indeed, Nathaniel Lee had so testified, precipitating thereby a crisis in the life of his son Jesse.[15] For Nathan Bangs, the reality of the forgiveness of sins, or justification, and of "holiness of heart and life," on condition of perseverance under God's grace, were matters of fact for honest observation:

> From all these facts — and that they are facts is attested by every person who is at all acquainted with our history — we conclude that this work was eminently the work of God. Who is to say it was not?[16]

The Methodist system of doctrine, then, recognized primarily as soteriology under the Wesleyan caption, the "Scripture way of salvation," was so general a consensus as to be the *rule of faith* in early American Methodism. As such it was acknowledged without argument by all representatives of the first generation whom we know from their memoirs or journals. Such literature as we possess from the early decades of the 19th century shows no departure or deviation from this *rule of faith*. However, it remains a fact that, apart from the writings of such authors as Bangs, Fisk, Holmes, Leroy Lee, Moses M. Henkle, and some episcopal addresses to the General Conference, doctrinal summations of the Methodist system of doctrine, or of "experimental and practical divinity," are scarce.

This may be due to the remarkable degree to which these Methodist preachers were familiar with the key writings of John Wesley. The purpose of those writings was not for instruction, but as a methodology of salvation; not for enlightenment, but for assimilation; not for optional response, but as the map of the way unto the great salvation for self and "precious souls," for which these were the rules of the road. Had not all Methodist preachers been coached in detail by Wesley's "Large Minutes," the crowning admonition of which was that "it is not your business to preach so many times, and to take care of this or that society; . . . but to bring as many sinners as you possibly can to repentance; and to build them up in that holiness without which no one will see the Lord"?[17] Wesley does not, therefore, relieve the preacher of responsibility for doctrinal instruction, he enjoins it: "If a man understand the fundamentals, speak what you perceive he most needs, either explaining further some doctrines, or some duty. . . ."[18] And as for the "fundamentals," Wesley, with variations, repeatedly marshalls them for prompt comprehension in the "Large Minutes." They cluster about the two foci: "Repentance toward God, and faith in our Lord Jesus Christ," and "holiness without which they cannot see the Lord."[19]

While Francis Asbury exercised leadership in the Methodist Episcopal Church, it is all but certain that all youthful Methodist preachers were, so to speak, raised on certain pivotal writings of John Wesley, among them the "Large Minutes"; for it was these that were employed by Coke and Asbury to order the *Form of Discipline* in 1785 and, subsequently, the *Doctrines and Discipline* beginning in 1792. These *Minutes of Several Conversations Between the Reverend Mr. Wesley and Others*, published in several successive editions from 1744 to 1789, were the preacher's "law and gospel" in America from 1773 onward. And two other works by Wesley were of major significance in a Methodist preacher's curriculum: *The Character of a Methodist* and *The Principles of a Methodist* (1742). The former was first in the list of books studied by Jesse Lee prior to his admission to Conference membership in 1779.[20] We noted in chapter 1 that the Conference of 1781 under Francis Asbury asked: "Ought not the Preachers often to read the *rules* of the Societies, the character of a Methodist, and the plain account [of Christian Perfection]?" To this question the answer was, of course, "Yes."[21]

This was the Conference which followed the narrowly avoided schism between Virginia and Maryland preachers and those northward, loyal to Asbury, in the controversy over the use of the sacraments. This Conference, according to John Dickens, editor of the *Minutes*, began with the decisive question:

> What Preachers are now determined, after mature consideration, close observation, and earnest prayer, to preach *the old Methodist doctrine*, and strictly enforce the discipline, as contained in the *Notes*, *Sermons*, and *Minutes*, as published by Mr. Wesley?[22]

Here once more we find evidence of the close coordination of doctrine and discipline. The phrase "the old Methodist doctrine" recalls the closing line of *The Character of a Methodist*, where Wesley acknowledges, to those who have come to understand "the marks of a true Methodist," as he names them, that it is nothing else than "the plain, old Christianity that I teach."[23]

This was Wesley's invariably affirmed "Scripture way of salvation," the soteriology exegeted from the New Testament, or his "experimental and practical divinity." It cannot be doubted that it was known and entertained as axiomatic in status by the Methodist preachers in Britain or America. That this was the case from 1773 onward through the founding of The Methodist Episcopal Church in 1784 and well into the 19th century is clear from the evidence presented thus far.

It is well known that Wesley's writings entered the colonies with Robert Williams in 1771. After 1785, editions of Wesley's writings appeared regularly from the press of the Book Concern. The story of Bishop Elijah Hedding's youthful conversion under Joseph Mitchell in 1798 is inseparable from the solicitious coaching of a Mrs. Bushnell, a former Congregationalist of Canaan, Connecticut, who welcomed the Wesleyan message of "salvation for all." She not only supplied young Elijah with some of Wesley's writings, but also made him public reader in the "class" over which she informally presided at the time of the arrival of the first Methodist itinerant preacher, Joseph Mitchell, in western Vermont.[24]

In addition to the surprisingly ready availability of the Wesleyan writings following 1785, due in great part to John Dickens, Book Editor — whose early death in 1798 was lamentable — we must credit both the classes and quarterly meetings of early Methodism for fostering and sustaining a well-defined "oral tradition" regarding the substance of what Nathan Bangs called the Wesleyan "experimental and practical religion."[25] Other things being more or less equal on the advancing frontier of American life, the observations of Leroy Lee strongly suggest that the Methodist "class-meeting," held under appointed and superintended leadership, provided for the Methodists a species of catechetical schools with corporate discipline and nurturing. This in great part accounted for, not alone the piety, but also the impressive doctrinal conversancy of Methodist people far into the 19th century. The vitality of the class in the Methodist connection was beginning to wane, however, by the measure of earlier performance, in the 1840s.

OF DOCTRINE COME TO LIFE IN *THE CHARACTER OF A METHODIST*

Two additional factors may have contributed to what we have described as a low profile of doctrinal consensus in early American Methodism. One of these has been our finding in these studies of experimental divinity, especially in chapter 2, that the truth of doctrine for the Wesleys is inseparable from the experience of saving grace, either in justification by faith, or in the sanctifying work of the Holy Spirit in the disciplined life of Christian perfection-in-process. A corollary is that, on principle, experimental and practical divinity — considered as a way of defining the methodology of saving faith — does not expect full validation of its theses or tenets apart from confirmation of the same in personal experience.

In some measure, therefore, experimental divinity, in addition to its descriptive function, is an invitation to all to claim the promises of God in Scripture. In some respects, accordingly, it is exhortation of persons to openness to God's justifying and sanctifying grace, as St. Paul always said, "through Jesus Christ our Lord." It is, perhaps, for this reason that John Wesley could regard his sermons as proclamation and exhortation but also as a compendium of doctrine. Practically all his sermons are promptings to decision, that is, to an appropriate response to prevenient grace as the Holy Spirit's working, according to a plan of salvation.

A second consideration of importance is elusive and rarely attended. It is intimately related to Wesley's twofold conception of the way of salvation; that is, embracing both justification by grace through faith, and the full renovation by grace of the subject of "living faith," who endeavors after entire sanctification of life in likeness to Christ. On this matter, we need to think of an ongoing dialogue between Wesley and Thomas à Kempis on the subject of the imitation of Christ. Wesley fully recognized this to be grounded in the Pauline gospel. It was Paul who exhorted the Corinthians: "Be imitators of me, as I am of Christ" (1 Cor. 11:1). We shall not be able to comprehend the role of Christian perfection in Wesley's experimental and practical divinity unless we grasp fully the import of Wesley's line in *The Character of a Methodist*: "By salvation he [a Methodist] means holiness of heart and life."[26] We have already noted how this phrase is recurrent in Nathan Bangs' various summations of distinctive Methodist doctrine.

To state the matter plainly, Wesley learned from St. Paul that it is more important that the truths of the "Scripture way of salvation" be embodied than that they merely be verbally professed. Further, Wesley learned from both St. Paul and the Homilies of the Church of England that unless these truths are embodied, that is, become constitutive of the "character" of a Christian, one can never attain more than nominal status as a Christian.[27] Wesley remembered the peroration of the Homily "Of Faith":

> A man may deceive himself, and think in his own phantasy that he by faith knoweth God, loveth him, feareth him, and belongeth to him, when in very deed he doeth nothing less [less than nothing]. For the trial of all these things is a very godly and Christian life.[28]

And *The Character of a Methodist* echoes with these further words from the Homily:

> Therefore, as you profess the name of Christ, good Christian people, let no phantasy and imagination of faith at any time beguile you: but be sure of your faith; try it by your living; look upon the fruits that cometh of it; mark the increase of love and charity by it toward God and your neighbor; and so shall you perceive it to be a true lively faith.[29]

In sections 1–16 of *The Character of a Methodist*, Wesley enumerates the multiple aspects of the "holiness of heart and life" whence comes salvation. Such is a summation of the second great work of grace, or "Christian perfection." Justification is presupposed in this essay. In section 17 comes the important summation with which, on the evidence, the early American preachers were uniformly familiar:

> These are the *principles* and *practices* of our sect; these are the marks of a true Methodist. *By these alone do those who are in derision so called, desire to be distinguished from other men.*[30]

Perhaps Wesley points to a doctrinal core? That matter I pass by for the moment to call attention to Wesley's statement that the enumerated "marks" of a "true Methodist" consist of both "principles and practices." Here is a pairing of great importance. "Principles" are for "practice," not alone for profession or declaration. Principles are not simply matters for belief and profession; they are for enactment in life, to become ingredients of Christian character. Wesley thus continues with the famous hypothetical observation:

> If any man say, "Why, these are only *the common fundamental principles of Christianity!*" thou hast said; so I mean; this is the very truth; I know they are no other; and I would to God both thou and all men knew, that I, and all who follow my judgment, do vehemently refuse to be distinguished from other men, by any other than the common principles of Christianity, — *the plain old Christianity that I teach*. . . .[31]

If, then, in *The Character of a Methodist*, Wesley has provided a summation of "the common fundamental principles of Christianity," two observations need to be made for the purposes of the current study. The first observation is that, by his own testimony, Wesley, in this tract or essay, has supplied us with a summation of those principles which belong to his doctrine of salvation so far as it is understood by his phrase "holiness of heart and life." This, in addition to "Christian perfection," necessarily also embraces justification by grace through faith, since the *Minutes of Several Conversations* make it clear that in 1737 the Wesleys saw that "holiness comes by faith" and that "men are justified before they are sanctified."[32] From this we conclude two things: (1) that *The Character of a Methodist* is a summation of Wesley's doctrine of salvation, or soteriology, and (2) that the *principles* of Christianity, according to Wesley, must be *practiced* if there is to be formation of Christian character, i.e., the character of a true Methodist.

The second observation is closely related to the first. Having affirmed that it is "the plain old Christianity" that he teaches, Wesley makes a statement so important that it must be quoted in full, since it is a summation of the character of a real Christian as Wesley reads Scripture:

> And whosoever *is* what I preach (let him be called what he will, for names change not the nature of things), he is a Christian, not in name only, *but in heart and life.* He is inwardly and outwardly conformed to the will of God, as revealed in the written word. He thinks, speaks, and lives, *according to the method laid down in the revelation of Jesus Christ.* His soul is renewed after the image of God, in righteousness and in all true holiness. And having the mind that was in Christ, he so walks as Christ also walked.[33]

There is, I suspect, no statement in all of Wesley's writings that more synoptically defines "Christian perfection," or "holiness of heart and life," or "final salvation." In this statement of salvation and its nature there is nothing exceptional to Wesley's prevailing views. In *The Farther Appeal to Men of Reason and Religion*, Wesley makes holiness as "renewal of our souls in the image of God" and "recovery of the divine nature" to be "synonymous" with "salvation." Holiness, in this sense, is "the thing itself," says Wesley.[34] Obviously, this recalls the Pauline "prize of the upward call of God in Christ Jesus" (Phil. 2:14), as well as Paul's exhortation: "What you have learned and received and heard and seen in me, do; and the God of peace will be with you" (Phil. 4:9). For Wesley as for Paul, the truth of the gospel is for enactment in life as well as recitation in word.

Just this stress is found in Wesley's statement that "whosoever is what I preach . . . is a Christian not in name only, but in heart and life." It could hardly be plainer that, for Wesley, the difference between nominal Christianity — "in name only" — and the real thing is the creed in flesh and blood, the incarnation of the Word. It is *principles* in *practice* in "the character of a Methodist." In my judgment, this accounts powerfully for the low profile of doctrinal utterance in early American Methodism. There can be no doubt that the early Methodist preachers, from Francis Asbury to Jesse Lee, estimated their Christianity by its vitality in their lives.

With this we have uncovered the grounds for the major premise of these studies in Wesleyan experimental and practical divinity: *that for the Wesleys and for the early Methodists in America, before and after 1784, doctrine is of little worth, in and of itself, unless — first, last and always — it is verified in experience and becomes more and more radiant in a Christian life.* The most convincing profession of the Christian religion Wesley learned from Paul and the Homilies is that of a fully formed Christian character — hopefully even the character of a Methodist. "By salvation," says Wesley, the Methodist means "holiness of heart and life." This is what Wesley means by Christian perfection. Here, it may be, is the true doctrinal standard.

How far afield is John Wesley in this from the manifest teaching of the Collect for Christmas Day of The Book of Common Prayer, which was quoted at the beginning of this chapter? Does the Collect not teach that, as Christ Jesus took upon himself our nature, for our salvation, so are we, being regenerate by justifying grace through the working of the Holy Spirit, to be daily renewed in the likeness of Christ? And are not here present, in addition to the Pauline teaching of "recapitulation," the two pillars of Wesley's "experimental divinity," namely, justification and Christian perfection? Undoubtedly, Wesley thought so. A like teaching certainly was current among the American Methodists well into the second quarter of the 19th century.

And so, in the final analysis, the "creed" is, as it were, the truly Christian life; and, conversely, the true Christian is, analogically, the self-authenticating Christian "creed." Such is, in fact, the "low profile" of "dogmatics" in Wesleyan "experimental divinity," however paradoxical this may seem. "Dogmatics" becomes significant for Wesley, in other words, only in "the character of a Methodist" (or any *bona fide* Christian). So far, Wesley is utterly in agreement with Thomas à Kempis.

CHAPTER 10

DOCTRINAL STANDARDS IN EARLY AMERICAN METHODISM, 1773–1794

DOCTRINE AND DISCIPLINE IN A SUCCESSION

George J. Stevenson, in "A Brief History of Methodism," observes that the Leeds Conference of 1769 was memorable for two things in particular. The first was the sending of Richard Boardman and Joseph Pilmore as "the first regular Methodist preachers in America." The second was Wesley's drawing up of a threefold Covenant of Union with the travelling preachers respecting procedures to be followed in the event of his death. This was to be read at three successive Conferences and signed by each preacher till all had done so.[1] The three *desiderata* agreed to and subscribed by all signers were:

> I. To devote ourselves entirely to God; denying ourselves, taking up our cross daily, steadily aiming at one thing, to save our own souls, and them that hear us. II. To preach *the old Methodist doctrines, and no other*, contained in the Minutes of the Conferences. III. To observe and enforce *the whole Methodist discipline*, laid down in the said Minutes.[2]

The first proposition reaffirms the presiding purpose of the Wesleyan preaching staff to advance the work of the United Societies, and affirms its cruciform nature and objective. The second and third propositions unite *doctrine* and *discipline*, or the *order* of salvation and the *way* thereof. Here is witnessed that closeness of doctrine and discipline that we found Freeborn Garrettson affirming to John Wesley in 1785.

And here also is found the historical antecedent for a position taken by the "preachers in connection with the Rev. Mr. John Wesley" in America, meeting at Choptank, Delaware, on April 16, 1781. It was but one year since, at the southern Conference at Manakintown, Virginia, the threatening division between the American Methodists

145

over the administration of the sacraments was narrowly avoided on grounds none could deny was of a divine leading.[3] Now at the Conference of 1781, appeal was made once more to the Covenant of Union of the 1769 Conference at Leeds, England. In a new context it became the basis of an open agreement among the American preachers "to preach *the old Methodist doctrine*, and strictly enforce the *discipline*, as contained in the notes, sermons, and minutes, as published by Mr. Wesley."[4]

Francis Asbury had attended the Leeds Conference in 1769. In 1781 he was Wesley's sole surviving Assistant in the colonies, all the others, including Rankin and Shadford, having left for Canada or returned to England. There is no doubt at all that the principles of "close union" and collegial fellowship among the early American preachers were, now under Asbury, adopted wholly from Wesley's Covenant of Union with his preachers in Britain of 1769 — the very year Boardman and Pilmore had begun their ministry in Philadelphia and New York. At the subsequent Conference, on April 17, 1782, in Sussex County, Virginia, this question was asked: "Do the brethren in conference unanimously choose Brother Asbury to act according to Mr. Wesley's original appointment, and preside over the American Conferences and the whole work?" The question was answered in the affirmative by all those present.[5] By this action of the Conference, Asbury was vindicated in his fidelity to the tradition represented by the 1769 Covenant of Union. Likewise, two vital principles — "the old Methodist doctrines" and "discipline" — were affirmed by corporate action of the assembled American preachers.

At the Conference of 1784, for the second time, another question arose: "How shall we conduct ourselves towards European preachers?" Because the answer has a direct bearing upon doctrinal standards, it is here quoted in full:

> If they are recommended by Mr. Wesley, will be subject to the American Conference, preach the doctrine taught in the four volumes of Sermons and Notes on the New Testament, keep the circuits they are appointed to, follow the directions of the London and American *Minutes*, and be subject to Francis Asbury as General Assistant, whilst he stands approved by Mr. Wesley, and the Conference, we will receive them; but if they walk contrary to the above directions, no ancient right of appointment shall prevent their being excluded from our connection.[6]

This succession of documents provides a clear indication that the criterion of doctrinal acceptability as between preachers under Wesley in Britain and those in America — also in connection with Mr. Wesley

— was very much the same. This, as our studies have made manifest, was attributable in great part to the fidelity of Wesley's delegated Assistants to Wesleyan doctrines and discipline. With these they were entrusted as emissaries of Wesley, and, therewith, of the "Scripture way of salvation." In the case of none in the period 1769–1784, from Boardman and Pilmore, Robert Williams and John King, to Rankin and Shadford — and one may include even the earliest volunteers, Embury, Webb, and Strawbridge — was there deviation or departure from "the old Methodist doctrines" or discipline save on the matter of the sacraments.

Nor should it be forgotten that the American Conference of 1782, in Sussex County, Virginia, acknowledged obligation and gratitude to Devereux Jarrett for his "kind and friendly services to preachers and people" and advised preachers in the South "to consult with him and take his advice in the absence of Brother Asbury."[7] Jarrett was at one with the Methodists, and notably with George Shadford, on doctrine and discipline. He knew John Wesley personally and corresponded with him. As we have seen earlier, Jarrett was committed to "experimental religion" as the gospel way of salvation.[8] This was well known to William Watters, Jesse Lee, Freeborn Garrettson, and indeed to all of the native American preachers of the early years.

THE OLD METHODIST DOCTRINES

The second mark of fidelity to the Covenant of Union set forth by Wesley in 1769 was, "To preach the old Methodist doctrines, and no other, contained in the Minutes of the Conferences." The final paragraph of the *Minutes* for the Leeds Conference states that the preachers "desired Mr. W. to extract the most material part of the *Minutes*, and send a copy to each Assistant, which he might communicate to all the Preachers in his Circuit."[9]

Wesley's phrase "contained in the *Minutes* of the Conferences" seems best interpreted broadly and so to include not only the *Minutes* of the various annual Conferences — which recurrently do contain both doctrinal and disciplinary matter of importance — but also the *Minutes of Several Conversations Between Mr. Wesley and Others*, or "Large Minutes" (1744–1789), and the earlier *Minutes of Some Late Conversations Between Mr. Wesley and Others* (1744–1747). The *Minutes of Several Conversations* are concerned primarily, though not exclusively, with disciplinary matters, while the *Minutes of Some Late Conversations* are concerned exclusively with doctrine.

The latter undertake to answer the question "What to teach?" and deal searchingly with what we have called the two chief pillars of Wesley's "experimental and practical divinity."[10] They also discuss the nature of faith, of repentance, divine assurance, Christ in believers as the mark of "living faith," and sanctification towards "inward and outward holiness." This approximates but does not quite embrace the full range of topics we have found inherent in Wesley's experimental and practical divinity. With the "Large Minutes" added, it is possible to regard "the old Methodist doctrines" as duly represented collectively in the *Minutes* of the several "Conferences" between "the Rev. Mr. John Wesley and others."

It is important to note the limitation stated by Wesley: "To preach the old Methodist doctrines, *and no others*." Methodist doctrines for preaching are here recongnized as *plural*. But we need to ask just what is meant by the phrase, "the old Methodist doctrines." This phrase recalls others appearing in the Wesleys' writings. Not unlike it are such phrases as "plain, old Bible Christianity," or "Bible-Christians,"[11] or "the plain old Christianity that I teach," or "the common fundamental principles of Christianity."[12] In the *Minutes of Several Conversations*, the doctrine of "the old Methodists" is identified with Christian perfection or entire sanctification seen as a work of God's grace, through faith, in this present life.[13] As we have seen, Christian perfection is the end-in-view of salvation, which has its indispensable start with justification. And these, together, are the pillars of the Methodist "plan of salvation."

The adjective "old" provides in fact some clue to Wesley's view of so-called Methodist doctrine. The adjective was functional from the time when Welsey recovered from the 1547 Homilies of the Church of England an understanding, as he says, "that justification by faith was the doctrine of the Church, as well as of the Bible."[14] This statement comes from Wesley's *Short History of Methodism*, in which he recalls the unfolding of early Methodism following upon the "conversion" of Charles and of himself in May, 1738. He continues:

> As soon as they believed, they spake; salvation by faith being now their standing topic. Indeed this implied three things: (1) That men are all, by nature, "dead in sin," and, consequently, "children of wrath." (2) That they are "justified by faith alone." (3) That faith produces inward and outward holiness: And these points they insisted on day and night. In a short time they became popular Preachers. The congregations were large wherever they preached. The former name was then revived; and all these gentlemen, with their followers, were entitled Methodists.[15]

In this self-exposure, Wesley has, in a measure, opened the way to a more defined summation of "the old Methodist doctrines." It was justification by grace through faith; but it was also the recovery in experience of the "living faith" taught by Cranmer in the first four Homilies and *recapitulated*, as we have seen, in the *experience* of both Wesleys and, thereafter, in multitudes of persons who became doers as well as hearers of the Word.

In my view, the most perceptive contemporary testimony to this "living faith" is found in Wesley's *Journal*, in the form of a statement, not by John Wesley himself, but by a hearer. It derives from a letter sent him by the Rev. Josiah Tucker, Vicar of All Saints, Bristol. Tucker went to hear Wesley preach in the fields at Bradford on October 23, 1739, in order to ascertain firsthand the nature of Wesleyan doctrine.[16] He was a discerning clergyman, capable of critical revision of his own opinions. Tucker's letter is not only a recantation of his conceded misunderstanding of Wesley and Wesley's teaching concerning justification by faith only as the doctrine of Christ, the Apostles, and the Church of England, but also the best extant synoptic account of "the old Methodist doctrines" by a competent outsider of the period:

> Man is by nature a sinner, the child of the devil, under God's wrath, in a state of damnation. The Son of God took pity on this our misery. He made himself man, he made himself sin for us — that is, he hath borne the punishment of our sin; "the chastisement of our peace was upon him, and by his stripes we are healed." To receive this boundless mercy, this inestimable benefit, we must have faith in our Benefactor, and through him in God. But then, true faith is not a lifeless principle, as your adversaries seem to understand it. *They and you mean quite another thing by faith. They mean, a bare believing that Jesus is the Christ. You mean, a living, growing purifying principle, which is the root both of inward and outward holiness; both of purity and good works; without which no man can have faith — at least no other than a dead faith.*
>
> This, Sir, you explained in your sermon at Bradford, Sunday, October 28, to near ten thousand people, who all stood to hear you with awful silence and great attention. I have since reflected how much good the clergy might do, if, instead of shunning, they would come to hear and converse with you; and in their churches and parishes would farther enforce those catholic doctrines which you preach, and which, I am glad to see, have such a surprising good effect on great numbers of souls.[17]

Tucker's letter witnesses that Wesley was preaching "the old Methodist doctrines" as early as 1739. Wesley published the letter without comment. None was needed; an honest and perceptive cleric had spoken. Although there undoubtedly were variations in emphasis, the core content of Methodist preaching well into the 19th century, both in Britain and in America, was "the old Methodist doctrines" so well summarized by Tucker. When Francis Asbury signed the Wesleyan Covenant of Union in 1769, well before his departure for the colonies in 1771, that action unquestionably signified his personal and lifelong commitment to "the old Methodist doctrines." Nothing we know of him, his message, his labors, or his discipline would suggest exceptions to this proposition.

An important corollary comes to focus in the Wesleyan conception of "true Christian faith," which Josiah Tucker has in part greatly illuminated. It recalls the definition of faith for which Wesley was indebted both to Peter Böhler and to Cranmer's Homily "Of Salvation," from which he quotes in *The Principles of a Methodist*:

> For the true Christian faith is, not only to believe that the Holy Scripture and the articles of our faith are true; but also to have "a sure trust and confidence to be saved from everlasting damnation by Christ," whereof doth follow a loving heart to obey his commandments. And this faith neither any devil hath, nor any wicked man. No ungodly man hath or can have this "sure trust and confidence in God, that by the merits of Christ his sins are forgiven, and he reconciled to the favour of God."[18]

As we have already seen in chapters 3 and 6, Wesley frequently quotes these passages from the Homilies after 1738. It is easy, however, to miss their point, to which Methodist preaching and doctrinal interpretation for more than a century is eloquent witness. It is this experience of a "sure trust and confidence" of sins forgiven, that is of justification, "whereof doth follow a loving heart to obey his [Christ's] commandments," that was in Wesley's view the distinguishing mark of "living faith" as taught, not by the Articles, but by the Homilies of the Church of England. And it was this "living and true faith" of the Homilies which manifested a "present salvation." This present salvation, learned first from Peter Böhler and confirmed by the Homilies, came to pass as a personal realization for the Wesleys in May, 1738. Thereafter they claimed it as a "promise" of Scripture: "because by faith we embrace the promise of God's mercy [in Christ] and of remission of sins, therefore the Scripture says, that faith does justify, yea, faith without works."[19] Living faith, for Wesley, is claiming God's promised mercy through Jesus Christ. It is promise faithfully received *now*. Therefore, it is *present salvation*. It is transformation of life, "new birth."[20]

The "old Methodist doctrines and no other," that Wesley prescribed to be preached in the Covenant of Union of 1769, include this dimension of the transformation of human existence by God's grace working through the Holy Spirit. In his answer to the Rev. Henry Stebbling's *A Caution Against Religious Delusion* (1739), Wesley gives a memorable description of the actualization of "living faith" in experience as the sign of transformation of inward life (again quoting from the Homilies):

> *To believe in Christ* [is] . . . not only an assent to the Articles of our Creed, but also "a true trust and confidence of the mercy of God through our Lord Jesus Christ."
>
> Now this it is certain a man may want, although he can truly say, "I am sober; I am just in my dealings; I help my neighbor, and use the ordinances of God." And, however such a man may have behaved in these respects, he is not to think well of his own state till he experiences something within himself which he has not yet experienced, but which he may beforehand be assured he shall, if the promises of God are true. That *something* is a living faith, "a sure trust and confidence in God that, by the merits of Christ, his sins are forgiven, and he reconciled to the favour of God." And from this will spring many other things, which till then he experienced not; as, the love of God shed abroad in his heart, the peace of God which passeth all understanding, and joy in the Holy Ghost. . . .[21]

This passage from Wesley's *Journal* illustrates his principle of verification in matters of doctrine. There is, Wesley allows, "sound divinity" where such matters are "agreeable both to Scripture and experience."[22] In this proposition, as previously discussed in chapter 2, is surely the foundation principle of "experimental religion." This is to say that, for Wesley, the validity of the New Testament gospel — the "Scripture way of salvation" — is verified fully only in experience, first, of regeneration and new birth, and second, by enlarging holiness of heart and life that becomes manifest outwardly in "fruits of the Spirit."

It becomes rather plain, then, what Wesley meant by the injunction incumbent upon all "to preach the old Methodist doctrines, and no other" in the Covenant of Union of 1769 — an injunction reasserted under Asbury at the Delaware Conference of 1781. These "old Methodist doctrines" cannot be distinguished from what we have in these studies described as Wesley's "experimental and practical divinity." Indeed, it is evident that precisely this "divinity" dominates the *Minutes* of the several Conferences of Wesley with others over the years 1744–1789. It is their quite distinctive doctrinal aim and stress. This is true also of the *Journal*, both *Appeals*, *The Principles of a Methodist*, and *The Character of a Methodist* as, manifestly, of Wesley's *Sermons*.

Thus, the findings of these studies concerning so-called *doctrinal standards* in early American Methodism are clear. The American itinerants of the first generation, 1773 to 1794, were doctrinally bred and nurtured on Wesley's "experimental and practical divinity." This they knew mainly as "experimental religion," or "heart-religion," or "the plan of salvation"; and they knew it always and only as the effectual working of the preventing grace of the Holy Spirit. Its currency was already evident in 1771 in the utterly Wesleyan comment of Nathaniel Lee, in the presence of his son, Jesse, that, "if a man's sins were forgiven him, he would know it."[23] This was, indeed, a watchword of the Wesleyan doctrine of "present salvation," although its source for Nathaniel Lee could well have been George Whitefield.

It was under the doctrinal umbrella of the experience of "present salvation" that doctrinal standards gradually acquired their identity in American Methodism. In a word, the *standard* was and had been "experimental religion," realized in its several aspects in living personal experience. Because of their unavoidable reference to this living personal experience of "saving faith," all doctrinal standards in early American Methodism were, in a sense, *ex post facto*. It was, probably, only as this experimental *prius* began to fade that the Twenty-Five Articles of Religion began to acquire place of particular interest. This sequence — the gradual ascendency of the creed as a defense of orthodoxy — had been the case from the third century of Christianity. What serves well enough as the rule of faith in the context of living and vital Christian community, resolves in its recession into "the Creed," and "orthodoxy" is born.

As the Wesleys discovered between 1735 and 1739, orthodoxy is mainly assent to pious opinions, usually received secondhand. They perceived that with the rise of such orthodoxy, doxology, or the glad witness to present salvation, has already retreated in the face of evidently needed and, at length, insistent concern for careful definition, quite as Thomas à Kempis had warned. This is to say, in the idiom of John Wesley, that the declaratory articles of faith, inherited and entertained at second- or thirdhand, presume to fill the place of "living faith" as Cranmer taught it and quite to dismiss "the character of a Methodist" as necessary for salvation.

In short, the Wesleys saw that in this manner, through the ages, "living faith" comes to take the shape of orthodoxy, and that the latter contentedly rests with the form without the power of godliness. As the Wesleys came to see, orthodoxy is a reputable and subtle process by which onetime "living faith" can properly be honored, even revered, without being shared. Yet to suggest, as some have done for long and others of late, that this translation to "orthodoxy" happened as soon as American Methodism became the Methodist Episcopal Church in

1784, by the espousal of the Twenty-Five Articles of Religion as chief doctrinal standards, is, I judge, badly to "get ahead of the game," as the saying is, as well as to be inexcusably ahistorical and ignorant of both the nature and history of doctrine.

OF DOCTRINE AND DISCIPLINE

The third proposition invoked by Wesley in his 1769 Covenant of Union enjoined "discipline" as well as "the old Methodist doctrines." It was "To observe and enforce *the whole Methodist discipline, laid down in the said Minutes*."[24] The meaning of "discipline" in Wesley's usage is not transparently clear, because his usage is broad and less than carefully defined. Yet it is not broad enough to embrace what "discipline" came to signify, perhaps necessarily, after the United Societies became churches, either in Britain or America. As Wesley used the term it did include instructions and rules for the labor of preachers and Assistants, as well as the *General Rules*, but it had little to do with ecclesiastical structures, orders of ministry, ordination, or liturgy and sacraments. Certainly it had nothing to say of Church boards or agencies, or the kind of educational and mission programs which unfolded in the 19th century It did, to be sure, include the order and administration of the Societies for their primary purpose: "to reform the nation, particularly the Church; and to spread scriptural holiness over the land."[25] In the Wesleyan sense of the term, therefore, "discipline" meant primarily the guidance of the Societies, with their classes and bands, as instruments of Christian nurture. For these ends, both exhorting and preaching were essential means for the salvation of souls.

The *Minutes of Several Conversations*, in referring to "God's design in raising up the preachers called Methodists," disavowed any intention "to form any new Sect."[26] When, much later, the formation of a new Church in fact occurred, at the Christmas Conference of 1784, the conception of discipline was to undergo not only vast expansion but radical transformation. More and more, discipline was to become concerned primarily with matters of ecclesiastical management. As this advanced, its original centerpiece, as conceived by Wesley in 1743, *The Nature, Design, and General Rules of the United Societies*, became less and less central. This development was not intentional, to be sure, but was perhaps inevitable, as ecclesiastical organization and management increasingly competed with the original objective — the salvation of souls. Eventually the built-in competition between ecclesiastical self-maintenance and the Wesleyan objective — human salvation — was, more and more, to obscure that objective. Every human system tends always to become its own end or sufficient reason for being. It is the law of institutional inertia, which is accompanied by a tendency for the operators of the system also to become their own sufficient reason for being. Such indeed was the case, it is widely acknowledged, with the 18th-century clergy of the Church of England who, hostile to trespass upon their domain, were chief foes of the Wesleyan Revival.

For Wesley, discipline was conceived as an instrument for the advance of "God's design in raising up the preachers called Methodists," namely (to state it once more), "to reform the nation, particularly the Church; and to spread scriptural holiness over the land." When Thomas Coke and Francis Asbury in *A Form of Discipline, for the Ministers, Preachers, and Members of the Methodist Episcopal Church in America* (1785) addressed the membership, they adopted, with some variation, this stated design as that of the new Church. "We believe," they declared, "that God's design in raising up the preachers called Methodists, in America, was to reform the continent, and spread Scripture holiness over these lands."[27] Unlike Wesley, their aspiration could hardly be to reform the Church of England but, voluntarily, to be the church in a land which, by constitutional provision, had banned ecclesiastical establishment on principle.

The newly formed Methodist Episcopal Church did in fact, however, incorporate virtually "the whole Methodist discipline, laid down in the said Minutes," that is, of the Conferences under Wesley in conversation with others. Of this matter, three things are but poorly comprehended. First, "the Methodist discipline," as it was conceived by Wesley, was and is summarized in the *Minutes of Several Conversations Between the Rev. Mr. Wesley and Others* (1744–1789), printed in several editions through 1789. Second, these *Minutes of Several Conversations*, early called the "Large Minutes," were the model employed by Coke and Asbury for the first *Discipline* of The Methodist Episcopal Church, published in 1785 as *Minutes of Several Conversations Between the Rev. Thomas Coke and the Rev. Francis Asbury and Others. At a Conference, Begun in Baltimore, Maryland, On Monday, the 27th of December, 1784. Composing A Form of Discipline For the Ministers, Preachers, and Other Members of the Methodist Episcopal Church In America.*[28] Third, the *Discipline* of the new Church continued to be published through 1791 under the title *A Form of Discipline* until, with the General Conference of 1792, a volume under the title *The Doctrines and Discipline of the Methodist Episcopal Church* replaced it as the eighth edition. This title remained unchanged through 1964. Beginning in 1968, the title became *The Book of Discipline of the United Methodist Church*, leaving open the surmise, perhaps, that discipline might now suffice for doctrine in the church. However, by action of the General Conference of 1972, a quadrennial report of the General Conference Commission on Doctrinal Standards was received and adopted as Part II of *The Book of Discipline*, under the title "On Doctrine and Doctrinal Statements."

At present, our primary concern is to understand the significance of the fact that "the whole Methodist discipline," as laid down in the "Large Minutes," was in fact not just incorporated in the earliest *Form of Discipline* of the American Church in 1785 but comprized its structure and most of its substance. This matter has not been adequately explored even by John J. Tigert, who discovered the fact, and Dr. Frank Baker, in his fine and much updated *From Wesley to Asbury: Studies in Early American Methodism*, has hardly scratched the surface.[29]

Throughout these studies, I have frequently urged and supplied evidence for the judgment that, for John Wesley, separation or divorce of doctrine and discipline is not possible by all the canons of "experimental and practical divinity." In that perspective, discipline serves doctrine for its incarnation in personal experience; and, conversely, doctrine supplies the rationale of discipline. For the Wesleys, the reality of salvation, which is the design and aim of the United Societies, cannot properly be separated from the supporting resource and way of salvation which the Societies provide and of which they prove themselves to be truly effectual instrumentalities. They do so through the classes, bands, and their leaders, under the supervision and guidance of appointed helpers, preachers, or assistants.

In this way the Societies are seen as instrumental, not merely as catechetical schools charged to instruct in valid doctrine. They provide a matrix of "living" and enlarging faith in persons who, together, form a community of Christian nurture. This, in concert with the Holy Spirit, may become the agency of an evangelical succession; it may serve to propagate the truth of doctrine, as St. Paul said, "from faith to faith" (Rom. 1:17, KJV). Where there is this "living faith," in the Wesleyan view, doctrine is not merely believed but becomes incarnate in the character of a Christian; indeed, such is a Methodist. The "incarnation" is some measure of "Christian perfection" — a lifelong goal. That is how and why the *imitatio Christi*, for the Wesleys, is the way in which the Methodist "works out his salvation with fear and trembling."

Accordingly, as we have seen, the truly engaged Methodist is not in pursuit of a *definition* of "compunction," as à Kempis put it, or of justification, or even of holiness of heart and life; a true Methodist is in pursuit of the *experimental reality*. And if he is alert to the Methodist *discipline*, he may have received guidance from the *Minutes of Several Conversations*. There he will have been warned that Methodists had, at times, "leaned too much to Calvinism" in doctrine, and that they should neither dismiss nor be ashamed of such a thing as "man's faithfulness" because our *final salvation* cannot do without it. He will have learned, further, that a real Christian "must work *for* life as well as *from* it, i.e., from justification and the new birth. And finally he shall be instructed that while, indeed, salvation is not through "the merit of works," it is "through works as a condition."[30] The Conference *Minutes* are also full of this kind of doctrinal understanding, instruction, and guidance. They are precisely the *discipline*, or the charted way, by which the awakened penitent may seek salvation, first, in justification and, second, in "holiness of heart and life."

Thomas Coke and Francis Asbury, having presided over the founding Conference of the new Methodist Episcopal Church at Baltimore in December, 1784, found it necessary to provide an instrument for conceiving and operating the newly-constituted Church — a Church that was possessed of an accepted Wesleyan authorization, but had been established by a corporate act of self-determination under God. These two chief leaders of the new Church found but one course of procedure: to adopt a long acknowledged and authoritative instrument already in use since the first authorized American Conference under Thomas Rankin of 1773, namely the *Minutes of Several Conversations*. That founding American Conference had asked the question: "Ought not *the doctrine and discipline* of the Methodists, *as contained in the Minutes*, to be *the sole rule of our conduct* who labour, in connection with Mr. Wesley, in America?" The answer was "Yes."[31]

To be noted at once is the explicit assertion that the *Minutes* contain both "doctrine and discipline." While the *Minutes* are not specifically identified, the reference is obviously to the *Minutes of Several Conversations*. Moreover, the "conduct" of which the *Minutes* are to be "the sole rule" is that of authorized preachers of the Methodist "doctrine and discipline." At the Baltimore Conference of 1781, following by a year the narrowly-avoided division of the United Societies over the matter of the Ordinances, a pledge of union was supplied by the preachers in attendance in answer to this question:

> What preachers are now determined, after mature consideration, close observation, and earnest prayer, to preach *the old Methodist doctrine*, and strictly to enforce *the discipline, as contained in the Notes, Sermons, and Minutes*, as published by Mr. Wesley . . . and firmly discountenance a separation among either preachers or people?[32]

Here again to be noted is the surprising assumption that the Methodist discipline to be "strictly enforced" is not restricted to the *Minutes of Several Conversations*, which we have now recognized as a *Discipline*, but is said also to be represented in Wesley's *Sermons* and *Notes on the New Testament*. Plainly, a sharp distinction between doctrine and discipline is not at all entertained — rather the contrary.

Our study arrives therefore at some interesting findings. First, Coke and Asbury, in making the "Large Minutes" the vehicle of Methodist doctrine and discipline, had behind them a precedent that was continuous back to the founding American Conference of 1773, and before that, to Wesley's several "Conferences" with others, beginning in 1744. Second, Coke and Asbury were in no way innovative in regarding the "Large Minutes" as adequately representative of both doctrine and discipline; this was a well-established principle in the Methodist tradition. Third, the "Large Minutes" were without question in their understanding both a doctrinal and disciplinary standard, or canon, fully conformable to the underlying conception of Wesley's "experimental and practical divinity." This, as we have seen, found the perfect and preferred declaration of faith, not in the form of creeds, but in the transformed character of a Christian life — in what Wesley had described as "the character of a Methodist."

DOCTRINES AND DISCIPLINE FOR THE AMERICAN CHURCH

The regular conjunction between doctrines and discipline in early American Methodism should have been easily recognized once John J. Tigert, in his *Constitutional History*, had proved beyond any doubt the near-complete parallelism between the 1780 edition of Wesley's *Minutes of Several Conversations*, or "Large Minutes," and *The Minutes of Several Conversations Between Thomas Coke and Francis Asbury and Others, Composing A Form of Discipline* (1785).[33] Coke and Asbury did rearrange the succession of questions and answers of the "Large Minutes" as seemed suitable to the management of the Societies that had become a Church. They did so following Wesley's topics but omitting some material no longer relevant to the new American situation. The Church now had orders of ministry, needed rules of governance, and required provision for the means of Grace. But, with unaltered objectives, it still utilized both classes and bands for the nurture of the old Methodist plan of salvation. Respecting this discriminating editorial task, we may remember that Thomas Coke, as a Doctor of Civil Law, had already served Wesley in that capacity and was, by experience, a master draftsman for the tasks of polity formation.

It is to be stressed that the *Minutes of Several Conversations* possessed the status of *norms* or *standards* for what a Methodist ought to think, believe, teach and do. They were, therefore, "articles" of distinctive Methodist affirmation and action suited to "God's design in raising up the Preachers called Methodists."[34] They may indeed be regarded as "doctrine," namely, the "Scripture way of salvation," implemented in a systematic plan called "discipline,"which is spoken of as "the Methodist plan."[35]

We shall now consider briefly two Questions and Answers, or articles. These are Q.68 and Q.69 in the Coke-Asbury sequence, as supplied by Tigert from the first edition of *A Form of Discipline* (1785). They parallel Q.50 and Q.51 in Wesley's *Minutes of Several Conversations* (both 1780 and 1789 editions). They are perpetuated in *The Doctrines and Discipline* of 1829 as §X and §VIII of chapter 1. These articles, set forth the prescribed method for examination and admission or rejection of candidates for membership in the Annual Conference, or ministerial orders. If the polity of the new Methodist Episcopal Church must necessarily invoke acknowledged doctrinal standards, it certainly should be the case in this instance.[36]

The examination prescribed here as providing the standards of admission or rejection of candidates for conference membership and ordination, beginning with the first *Form of Discipline* of 1785, continued in essentially unaltered form through at least the General Conference of 1872 both in the Methodist Episcopal Church and (after 1844) in the Methodist Episcopal Church, South. There was relocation and realignment with related materials, such as the rules for and duties of preachers elsewhere included in Wesley's *Minutes*. But these doctrinal prescriptions, in the form of required answers to doctrinal norms for admission to conference membership in the Methodist Episcopal Church, persisted into the 20th century. It is true that not all of the questions found in Q.50 of the "Large Minutes" (1780) or Q.68 of the *Form of Discipline* (1785) have been retained. Yet certain of the original questions do survive today, such as: Have you faith in Christ? Are you going on to perfection? Do you expect to be made perfect in this life? Are you earnestly striving after it? Conspicuous by their absence are questions relating to justification by faith through grace, regeneration or the "new birth," etc. Nevertheless the former questions, with others regarding the *General Rules* and "our doctrines" and their "harmony with the Holy Scriptures" may be found in ¶424 of *The Book of Discipline, 1984.*

A Form of Discipline (1785)

Q. 68. How shall we try those who think they are moved by the Holy Ghost to preach?

A. Inquire, 1. Do they know God as a pardoning God? Have they the Love of God abiding in them? Do they desire to seek nothing but God? And are they holy in all manner of Conversation? 2. Have they *Gifts* (as well as *Grace*) for the Work? Have they (in some tolerable Degree) a clear, sound Understanding? Have they a right Judgment in the Things of God? Have they a just Conception of Salvation by Faith? And has God given them any Degree of Utterance? Do they speak justly, readily, clearly? 3. Have they *Fruit*? Are any truly convinced of Sin and converted to God by their Preaching?

As long as these three Marks concur in anyone, we believe he is called of God to preach. These we receive as a sufficient Proof, that he is *moved thereto by the Holy Ghost.*

Q. 69. What Method may we use in receiving a New Helper?

A. A proper Time for doing this, is at a Conference after solemn Fasting and Prayer.

Every Person proposed shall then be asked (with any other Questions which may be thought necessary by the Conference) the following, viz.

Have *you* Faith in Christ? Are you *going on to Perfection*? Do you expect to be *perfected in Love in this life*? Are you groaning after it? Are you resolved to devote yourself wholly to God and to his Work? Do you know the *Methodist-Plan*? Do you know the *Rules of the Society*? Of the *Bands*? Do you keep them? Do you take no *Drams*? Do you constantly attend the *Sacrament*? Have you read the *Minutes of the Conference*? Are you willing to conform to them? Have you considered the Rules of a *Helper*? Especially the first, tenth, and twelfth? Will you keep them for Conscience'

The "Large Minutes" (1780)

Q. 50. How shall we try those who think they are moved by the Holy Ghost to preach?

A. Enquire, 1. Do they know God as a pardoning God? Have they the Love of God abiding in them? Do they desire to seek nothing but God? And are they holy in all manner of Conversation? 2. Have they *Gifts*, (as well as *Grace*) for the work? Have they (in some tolerable degree) a clear, sound Understanding? Have they a right Judgment in the things of God? Have they a just conception of Salvation by Faith? And has God given them any degree of Utterance? Do they speak justly, readily, clearly? 3. Have they *Fruit*? Are any truly convinced of sin and converted to God by their Preaching?

As long as these three marks concur in anyone, we believe he is called of God to preach. These we receive as a sufficient proof, that he is *moved thereto by the Holy Ghost.*

Q. 51. What Method may we use in receiving a New Helper?

A. A proper time, for doing this, is at a Conference after solemn Fasting and Prayer.

Every person proposed is then to be present; and each of them may be asked,

Have *you* Faith in Christ? Are you *going on to perfection*? Do you expect to be *perfected in love in this life*? Are you groaning after it? Are you resolved to devote yourself wholly to God and to his work? Do you know the Methodist-Plan? Have you read the *Plain Account*? The *Appeals*? Do you know the *Rules of the Society*? Of the *Bands*? Do you keep them? Do you take no Snuff? Tobacco? Drams? Do you constantly attend the Church and Sacrament? Have you read the *Minutes of the Conference*? Are you willing to conform to them? Have you considered the Rules of an *Helper*?

A Form of Discipline (1785)

sake? Are you determined to employ *all* your Time in the Work of God? Will you preach every Morning at five o'Clock wherever you can have twenty Hearers? Will you endeavour not to speak too long or too loud? Will you diligently instruct the Children in every Place? Will you visit from House to House? Will you recommend Fasting both by Precept and Example? Are you in Debt?

We may then, if he gives Satisfaction, receive him as a Probationer by giving him the Minutes of the Conference inscribed thus:

To A.B.

"You think it you[r] Duty to call Sinners to Repentance. Make full Proof hereof, and we shall rejoice to receive you as a Fellow Labourer."

Let him then read and carefully weigh what is contained therein, that if he has any Doubt, it may be removed.

Observe! Taking *on Trial* is entirely different from *admitting* a Preacher. One on Trial, may be either admitted or rejected without doing him any wrong. Otherwise it would be no Trial at all. Let every Assistant explain this to them that are on Trial.

After two Years' Probation, being recommended by the Assistant and examined by the Conference, he may be received into full Connexion by giving him the Minutes inscribed thus:

"As long as you freely consent to, and earnestly endeavour to walk by these Rules, we shall rejoice to acknowledge you as a Fellow-Labourer."

Mean time let none preach or exhort in any of our Societies without a Note of Permission from the Assistant: Let every Preacher or Exhorter take care to have this renewed yearly: And let every Assistant insist upon it.

The "Large Minutes" (1780)

Especially the first, tenth, and twelfth? Will you keep them for Conscience' sake? Are you determined to employ *all* your Time in the work of God? Will you preach every Morning and Evening: Endeavouring not to speak too long or too loud? Will you diligently instruct the Children in every Place? Will you visit from house to house? Will you recommend Fasting both by Precept and Example? Are you in Debt?

We may then receive him as a Probationer by giving him the Minutes of the Conference inscribed thus:

To A.B.

"You think it your Duty to call Sinners to Repentance. Make full proof hereof, and we shall rejoice to receive you as a Fellow-labourer."

Let him then read, and carefully weigh what is contained therein, that if he has any Doubt, it may be removed.

Observe! Taking *on trial* is entirely different from *admitting* a Preacher. One on trial may be either admitted or rejected, without doing him any wrong. Otherwise it would be no trial at all. Let every Assistant explain this to them that are on trial.

At the next Conference, if recommended by the Assistant, he may be received into full Connexion, by giving him the Minutes inscribed thus:

"As long as you freely consent to, and earnestly endeavour to walk by these Rules, we shall rejoice to acknowledge you as a Fellow-labourer."

Mean time let none exhort in any of our Societies without a Note of Permission from the Assistant: Let every Exhorter take care to have this renewed yearly: And let every Assistant insist upon it.

The real question before us is, whether these questions, solemnly asked of candidates for the Methodist ministry in 1785, did not have the status of genuine doctrinal standards in the mind of John Wesley and his immediate successors, Thomas Coke and Francis Asbury and their ministerial contemporaries. There is no mention whatever of the Twenty-Five Articles of Religion. Let us consider specifically what is asked by Question 68.

Concerning those who think they are moved by the Holy Ghost to preach, the inquiry aims to validate the truth or falsity of that presumption. Evidently the claim, if valid, would be grounds for acceptance of the candidate for further trial. The supposition of the claimant may be weighed by certain prescribed considerations: Does the individual know God as a pardoning God? This is precisely the evidence of justification, forgiveness of sins and the "new birth." In that case, Wesley's "experimental religion" would manifest its vitality in an inward disposition to the love of God and of neighbor, for that is what the phrase "the love of God abiding in them" implies. In that case, the first commandment to love God with "all the soul, mind and strength" would begin to have some function in holiness of heart and life.

The second criterion is sound understanding. For instance, do candidates have "a just conception of salvation by faith?" And gifts of clarity of mind and utterance? In the third place, have they fruit? That is, "Are any (persons) truly convinced of sin, and converted to God, by their preaching?" This matter is central in the "Rules of a Helper," i.e., a preacher:

> You have nothing to do but to save souls. . . . It is not your business preach so many times, and to take care of this or that society, but to save all the souls you can; to bring as many sinners as you possibly can to repentance, and with all your power build them up in that holiness without which they cannot see the Lord."[37]

When we look more closely at Question 69 regarding the method of receiving a preacher on trial, the doctrinal stress becomes more emphatic while, at the same time, it is intimately related to the disciplinary vehicles for its realization in human lives, both of preachers and people. Furthermore, the inquisition to which the candidate is subjected in the Conference session, after fasting and prayer, tests both his understanding of and aptitude for what is called "the Methodist plan," that is, the plan of salvation in two stages: justification and Christian perfection that should be in process. As we have frequently noted, these are the two main pillars of "experimental religion." The queries become direct cross-examinations of the candidate: "Have you read the *Plain Account* [*of Christian Perfection*]? The *Appeals* [*to Men of Reason and Religion*]? Do you know the *Rules of the Society* [that is, the *General Rules of the United Societies*]? [The *Rules*] of the Bands? Do you keep them?"

If, in fact, the candidate did know the *Rules* of the bands, he would know that admission to the bands presupposed much on the part of the person admitted: forgiveness of sins, peace with God through our Lord Jesus Christ, the witness of the Holy Spirit to adoption as a child of God, the love of God shed abroad in the heart ("heart-religion"), and dominion over inward and outward sin.[38] In this way the bands were reserved for "Eagle Scouts" in Methodism. They were essential to assist justified persons "not to rest in being half Christians," as Wesley described the matter to Freeborn Garrettson. The bands were essential to what he enjoined as "the whole Methodist plan."[39]

I have attempted here to make it clear that in the passages appropriated by Coke and Asbury from Wesley's "Large Minutes" as the substance of their *Form of Discipline* for the governance of the new Methodist Episcopal Church, there is in fact a republication of the chief tenets of Wesley's "experimental and practical divinity." In the next chapter an effort will be made to reappraise, in the light of the findings of these studies, the meaning and identity of early Methodist doctrinal standards. It is difficult indeed not to suppose that, in the trial of persons for conference membership and orders in the new Church, the norms of doctrines and discipline would not be used and enforced as criteria of acceptable candidacy for authorized ministerial status in the new Methodist Episcopal Church.

If ruling doctrinal standards are not invoked as norms, both for qualification of acceptability for ministry and for its assessment after the fact, where, it may properly be asked, would doctrinal norms be appropriate and applied? If, indeed, they are applied in such cases, we may, in the several doctrines of Wesley's "experimental divinity," have, at last, proper referents for the second phrase of the First Restrictive Rule of May 24, 1808, namely, "nor establish any new standards or rules of doctrine, contrary to our present existing and established standards of doctrine."[40]

CHAPTER 11

THE METHODIST EPISCOPAL CHURCH: DOCTRINAL STANDARDS, 1785–1816

Contrary to the notion that the establishment of the Methodist Episcopal Church entailed something in the nature of a break with its doctrinal antecedents, the findings of these studies rather plainly indicate the opposite. Our indications suggest that the founding of the new Church at the Christmas Conference of December, 1784, with the succeeding leadership of Thomas Coke and Francis Asbury, was of virtually no consequence either in muting or changing "the old Methodist doctrines and discipline." These were the same that had guided preachers and the Societies, officially, since 1773.

Evidence of this continuity is the fact that the stated purpose of the new Church, namely, "to reform the continent, and spread Scripture holiness over these lands,"[1] was but a translation and transference of the "design" of the United Societies to that of a voluntary and separate church in the new Republic. It is of the utmost importance to recognize that this *desideratum,* in point of fact, defined for Wesley, as for Freeborn Garrettson, the difference between a "half Methodist" and the "whole Methodist plan" of human salvation.[2] It was the difference between salvation as justification by grace through faith only — that an Antinomian might claim — and "holiness of heart and life" understood as an essential "condition" of salvation and of the *bona fide* "character of a Methodist."[3]

WESLEY'S EXPERIMENTAL DIVINITY AS THE RULE OF FAITH

Because of the magnitude of our subject matter in this chapter and limitation of space, I shall, under this heading, proceed by way of propositions I judge to be well grounded in our findings regarding early American Methodist history and doctrine.

Proposition 1. The prompting and controlling doctrine of early American Methodism until 1852 — to set a somewhat arbitrary date — was in fact primarily the sum of Wesley's experimental and practical divinity. As that body of divinity was from 1740 onward the formative and constitutive rationale of all the United Societies under Wesley, so it continued to be so long as the language of Methodism, whether British or American, still reflected the organization and the aspiration of the Societies. This, it appears, persisted in America perhaps until the middle of the 19th century.

Proposition 2. The Methodist Bishops in their official role and address to the British Methodists in 1840 stated that "The General Rules of the United Societies . . . are of constitutional authority in our Church."[4] The *General Rules* were also the presiding rationale for the *Minutes of Several Conversations* (1744–89), which supplied the organizational structure, directives, and the doctrinal tenets of the Societies from the beginning. Those *Minutes* had always been, in fact, doctrines and discipline. We saw that they were acknowledged as such in the American Conference *Minutes* of 1773, 1781, and 1784. Complementary to this was Wesley's unfolding "experimental divinity" as more amply conveyed in the *Sermons*, the *Notes on the New Testament*, the *Plain Account of Christian Perfection*, *The Character of a Methodist*, the *Appeals*, and other writings. These things were still generally acknowledged in American Methodism in the 1840s.

Proposition 3. The sum of "experimental and practical divinity" as expounded in these essays was largely the Wesleyan emendation of the received doctrine of the Church of England, especially as grounded in the Edwardian Homilies and the Book of Common Prayer. It was altered to conform with "The Scripture Way of Salvation." This was possessed of certain accents and some alterations of the received Anglican doctrinal tradition. Its distinctive accents were:

(1) Justification was understood as attended by full penitence; entire surrender; forgiveness of sins; assurance of pardon, acceptance with God, or reconciliation; and joy in the Holy Spirit. Comprehensively, this entailed newness of life, or regeneration.

(2) Emphasis was placed upon the immediate, indispensable and present saving work of the Holy Spirit.

(3) Through the work of the Holy Spirit came the hope of extrication from the bondage of original sin.

(4) As justification made way for the "new birth," so the uniform vocation of the justified person carried with it a mandate for progressive sanctification, or holiness of life as the "condition" of final salvation.

(5) Against Calvinism, the "Scripture way of salvation" was opened to all, i.e., God's election was universalized, and, with it, the love of God was "shed abroad in the hearts" of all those who received it, and as a mark of the new life.

(6) The saving work and vicarious sacrifice of Christ — his atoning work — was made applicable and available to all who received his grace by faith.

The innovations or alterations of received Anglican doctrine which it made were:

(1) The "Scripture way of salvation" itself was understood as the realization in experience of God's "promises" in Scripture — "proof" open to the experience of all who, in faith and trust, enter upon and keep to God's revealed way.

(2) Corresponding to this was the verification and vindication of the truth of Scripture as containing "all things necessary to salvation" and as the standard for setting aside what was merely "opinion" and either "controversial" or "speculative divinity."

(3) The "living sacrifice," the cruciform life of faith, or "Christian perfection," was conceived as the norm and goal of "saving faith."

(4) "Perfect love" of God and neighbor, to the extent of "entire sanctification," was held to be attainable in this life, at least, on principle.

These ten doctrines comprise the sum of the Wesleyan "experimental and practical divinity." This experimental divinity or "heart religion" was presupposed by Thomas Coke and Francis Asbury in the first edition of *A Form of Discipline For Ministers, Preachers, and Members, Now Comprehended in the Principles and Doctrines of the Methodist Episcopal Church in America*. If, in fact, they invoked the above title as indicative of the event, then the burden of proof lies heavily upon any who affirm that "the principles and doctrines" mentioned were not understood by the founders in 1784 as including the sum of Wesley's experimental divinity.

Proposition 4. "Living faith," as we saw in chapter 1, passes from doxology, through *homologia*, or glad personal witness in agreement, to declaration in testimony, hymn, or preaching, onward to expression in a *consensus fidelium*. Historically considered, that consensus first issues in the corporate *rule of faith* as the intra-mural verbal consent to the common faith. It is not yet a published creed. That is, it has not yet been objectified, or declared in the indicative mood as a statement of fact for belief or rejection. Rather it is allowed to remain a confession of faith by confessors. Yet the rule of faith speaks the common mind and heart of the group, and provides its mutually acknowledged self-understanding. It is also the norm for determining membership in the Society or Church.

This was precisely the status of Wesley's "Scripture way of salvation" in the ongoing 18th-century Revival, as Nathaniel Burwash suggests. It was in 1773, and again in both 1781 and 1783, acknowledged as *constitutive* of the very existence of the United Societies, their reason for being in America. It was the substance of preaching, of its objectives, and of the mode of its propagation and nurture as in *The General Rules of the United Societies* and in the "Large Minutes." Its tenets, while not systematically codified or expounded, even by Wesley, were, nevertheless, embodied in all his writings, some few of which were singled out for their emphatic exposition of the same "Scripture way of salvation."

It both *is* and *is not* an historical accident that the "rule of faith," which I find ample reason to embrace under the title of Wesley's early sermon, "The Scripture Way of Salvation," always remained only an intramural "rule of faith" and never acquired summary creedal status. This circumstance *is* an historical accident in that, after the death of John Fletcher, August 14, 1785, Wesley evidently had no theological interpreter of his soteriological system adequate to the task in either British or American Methodism. It is *not* an historical accident, however, because Wesley himself never formulated a summation *as such*, but preferred to see the "Scripture way of salvation" *recapitulated* in human lives — as described particularly in chapters 2, 6 and 7 — rather than offered as a creedal formula to the curious or to the speculative theologian. At the same time, instances of such summation are scattered here and there throughout Wesley's works.[5]

Proposition 5. The address of Bishops Coke and Asbury "To the Members of the Methodist Societies in America" — printed as the preface to each successive edition of *A Form of Discipline* (1785–1791) and, thereafter, to *The Doctrines and Discipline* (beginning in 1792 and continuing until the end of the 19th century) — states that "We humbly believe that God's design in raising up the preachers called Methodists, in America, was to reform the continent, and spread Scripture-holiness over these lands." In the 1792 edition, they added that while some "alterations" have been made, they are "such as affect not in any degree the essentials of our doctrines and discipline."[6] Manifestly, this statement could not have intended by "doctrines" reference to the Articles of Religion.

It would seem to be plain, then, that Coke and Asbury are disposed — if in the new setting — to summon the same rationale for the Methodist Episcopal Church that Wesley adopted for the United Societies as early as 1743. Holiness was their aim and their reason for being, for it was one with salvation itself. This time, however, the aim is not to reform the Church of England, but, perhaps, to *be* the Church in America after 1784 and so "to spread," as they said, "Scripture-holiness over these lands." And one would be either ignorant or dull indeed to overlook Wesley's discovery and insistence that holiness waits upon taking the "Scripture way of salvation" as the preferred route. Coke and Asbury were certainly familiar with words from *The Character of a Methodist*: "By salvation he [a Methodist] means holiness of heart and life. And this he affirms to spring from true faith alone."[7] The inseparability of justification by faith and holiness of heart and life had long since been a Methodist axiom. They were, as we have recurrently noted throughout these studies, the two poles in the ellipse of experimental divinity.

On the matter of the transition from United Societies to the new Methodist Episcopal Church, and the carry-over to the latter of the design of the former as defined by the *General Rules*, we ought to hear from Thomas Ware, one of the wisest and most disciplined of Methodist preachers of the succeeding generation, who reflects thus on his presence at the founding Conference:

> At the Christmas conference we met to congratulate each other, and to praise the Lord that he had disposed the mind of our excellent Wesley to renounce the fable of uninterrupted succession, and prepare the way for furnishing us with the long-desired privileges we were thenceforth expecting to enjoy. The announcement of the plan devised by him for our organization as a Church filled us with solemn delight. It answered to what we did suppose, during our labours and privations, we had reason to expect our God would do for us, for in the integrity of our hearts we verily believed his design in raising up the preachers called Methodists, in this country, was to reform the continent, and spread scriptural holiness through these lands. . . . We therefore, according to the best of our knowledge received and followed the advice of Mr. Wesley, as stated in our form of Discipline.[8]

From these observations of Thomas Ware, who was for near fifty years following the Christmas Conference a Methodist preacher who battled Satan in the lives of persons with nerve, astuteness and literate power, we 20th-century Methodists may learn much. We shall return to him shortly on the matters of reformation, the sacraments, and ministerial orders.

THE REFORMING RULE OF THE NEW CHURCH AND ITS DOCTRINE

In this section I propose to deal successively, under the theme of "reformation," with three factors in ferment in American Methodism of the 1780s. For this urgency, Wesley's plan for organization of a Methodist Episcopal Church by way of ordination of a ministry (including a General Superintendent) was profoundly needed and received with gladness. As Ware put it with his customary felicity, "The announcement of the plan devised by him (Wesley) for our organization as a church filled us with solemn delight."

In his eyewitness account of the Christmas Conference, Ware — then a new preacher "on trial" — spoke of John Dickens with high approbation. Thomas Coke's *Journal* tells how Dickens, as preacher in charge at New York, received Dr. Coke in November 1784. When informed of Wesley's plan Coke reports that

> . . . brother Dickens, traveling preacher stationed at this place . . . highly approved of it, says that all the preachers most earnestly long for such a reformation, and that brother Asbury, he is sure, will consent to it. He presses me earnestly to make it public. . . .[9]

Dr. Coke, however, declined to give public notice of Wesley's plan until he had become acquainted with the work in Philadelphia and was ready to make his way to County Kent, Delaware, to meet with Francis Asbury.

The manner in which the early American Methodists understood "reformation" and attributed it in several respects to their own movement is not always recognized. Methodism as God's instrument of "reformation" finds expression, as already noted, in utterances of both William Watters and Freeborn Garrettson. We recall that in 1778 Philip Gatch remarked casually of the Virginia family into which he married that "previous to the reformation in Virginia," it belonged to the Established Church.[10] It is quite apparent that Watters, Garrettson, and Gatch — all reared in the parishes of the Church of England — were, for a number of reasons (including its decadent and even dissolute clergy), sure of the need of its reformation. For them, the stated design in Article 3 of the "Large Minutes," "to reform the nation, particularly the Church," was hardly debatable.[11]

One principal meaning of "reformation" for these leading Methodist preachers is summed up in the rejoicing of Thomas Ware. His "solemn delight" of the Christmas Conference was in the ordination of elders and deacons as well as that of a General Superintendent. The administration of the sacraments was now at the disposition of duly ordained Methodist elders. As Ware put it, "Many, very many, who had been brought to the knowledge of God through our instrumentality were kept from uniting with us because we could not administer to them all the ordinances."[12] It was for the same reasons that William Watters reported that

> . . . the Plan of Church Government, which the Doctor [Coke] brought over recommended by Mr. Wesley . . . was adopted, and unanimously agreed to with great satisfaction, and we became instead of a religious society, a separate Church under the name of the Methodist Episcopal Church. . . . This change gave great satisfaction through all our societies in America . . . particularly, to those who had some time past thought it their duty to administer the ordinances . . . [and] also to those who had long felt scruples of conscience in receiving them from men whom they could not believe were sent by the Lord Jesus to minister in holy things, whose lives were immoral.[13]

In these matters William Watters speaks of what he fully knows. His whole family had been members of the Church of England; his father had been before his death chief vestryman, as also had an elder brother. In addition, he had been the principal and probably most effective mediator in the conscientious but destructive division between northern and southern preachers during the ordinance controversy of 1778–1780. This had been disquieting and unresolved until, at last, Wesley made his decision. Watters, therefore, shared with Thomas Ware in praising God

> that he had disposed the mind of our excellent Wesley to renounce the fable of uninterrupted succession, and prepare the way for furnishing us with the long-desired privileges.[14]

Concerning the "humiliating" and impeding effects of the want of ecclesiastical orders and status, Ware had written at length, observing that there was

> not a man in holy orders among us . . . and though the work of God was prospering, and the Societies increasing more rapidly than any other denomination . . . the want of orders had a tendency to paralyze our efforts.[15]

These words, from a clear-headed and discriminating witness fully positioned to know, will indicate the reasons why the whole body of Methodist preachers, both south and north, received the plan of Wesley for ordination and, therefore, sacramental authorization with profound gladness and thanksgiving. If we ask what indeed, then, was the "reformation" spoken of as a part of the design of the Methodist Episcopal Church, the answer is not simple but at least fourfold.

(1) For those, such as Gatch, Watters, Garrettson, and Jesse Lee, who were baptized and confirmed under clergy of the Church of England, the message and work of the Methodist preachers and the Societies were viewed as of themselves "reformation," since its representatives, sent and authorized by Wesley, were Church of England people. If of a lay status, they were, nonetheless, authorized by the eminent churchman, John Wesley.

(2) Ordination was, for the first generation of Methodist preachers, authorization to administer the sacraments and so to fulfill the ministerial task. Therefore, also, it was appropriate to claim the prerogative entailed by Article XIII of the Articles of Religion supplied by Wesley along with with the *Sunday Service*, which included a liturgy of ordination called the "Ordinal." The full title is: "The Form and Manner of Making and Ordaining of Superintendents, Elders, and Deacons."[16] To this day, this form of ordination is used, with some small changes, in The United Methodist Church. It has been and remains a part of our *Doctrines and Discipline*. It is a part of our so-called doctrinal standards, as are also the liturgies of the sacraments and other services.[17]

If we examine the "Ordinal,"it quickly becomes apparent that the Articles of Religion which Wesley made immediately to follow it are necessarily involved and invoked therein. The questions put to the candidates for deacon's and elder's orders are answerable only by reference to standards held to be normative by the Church, which also certifies them as stipulations for a ministerial office within its charge. For example:

> 1. Do you trust you are inwardly moved by the Holy Spirit to take upon you this office, etc?
> 2. Do you believe the canonical Scriptures of the Old and New Testaments?
> 3. Do you think you are truly called, according to our Lord Jesus Christ, to the ministry of the church?
> 4. Will you apply all your diligence to frame and fashion your own lives, and the lives of your families . . . according to the doctrine of Christ?[18]
> 5. Will you . . . give your diligence, always to minister to the doctrine and sacraments, and the discipline of Christ?
> 6. Will you be ready with all faithful diligence to banish . . . all erroneous and strange doctrines contrary to God's word. . . ?[19]

By these questions, and by the exhortations and the prayers of the superintendent, the following Articles of Religion are invoked: I. Of

Faith in the Holy Trinity; II. Of the Word, or Son of God, who was made man; IV. Of the Holy ghost; V. Of the Sufficiency of the Holy Scriptures for Salvation; VI. Of the Old Testament; XIII. Of the Church; XV. Of Speaking in the Congregation in such a Tongue as the People understand; XVI. Of the Sacraments; XVII. Of Baptism; XVIII. Of the Lord's Supper; XIX. Of both Kinds; XX. Of the One Oblation of Christ; XXI. Of the Marriage of Ministers; XXII. Of the Rites and Ceremonies of Churches.

Thus we may say that the questions for ordination of deacons and elders invokes the norms of thirteen Articles. While Wesley and his preachers built and nurtured only "United Societies," there was small need for and little reference to such norms, and, surely, no explicit dependence upon them. This is why they had no place in the "Large Minutes." For the establishment of the ordained ministry of a Christian church, however, it was self-evident that Articles touching upon the church, the ministry, and the sacraments were prerequisites. Wesley's edited version of the Thirty-Nine Articles of Religion of the Church of England was, therefore, a resource to which, conscientiously, he could and did defer in founding a "Methodist Episcopal Church."

The liturgies of the sacraments and other services of the Church appear in Wesley's *Sunday Service* following the collects and Scripture lessons of the Christian year for morning and evening prayer. They begin with the Order of Administration of the Lord's Supper and proceed to the Ministration of Baptism of Infants, and to those of Riper Years. There follows the Form of Solemnization of Matrimony; the Communion of the Sick; and the Order for the Burial of the Dead.[20] This liturgy invokes the following Articles: III. Of the Resurrection of Christ; VII. Of Original or Birth-Sin; VIII. Of Free-Will; X. Of Good Works; XI. Of Works of Supererogation; XII. Of Sin after Justification.

Further, these liturgical offices presuppose the chief pillar of Protestant reformation doctrine, in this instance, Article IX. Of the Justification of Man. In Wesley's recension there is a bare minimum statement of that doctrine so central to the Wesleyan "reformation"; there is nothing at all of the overwhelmingly important Wesleyan stress upon salvation as invoking both justification and sanctification of life in the likeness of Christ, or "Christian perfection." If we were to rely upon them for Wesley's doctrine of saving faith and of salvation we would fail for want of essentials.

Above all, it is to be recognized that John Wesley's *Sunday Service* was provided as an instrument for the proper authorization and establishment of a Methodist Episcopal Church in which, as the condition *sine qua non*, normative statements on the parts of worship, including the sacraments, had to be supplied. A sacramental theology, was, it seemed, indispensable to a doctrine of the church! Only by prior acknowledgment of such norms by a church as an ordaining body, as Wesley knew, was it possible to specify certain doctrinal standards on church and sacraments by which candidates were to be judged when on trial for holy orders.

The United Societies had no such canons. Wesley volunteered, under necessity, to supply them, and for obvious reasons used the Thirty-Nine Articles of Religion of the Church of England. This doctrine he both owned and had been amending for half a century. The amendment had included also certain of the Articles. These, at length, appeared as Wesley's Twenty-Four Articles, and as a part of the *Sunday Service*, the "Book of Common Prayer" of the Methodists. This, too, in a sense, might be viewed as "reformation."

Thus it was the case that, while all Articles pertaining to the Wesleyan doctrine of salvation were provided, on principle, in Wesley's soteriology, those relating particularly to church, ministry, and the sacraments had not been needed while Wesley's preachers presided over only the United Societies. Now, with the addition of Articles on the church, ministry, and sacraments, it may be seen that additional doctrinal standards have been provided in a manner comparable to Protestant Churches generally. As Coke and Asbury were to say of the Articles incorporated also in the *Form of Discipline* for 1789 and following, viz., the Articles "are maintained more or less, in part or in whole, by every Reformed church in the World."

Another probable meaning of "reformation" recognized by the early Methodists as attaching to Wesley's plan for the establishment of the Methodist Episcopal Church requires only passing attention. It was, doubtless, their widespread relief from suffering an awkward dependency upon the ordained ministry of other churches, whether Presbyterian or Episcopolian. In 1784, the Church of England was no more in the United States, and the Protestant Episcopal Church was yet to be.

Perhaps the most encouraging, if not fundamental, factor in the "reformation" incident to the creation of an ordained ministry of a separate church is that Methodist preachers were now possessed of the essential ministerial competence. Thomas Ware both described this, and complained of its lack, prior to the Christmas Conference of 1784. With ordination, whether as elders or deacons (and under a presiding elder), the Methodist ministers were possessed of an authority and competence to discharge (in a context now devoid of any religious

establishment but under constituted ecclesial authority) their acknowl-
eged divinely conferred calling. And that was in essence the same with
which they began in 1773 — "to reform the continent, and spread
Scripture holiness over these lands." Thomas Coke and Francis Asbury
reaffirmed that divine mandate in *A Form of Discipline*. In 1790 it was
published under this title:

> *A Form of Discipline for the Ministers, Preachers and Members (now com-*
> *prehending the Principles and Doctrines) of the Methodist Episcopal Church*
> *in America, considered and approved at a Conference Held in Baltimore, in*
> *the State of Maryland On Monday the 27th of December, 1784: In which*
> *Thomas Coke and Francis Asbury, Presided; Arranged under proper Heads,*
> *and methodized in a more acceptable and easy manner.* The Sixth Edition.
> Philadelphia: Printed by R. Aitkin & Son, and sold by John Dickens.
> No. 43. Fourth Street, MDCCXC.[21]

The divine calling which Coke and Asbury acknowledged in the
prefatory address continued to be republished in the Episcopal Address for more than a century, and a part of the line is still retained in
the present *Book of Discipline*. For our purposes at the moment it is
important to stress the point that the mandate "to reform the continent and spread Scripture holiness over these lands" had been since
1744, and was still in 1790, the ruling purpose of the Wesleyan "experimental and practicial divinity." It had been advanced by the agency of the United Societies in both Britain and America. In America,
after the Christmas Conference of 1784, it was to be advanced by the
Methodist Episcopal Church. This was clearly the understanding of
the founding fathers and mothers, if we can rely upon the testimony
of such veterans of total fidelity as Freeborn Garrettson or Thomas
Ware.

SOME CONCLUDING OBSERVATIONS

I am well aware that the proper subject matter of this chapter has
not been exhausted. In conclusion, however, some attention must be
directed to the expressed judgment of Thomas Coke and Francis
Asbury on yet another feature of the Methodist "reformation," namely, its reformulation and enforcement of Christian discipline where, in
their view, the established Church had conspicuously faltered, if not
quite failed.[22]

This judgment and viewpoint was to find expression in the new
title of the *Form of Discipline* which, following upon the Methodist
General Conference of 1792, became *The Doctrines and Discipline of the
Methodist Episcopal Church*. It so remained, as noted earlier, through

1964. In that title the distinctive genius of the Wesleyan understanding and proclamation of the "Scripture way of salvation" was, at least nominally, perpetuated in American Methodism into the 20th century. This, I believe, is indicated insofar as these studies have disclosed and verified the inseparability, in authentic Christian experience, of doctrine and the demanding vocation embraced in the phrase "the character of a Methodist," or "a Christian." The evidence is plain that the Wesleys, in the succession of St. Paul, saw the Christian life as "a living sacrifice" and so practiced it.

We are probably warranted in the judgment that John Wesley, more thoroughly and more cogently than any Christian thinker since St. Paul, exposed the vanity, flaccidity, and spiritual futility of an identification of Christian truth and piety with its mere intellectual formulation as creed, or its indoctrination conceived as the way of salvation. He was at one with the words: "Charity never faileth: but whether there be prophesies, they shall fail, whether there be tongues they shall cease, whether there be knowledge, it shall vanish away" (1 Cor. 13:8, KJV). With Paul, Wesley was advocate of experimental religion of the heart (Rom. 10:10). This absent, the vacancy was filled with idols of man's love and making. With these things in mind, I want to make a few concluding observations.

(1) If we mean to speak about the identity of early Methodist doctrinal standards of the years 1773 to 1816, we are obliged to recognize that, while they were all Wesleyan, we come upon them in layers, and possibly such was the case for the Methodists of that era also. This was, in some respects, the case for John Wesley himself.

With Wesley the verity of the Nicene or Calcedonian Creeds was no more at issue than with his Anglican predecessors from Thomas Cranmer to Bishop John Pearson, well known to Wesley in the latter's classical *An Exposition of the Creed* (1659). However, as Wesley discovered, in the autumn of 1737, this orthodoxy which he had inherited and esteemed somehow did not save, and, surprisingly, was not at all identical with something Thomas Cranmer described as "living faith." Therewith, under the prompting of Peter Böhler, he made the discovery, against his will, of "experimental religion" in which the point at issue was no longer right belief, but, first of all, right relation to God through Jesus Christ and by way of the intervention of the Holy Spirit; and, second, salvation entailed a right relation to neighbor. Then in 1784, in order to establish in America a church with a ministry authorized both to preach the gospel and to administer the sacraments, something was needed not-hitherto supplied to the United Societies. It was acceptable definitions of the church, the ministry, and the sacraments. It was, in short, an ecclesiology, or doctrine of the church. By such standards — understood in common and mutually acknowledged by the acting ministry, the members, and candidates for orders — and therefore publishable, it was possible for the church, through its designated agents, to examine candidates for holy orders; and, conversely, for candidates for orders to understand by what standards they were fairly judged as acceptable for ordination.

(2) As one reflects upon this layered set of historical circumstances, a second observation offers itself in the light of our study, especially in chapter 6, of "living faith" vis à vis "orthodoxy" in Wesley's teaching. On the one hand, Wesley proves times without number that "orthodoxy" does not save. On the other hand, Wesley's mandate of 1784 respecting the American Methodists and their urgent needs strongly suggests that orthodoxy is not finally dispensable, but, to the contrary, is indispensable. Are we faced, then, with an insoluble paradox, or apparent contradiction?

(3) Paradox it may well be, yet, in this seeming contradiction, we are again faced with that obscure, subtle, and recurrently overlooked reality in faithful Christian experience. We have touched upon this reality in the study of Philip Melanchthon and Thomas Cranmer in chapters 3 and 7. The reality mentioned involves two distinct but complementary forms of faith. The first was called "saving faith." It is St. Augustine's *fides qua creditur*. By this, he means (and Melanchthon and Cranmer agree) *the faith by which what is believed proves believable* through an intervention of the Holy Spirit. Wesley, likewise, taught that "saving faith" is experienced as a work of God in the soul. It is an inner event caused by grace and appropriated in faith. We are, then, once more in the precincts of "experimental religion."

On the other side, the complementary, not contradictory, mode of faith which Wesley, it appears, must rely upon for a workable ecclesiology, i.e., a doctrine of the church, ministry, and sacraments, is the *fides quae creditur*. It is *the faith that is believed* and positively stated. In its evident indispensability for the establishment of the Methodist Episcopal Church in 1784, it must be reckoned as an enabling part of the system of doctrinal standards acknowledged by that Church, or any church, as constitutive of its corporate existence.

(4) If these two kinds of faith are complementary, then, are they not equally fundamental? These studies as a whole have been concerned to answer that question. Whenever the articulated corporate confession of Christian faith is published, in whatever form, and becomes *itself* the object of faith, then "faith" becomes "secondhand," or affirmation of the received tradition, instead of the "living faith" by

which doctrine becomes incarnate. It is then that the Christian religion may lapse into "the form without the power of Godliness." Therewith it may become, and is always tending to become, "second-hand religion," an inherited bit of public propriety perhaps, a piety affirmed not for intrinsic but for extrinsic reasons.

The bearing of these studies has been that without the recurring recovery of the *fides qua creditur*, Cranmer's "living faith," the Wesleys are everlastingly right concerning the urgency of "experimental religion." In its absence, Christianity is continually in the process of becoming defunct, and needs reformation. Without the renewing work of the Holy Spirit, the surviving tradition — that is indeed a divine inertia — nevertheless wanes. It commonly does so either in the direction of doctrinal *indifferentism* in the churches, or, in aroused defensiveness, it takes on the form of its opposite, bigoted orthodox *dogmatism*. It is indeed a pressing question whether these opposites are not living realities among us today, in our midst here in America.

The Wesleys can still assist us in understanding that, in the absence of "living faith" or "experimental religion," the always incipient and characteristic alternatives are unwholesome extremes. They tend to be either progressive doctrinal indifference, confusion, and acculturation of Christianity, or its opposite — a reactionary orthodoxy that veers toward bigotry, or even fanaticism. Bigotry becomes menacing insofar as it supposes orthodoxy is enforceable and ought to be for such extrinsic reasons as, perhaps, the good of the nation. If there are some strong grounds for believing that 19th-century Methodism was a principal moral tonic of American society, the explanation lies both in its doctrinal standards and even more in the fact that the latter did find some considerable expression in "the character of a Methodist" in that century.

EPILOGUE

As a Greek derivative, the word "epilogue" refers to a writing supplementary to the main body of an already completed work. As a supplement, it may also be a brief recapitulation of the original. This latter aspect will have but modest occurrence in this instance. For the most part, and presupposing our findings respecting Wesley's "experimental and practical divinity," we shall here consider briefly a few implications of these findings for a now somewhat prolonged endeavor on the part of the United Methodist Church to clarify its doctrinal standards.

SOME ISSUES BEFORE US

Two decades have passed since the General Conference of the newly-constituted United Methodist Church authorized, in 1968, a designated Commission to investigate its doctrinal standards. The assignment was made in the light of the union of two churches — with a longtime kinship — and the status of doctrinal norms in the face of "pluralizing" influences judged to be resident in the united Church. Yet again in 1984 a reassessment, under yet another Commission of the General Conference, was enjoined and authorized to report to the General Conference of 1988. The initial exploration and recommendations had occupied the work of a Commission which pursued its task during the quadrennium 1968–1972 and made an important report to the General Conference in 1972.

The study and report of the quadrennial Commission of 1968–1972 was done with conspicuous learning in the sphere of Wesleyan and historic Methodist doctrine, and with alertness to an altering doctrinal climate not without representation in the churches. The study was marked both by discretion and conservation of mind and spirit, and with no little proficiency in historical assessment of the role and function of doctrinal standards in the Methodist tradition. The report of the Commission was adopted by the General Conference of 1972, and with a few emendations remained as Part II of *The Book of*

Discipline — and thus as the official statement on doctrinal norms of the United Methodist Church — until 1988.

In its recovery, with approval and recommendation, of the so-called Wesleyan "quadrilateral" of doctrinal norms (Scripture, tradition, experience and reason) the General Conference Commission in 1972 laid permanent new groundwork, in my view, for any further responsible official Methodist doctrinal study or reformulation. This "quadrilateral" has been reaffirmed, in substance if not in name, in the report of the most recent Commission, which was approved by the General Conference of 1988.

Following a motion by its Committee of Revisals, the General Conference of The Methodist Episcopal Church in 1870, and again in 1874, declined to authorize official restudy of standards or any doctrinal reformulation. In 1876 it was confirmed in this stand by the Council of Bishops, which found the previous proposals of the Committee of Revisals inadequately cognizant of the First Restrictive Rule, on the one hand, and, on the other, cautioned that the "work of formulating theological truth into an authoritative declaration of faith" could be hoped for only by "the concurrence of many minds, after patient and laborious research."[1]

Thus, until 1968, no officially authorized reexamination of doctrinal standards had been ventured by the two original branches of American Methodism, north or south, since 1808.[2] As the present studies have shown, the First Restrictive Rule of that early General Conference was mainly a declaration and a safeguard of the actually operative doctrinal fabric. We have seen that the working core of that doctrinal fabric in 1808 was John Wesley's "experimental and practical divinity" together with the *General Rules* of the United Societies, and, after 1784, Wesley's *Minutes of Several Conversations*, the Articles of Religion, and the liturgy of Wesley's *Sunday Service*. Alteration of any or all of these was proscribed by the First Restrictive Rule, which prohibited revocation or change of the Articles of Religion or establishment of "any new standards or rules of doctrine contrary to our present existing and established standards of doctrine."

MULTIPLE REFERENCE OF THE FIRST RESTRICTIVE RULE

It was the *Minutes*, the Articles and the liturgy of the *Sunday Service*, as we have seen, which provided to the new Methodist Episcopal Church in 1784 its doctrine of the church, of the sacraments, and of the ministry. To this ecclesiology, Wesley's "experimental divinity" had neither attempted nor made any direct contribution. Such was not its purpose. Rather, the latter always presupposed for Wesley the standing ecclesiology of the Church of England. From this Wesley himself never departed, and he conveyed it to the Methodist Episcopal Church in America by Thomas Coke as his agent in 1784.

Once these matters become clear, it also becomes clear that the often controverted referents of the First Restrictive Rule must be multiple to embrace the range of doctrine and discipline normative for the Methodist Episcopal Church in the United States in 1808. The discipline that was embodied in the *General Rules* and in Wesley's *Minutes of Several Conversations* (1780) was as fully embraced as were the Articles (declarative of the doctrines of the trinity, Scripture, church, sacraments, and ministry) or Wesley's distinctive doctrine of salvation (soteriology) — his "experimental and practical divinity." The latter had been and still was the particular mark and "character" of Methodism — its *animus*, its reason for being. To subscribe to the Articles only was to remain in those days — as, perhaps, even now — an "unreformed" Anglican. Certainly, as these studies have shown, such was the view of William Watters, Jesse Lee, Freeborn Garrettson, or Francis Asbury.

DOCTRINAL STANDARDS AND THE TRADITION

With the background of this brief summation, let us return to the first officially authorized assessment and examination of United Methodist doctrinal standards of 1968–1972. It is to be recalled that the work of the authorized Commission became, by action of the 1972 General Conference, the present Part II of *The Book of Discipline*, entitled "Doctrine and Doctrinal Statements and General Rules." According to a 1972 ruling of the Judicial Council of The United Methodist Church, Section 1, "Historical Background," and Section 3, "Our Theological Task," are "legislative enactments and neither part of the Constitution nor under the Restrictive Rules."[3]

This ruling, contemporaneous with General Conference action in Atlanta in 1972, appears two-sided in its import. On the one hand, the ruling appears to deny Sections 1 and 3 either actual or intended normative doctrinal status, so as not to invoke the First Restrictive Rule of 1808. On the other hand, the ruling may, it appears, be interpreted to mean that the so-called "Landmark Documents" of Section 2 — namely, the Twenty-Five Articles of Religion, The Confession of Faith of the former Evangelical United Brethren Church, and the *General Rules of the United Societies* (1743) of the original Methodist Episcopal Church (received with the Articles, *Sunday Service*

179

and Wesley's *Minutes* of 1780) — are regarded by the Judicial Council as possessing constitutional status as essential norms of doctrine, both by right of tradition or unbroken usage and by prescription of the First Restrictive Rule (if properly understood).[4] However, so far as I am aware, the Judicial Council has never said so specifically, nor has the Council of Bishops ever spoken to the point.

In the initial *Form of Discipline* (1785–1791) by Coke and Asbury, both the *General Rules* and the Articles of Religion were included, not at the beginning of the document, but as §XXXIV and §XXXV. With the first edition of *The Doctrines and Discipline of The Methodist Episcopal Church* (1792), however, the Articles were made to constitute §ii of chapter 1. Thus, they were, in effect, advanced to constitutional rank. Not until 1846, in the Methodist Episcopal Church, South, and 1852, in the Methodist Episcopal Church [North], did the *General Rules* take their place as §iii of chapter 1 of the *Discipline*, immediately following the Articles. As central to discipline, however, they were always paired with the doctrine which they implemented by a truly practicing Methodist.

The question now returns afresh: what is the officially acknowledged obligation, if any, to the *traditioned* Methodist doctrinal commitment by present-day United Methodism in America? By *traditioned* doctrinal commitment I refer to a constellation of doctrinal affirmations we have already found plainly constitutive of early American Methodism from 1773 through 1794. These refer us to matters treated at length in chapters 1, 2, 3, 5, 10, and 11 of these studies, and concern not only Wesley's "experimental divinity" or his published *Sermons* and *Notes Upon the New Testament*, but also his *Minutes of Several Conversations* (1780), the *General Rules* (formally enjoined in 1773), and specifically, beginning in 1784, both the Articles of Religion and the *Sunday Service*, along with the *Collection of Hymns* of 1780.

In my view, it is obvious that the First Restrictive Rule was in fact possessed in 1808 of this range of reference. To suppose otherwise is, as these studies have shown, to be found carelessly or intentionally ignorant. How else are we to comprehend the "plurality" of the First Restrictive Rule? It reads:

> The General Conference shall not revoke, alter or change our articles of religion, nor establish any new standards or rules of doctrine contrary to our present existing and established standards of doctrine.[5]

Is it the case, then, that in its ruling of May, 1972, the Judicial Council, in not excluding Section 2, "Landmark Documents," from conformity with the First Restrictive Rule, was in fact recognizing the substance of those documents as even yet "established standards of doctrine"? I would suppose so, because to deny the constitutional status of these documents would be to ignore historical fact, and would amount to repudiation of the First Restrictive Rule itself, which defends both the Articles of Religion and the *General Rules*, and, as we have seen, much more, namely, Wesley's "experimental divinity." This, perhaps, underscores the predicament confronting the Judicial Council in any departure of an authorized Commission on Methodist doctrinal standards from the received, traditioned, and established standards or "canons of doctrine" of 1808.

One long-standing way to avoid the force of this impasse has been, for a century and more, something between disinterest and ignorance as to what, indeed, these early "canons of doctrine" in fact were to the General Conference of 1808. To clarify this impass it has seemed necessary to me to recover the substance of Wesleyan "experimental divinity" and, in turn, to understand its particular need for a supporting ecclesiology authorized by the Articles, *Minutes*, and *Sunday Service*, which Wesley saw so clearly. Wesley understood their necessity for constituting, not "Societies" as earlier, but, in 1784, for constituting a church as their successor. After prolonged consideration, and with this objective in mind, Wesley had completed elaborate provisions With Thomas Coke as chief agent, Wesley sought to commend his plan of a church to the American Methodists. He had become convinced that Methodism in the colonies, now severed from Britain, was faced either with becoming a self-perpetuating church or with the final dissolution of the Societies formed under his guidance and authority in 1773 for church reform.

CANONICAL STANDARDS OF DOCTRINE AND DISCIPLINE

Suppose, then, that what the Judicial Council recognized in the so-called "Landmark Documents" of §2 of Part II of *The Book of Discipline* as evidently "established standards of doctrine" (according to the First Restrictive Rule) also applies in actual fact to a far wider range of "established standards." May we suppose further that a failure of memory in later 19th-century Methodism obscured the place and doctrinal role, not only of Wesley's "experimental divinity" but also of Wesley's *Sermons* and *Notes Upon the New Testament*, the liturgy of the sacraments and ordination of the *Sunday Service*, and, above all — as has been shown in these studies — the "canonical" summations of the 1780 *Minutes of Several Occasions*? This it was that supplied the substance of the *earliest Form of Discipline* and, successively, that of *The Doctrines and Discipline* of 1792 and thereafter.

This last matter, as we saw in chapter 10, was fully demonstrated for the first time by John J. Tigert in the last decade of the 19th century.[6] Yet, before and since that time, the canonical history of American Methodism in this matter appears to have remained largely unknown to the heirs.[7] In some respects, this is strange, for, from the publication of the earliest *Form of Discipline* in 1785, and continuing for more than a half century, the inaugural message of the first General Superintendents — shortly to be called bishops — namely, Thomas Coke and Francis Asbury, and then also Richard Whatcoat and William McKendree, carried this counsel and exhortation to all Methodist members:

> Far from wishing you to be ignorant of any of our doctrines, or any part of our discipline, we desire you to read, mark, learn, and inwardly digest the whole. We know you are not in general able to purchase many books: but you ought, next to the word of God, to procure the Articles and Canons of the Church to which you belong.[8]

The import of this episcopal counsel to the general membership of the early Methodist Episcopal Church has had little attention and no recent commentary. It is manifest that this exhortation presupposes a plurality of Methodist doctrines with which members are presumed to need conversancy. Next to "the word of God" in Scripture these are commended and in their entirety. Plainly, then, there is a received doctrinal tradition in which members are expected to stand; and it is certain from our acquaintance with Wesley's "experimental and practical divinity," or "experimental religion," that this tradition of "living faith" is given to be claimed in the personal experience of individual believers.

Such experience, as we have seen, entailed a vital doctrine of the present working of the Holy Spirit. It was in and with such experience of the divine agency that both the "promises" of God's word in Scripture were personally claimed and the truth of doctrines respecting the "Scripture way of salvation" were "proved," that is, verified immediately in experience. Forgiveness of sins and reconciliation to God were supplied assurance through an inner witness of the Spirit. For, as we have seen, Wesleyan Methodists were at one with St. Paul's point that "it is the Spirit himself bearing witness with our spirit that we are the children of God" (Rom. 8:16). And by the same witness does the justified person know God as Abba, Father.

As the early Methodists well understood, such cognizance as this was, what John Wesley had called, following the Edwardian Homilies of the Church of England, "living faith" and, likewise, faith's confession. This was eager and joyous consent, perhaps, to "our present existing and established standards of doctrine" as exampled elsewhere, in Wesley's *Sermons on Several Occasions*. It was, therewith, glad sharing in the Methodist *consensus fidelium* — the common consent or declaration of the faithful. It was something eagerly acknowledged and thankfully shared in faith, and hope, and love.

In this way, the members of the United Societies recognized themselves as participants in a community of the faithful. They understood themselves as united in sharing Wesley's "little body of divinity" — the "Scripture way of salvation" — and this, not as a doctrinal schema, but a new way of being in relation, first, to God the Father, through Jesus Christ, and, then, to neighbor. It was the twofold Great Commandment, not merely applauded but reinacted.

Thus, as the Wesleys taught and their colleagues in faith understood, the sum of the "Scripture way of salvation" was repeatedly being verified in experience as persons entered upon it. So, also, it began to be confessed as "our present existing and established standards of doctrine," according to the phraseology of the First Restrictive Rule of 1808. In short, that range of propositions was becoming "doctrine" to be confessed but on the supposition that, by the redemptive intervention of God's Holy Spirit, they were given and received biographical representation in human lives, for their salvation.

Only in this light can we comprehend the episcopal message of the earliest Methodist Bishops to their membership, and their counsel that "next to the Word of God" are "the Articles" and the "Canons of the Church to which you belong." The connection between these words and those of the First Restrictive Rule deserves attention. It is, moreover, the kind of admonition that American Methodists of the 20th century have not heard often, I believe, in their time.

But what is meant by the Bishops' phrase, "Canons of the church to which you belong"? What are canons? The word "canon" derives from the Greek, *kanon*. It means rule, or measure, or standard, or norm. In its ecclesiastical usage *Webster's Unabridged Dictionary* defines "canon" as "A law or rule of doctrine or discipline . . . made by ecclesiastical authority."

It might have been defined as a "standard" or "rule" or a "norm" of doctrine or discipline. In either case, the definition comes close indeed to the views of Thomas Coke and Francis Asbury. We have recurrently seen that for Wesley and his successors, doctrine called for, or presupposed, an appropriate discipline by which its truth might be nurtured and become a *biographical* reality. With the Wesleys, and thereafter, with their succession, doctrine and discipline were insep-arably allied.

So essential was the mutuality of relation as between doctrine and discipline for Asbury that, as his autobiography reveals, he could scarce consider them in isolation. The reason was clear to him: If the truth of doctrine, namely the "Scripture way of salvation," waited upon its actualization and, thus, verification in personal experience — as a *present*, not a postponed, salvation — then it was plain that the instrumentalities or *means of grace*, including Christian discipline, were inseparable from the cognate truths of "saving faith." Accordingly, for Asbury, the *General Rules of the United Societies* were also "canonical" and belonged to the sum of what Asbury and Coke called the "Canon," that is, the authoritative doctrine and discipline of the Methodist Episcopal Church.

Meanwhile, Thomas Coke was Asbury's highly educated collab-orator in the collation and summation of the doctrinal and disciplinary fabric of the new Church. It is all but certain that, as a Doctor of Civil Law, Dr. Coke was fully conversant with the nature and function of the "constitutions and canons ecclesiastical" of the Church of England. These had been drawn up by Convocation of the Church and ratified by James I in 1603; and they remained in force in the 18th century and thereafter. Here was antecedent enough for the conception of a "canonical" rating of doctrines and discipline as entertained, it ap-pears, by Coke, Asbury, Whatcoat, and William McKendree from 1784, certainly to the death of Asbury in 1816 — and, surely, a firm precedent for the succession presupposed by the General Conference of 1808.

The language of the First Restrictive Rule of 1808 is rather plainly congruent with this "canonical" view of doctrines and discipline. It is so with reference to prohibition of "any new standards or rules [canons] of doctrine contrary to our present existing and established standards [canons] of doctrine." Because these are acknowledged al-ready as *normative*, that is, *canonical*, and "presently existing and *estab-lished* standards [canons] of doctrine," any new and contrary "canons" are forbidden, or proscribed. Is this not, then, *already* an established confession of faith — a *consensus fidelium*? And is not this consensus of the faithful as witnessed and declared in the doctrine and discipline identified in these studies as a *regula fidei*, a "rule of faith," to which Coke and Asbury expected of Methodists both conversancy and ad-herence? And was this not much like the state of doctrinal witness prevalent in the ante-Nicene Church? I judge it so.

Does this not suggest a probable error of fact, and of judgment, in the view declared in §1 of Part II of our *Discipline* from 1972 through 1984; namely, that the founding fathers "declined to adopt any of the classical forms of the 'confessional principle' — the claim that the essence of Christian truth can, and ought to be, stated in precisely defined propositions?"[9] Such a disclaimer of the so-called "confessional principle" can hardly be squared, it appears, with the prominent message of the earliest Methodist leaders in their preface to the *Form of Discipline*, which was continued as the *Doctrines and Discipline* to 1888.

It is one thing, today, to propose conciliar dialogue as a model for doctrinal formation in place of the "confessional tradition," (which was the distinctive innovation of Part II of the *Discipline* from 1972 through 1984).[10] It is quite another to misread the absence of the "confessional principle" in early American Methodism that appears to be presupposed by the Restrictive Rules themselves. The vicissitudes — ecclesiological and theological — and the course and timing by which, in the later 19th and the 20th century, the "confessional principle" dwindled to near insignificance in American Methodism is quite another story which can have no treatment here.

OF THE AUTHORITY OF EARLY DOCTRINAL STANDARDS

At this point, another question that is related to the so-called "confessional principle" demands attention: What were the role and the authority of the canons, rules, or norms of doctrine and discipline which, in the Bishops' preface to the early *Discipline*, were apparently enjoined for express acknowledgment by the members of the Church? More particularly, we might ask: Can it be that these "doctrines and discipline" — such is the very title of the Methodist book of order after 1792 — which were generally acknowledged, were also declared authoritative, or canonical, by the instrument of the Restrictive Rules of 1808?

If, as appears likely, the Restrictive Rules, particularly the First, were, in part, enacted to preserve both the role and the authority of Methodist doctrines and discipline in the Church, then presumably those doctrines and discipline were perceived as normative, or "canonical." As such they were also conceived as defining the reason for being of the Methodist Episcopal community of believers, and with such finality as would enforce the definition and, therewith, the identity of "the people called Methodists." In this way, it becomes fairly evident that without a "canonical," or normative declaration of doctrines and discipline, the early Methodist Episcopal Church in America would have lacked self-understanding and self-identity, without which, doubtless, erosion of purpose would follow.

At this point we arrive at some comprehension of the need for and constructive function of a confession of faith or the rationale of a *consensus fidelium*. Precisely this is what we have found to be implicated in that species of faith long known as *fides quae creditur*, the faith *that* we believe. Further, it may be said that in one perspective, the measure of doctrinal authority in a given church is the degree to which the *consensus fidelium* is constitutive of the church, and becomes the principle and ground of its self-identity. In State churches of earlier times men and women were, so to speak, "born" Christians of the reigning denomination and were assured membership by baptism. In State churches, therefore, the *consensus fidelium* tends to become merely nominal and not constitutive. Where church membership is voluntary, as in the so-called "free" Protestant churches, the faith confessed tends to be constitutive or "constitutional." That is to say once more, that the *consensus fidelium* — whether of the early Church in the Roman Empire or Protestant churches in America — tends to be truly constitutive because voluntary and because the consensus defines the reason for being of the several churches.

Three consequences emerge from these considerations:

(1) In the "free churches" the authority of "the canon of doctrines and discipline" is proportionate to the measure in which that canon defines the acknowledged reason for being of the church, i.e., is *constitutional*.

(2) The more the canon is, in fact, acknowledged as *constitutional*, the more justified is the Church in expecting of its members positive adherence to the canon, as did Coke and Asbury.

(3) If "the canon of doctrines and discipline" embodies the "sufficient reason" for the church's being, the dimming, or decline, or erosion of that rationale (that is, the *consensus fidelium*) is a negative prognosis for the survival of that church, particularly in modern secular society.

It is, then, to be pondered, whether in the absence of a *consensus fidelium* (that is, a canonical sum of doctrines and discipline acknowledged by most) a Christian community can attain to or retain a manifest identity and self-understanding, or convey a recognizable or enduring message, or, indeed, survive at all.

I think it is not straining the truth to suggest that, by express intention, the First Restrictive Rule of 1808 undertook to secure a *consensus fidelium* of the Methodist Episcopal Church conformable, on principle, to the exhortation of the presiding bishops of that day for understanding and adherence to "the Articles and Canons of the Church" on the part of the constituency. Apparently, for Bishops Coke, Asbury, Whatcoat, and McKendree, a *consensus fidelium*, or adherence to acknowledged standards of doctrine and discipline, was expected on the part of the members of the new Church. Neither was this a departure from expectations of members of the earlier Societies. Rather was it, in plain fact, an extension of that requirement from the former United Societies to the voluntary membership of the new Methodist Episcopal Church.

This canonical faith was never proposed by the early Methodist preachers or superintendents as an "absolute." Rather was the consensus of the faithful normative for those who, following upon the "Scripture way of salvation" and through the inner working of the Holy Spirit, had come to share, or were seeking, that renovation of life published by John Wesley's "experimental divinity." It denoted a synergistic process of which, as we have seen, the two principal doctrines were justification by grace through faith and sanctification as the lifelong quest for "inner and outward holiness in heart and life," and in the likeness of Christ.

OF LIVING FAITH AND CANONICAL DOCTRINE

Our rather extended exploration of John Wesley's "experimental and practical divinity" has made it plain that, for Wesley and the early Methodists, "living" or "saving faith" is different from canonical doctrine. Such canonical doctrine is essential for organized voluntary Christianity — that is, in defining the distinctive reason for being of the several churches, determining a measure of their identity, and advancing their self-understanding. Yet, for Wesley and his authentic succession, mere orthodoxy or canonical doctrines and discipline may screen out the vitality of "living faith," the new creation, and a dedicated life going on to perfection.

As we have noted, especially in chapter 6, when, as in *The Character of a Methodist*, Wesley teaches that "the distinguishing marks of a Methodist are not his opinions of any sort" he is in some measure dismissing what we have come to term "canonical doctrine" or theology.[11] This is part and parcel of his discreditation of "orthodoxy," which tends to exhaust Christian fidelity in fervent, and often rigid, adherence to a certain system of thought, opinion, or of creed.

Such "orthodoxy" often confounds addiction to a dogmatic system for living Christian faith, whereas, for Wesley, "living faith" presupposes a life wholly engrossed in a renovated relation to both God and man, as in the twofold Great Commandment of Mark 12:29–30. "Living faith" is manifested in faith, hope, and love as *a way of being in the world* after the likeness of Christ. "Living faith" was for Wesley and his associates a life-vocation as a "living sacrifice," as in Romans 12:1. "Living faith" for the early Methodists was the outcome of an encounter with Christ crucified in which the Holy Spirit had been victor. Salvation was not the end of an untraveled and unknown road but a present reality, traumatic no doubt, but fruitful of radical revision of life's incentives and direction. When, therefore, Wesley depreciates "orthodoxy" or a religion that justifies itself by the claim to possession of true opinions, he discounts it as a species of Pharisaism which takes pride in not being wrong, as are other men.

For Wesley, then, the distinguishing marks of a Methodist are not his "opinions" of any sort, even true ones, because the truth of the Christian religion is not something worked out by keen assessment. *For Wesley and his successors the truth of the Christian religion has its verification only by way of the experience of God's saving grace in Christ opened to acceptance by the inner working of the Holy Spirit.* It is received as justification by faith and the forgiveness of sins. To be sure, if there are no sins, there will be no relevance of this gospel. For the early Methodists, however, this gospel was relevant, since sin was rampant. Accordingly, the Methodists held that the truth of this gospel is truly and decisively known only by "taking the cure."

In a word, we have uncovered again the distinction previously made between the *fides qua creditur*, that is "living" or "saving faith" and the *fides quae creditur* — the faith that is believed. We have seen that with the early Methodists the former kind of faith has primacy — the faith *by which* we believe. But it does not negate nor dispense with the latter. And the latter is what we have come to call "canonical." It may be either the *consensus fidelium* or it may be "the rule of doctrine and discipline" — "the Canons of the Church" which Coke and Asbury regarded as "next to the word of God" in claiming the adherence of the membership.

In the measure members of the Church settle for only the consensus fidelium and fail to "take the cure," they are precisely where Wesley found the churches in the 18th century — possessed of "the form without the power of Godliness." Without doubt Wesley recognized fully the paradox of "orthodoxy." It was censurable when it substituted "the form" (whether of creed or of ceremony) for "the power of Godliness"; or "right belief" or "true opinion" for "saving faith" and the "new creation." But Wesley never supposed that a Christian church could dispense with its *consensus fidelium*, i.e., the consensus of faith that is affirmed. Perhaps the problem in present-day Methodism resides in its history. By the close of the 19th century Wesley's "experimental divinity" — the "Scripture way of salvation" — had lost currency. By the third quarter of the 20th century a *consensus fidelium* was not regarded by many, perhaps by most, as essential and its affirmation was seen as controversial.

Meanwhile, the spectacular decline of membership in the United Methodist Church during the past decade and more may suggest that very many have wearied beyond endurance with a church that manages mainly "the form of Godliness," on the one hand, and seems doctrinally shapeless, on the other.

ABBREVIATIONS

Appeals	*The Works of John Wesley*, Volume 11: *The Appeals to Men of Reason and Religion and Certain Related Open Letters*, ed. Gerald R. Cragg (Oxford: Clarendon Press, 1975).
Creeds	*The Creeds of Christendom, With a History and Critical Notes*, ed. Philip Schaff, 3 vols. (New York: Harper and Brothers, 1877).
Homilies	*Certain Sermons or Homilies Appointed to Be Read in the Church of England* (London: S.P.C.K., 1899).
Hymns	*The Works of John Wesley*, Volume 7: *A Collection of Hymns for the Use of the People Called Methodists*, ed. Franz Hildebrandt and Oliver A. Beckerlegge with James Dale (Oxford: Clarendon Press, 1983).
Journal	*The Works of John Wesley*, Volume 18: *Journal and Diaries I (1735–1738)*, ed. W. Reginald Ward and Richard P. Heitzenrater (Nashville: Abingdon Press, 1988).
Journal (Curnock)	*The Journal of the Rev. John Wesley, A.M.*, ed. Nehemiah Curnock, 8 vols. (London: Epworth Press, 1909–16).
Minutes (American)	*Minutes of the Methodist Conferences Annually Held in America, from 1773 to 1794, Inclusive* (Philadelphia: Printed by Henry Tuckness, Sold by John Dickens, 1795).
Minutes (British)	*Minutes of the Methodist Conferences from the First Held in London . . . in 1744*, Volume I: *1744–1798* (London: Thomas Cordeaux, at the Conference Office, 1812).
Sermons	*The Works of John Wesley*, Volumes 1–4: *Sermons I, 1–33*; *Sermons II, 34–70*; *Sermons III, 71–114*; and *Sermons IV, 115–151*; all ed. Albert C. Outler (Nashville: Abingdon Press, 1984–87).
Works	*The Works of the Rev. John Wesley*, ed. Thomas Jackson, 3rd ed., 14 vols. (London: Wesleyan Methodist Book Room, 1872; reprinted Grand Rapids: Baker Book House, 1979).

NOTES

PREFACE

1. *Hymns*, Preface, §4, pp. 73–4: "[This hymn book] is large enough to contain all the important truths of our most holy religion, whether speculative or practical; yea, and to illustrate them all, and prove them both by Scripture and reason. . . . So that this book is in effect a little body of experimental and practical divinity."

2. Gerald O. McCulloh, "Christian Experience," in *The Encyclopedia of World Methodism*, ed. Nolan B. Harmon, 2 vols. (Nashville: The United Methodist Publishing House, 1974), 1:822.

3. *The Book of Discipline of the United Methodist Church, 1984* (Nashville: The United Methodist Publishing House, 1984), ¶69, p. 45.

4. Thomas Williams, *An Historic Defense of Experimental Religion in Which the Doctrine of Divine Influences is Supported by the Authority of Scripture and the Experience of the Wisest and Best of Men in All Ages*, 2 vols. (London: Printed by Wm. Taylor for T. Heptinstall and W. Button, 1795).

5. Ola E. Winslow, *Jonathan Edwards, 1703–1758* (New York: Macmillan, 1941), pp. 232–4.

INTRODUCTION

1. Francis Asbury, *The Journal and Letters of Francis Asbury*, ed. Elmer T. Clark, J. Manning Potts, and Jacob S. Payton, 3 vols. (Nashville: Abingdon Press, 1958), 2:294. Despite the cautions of the editors, the cumulative evidence for the priority of the work of Strawbridge seems conclusive.

2. Ibid., 1:46.

3. St. George's, the "Old Cathedral" of Methodism, was purchased by Miles Pennington in an unfinished state from the German Reformed Church. Pennington was a charter member of the first class formed by Captain Thomas Webb in 1767. Joseph Pilmore's *Journal* shows that the shell of a church was purchased in November, 1769, and was first occupied for preaching November 23; see *The Journal of Joseph Pilmore (1769–1794)*, ed. Frederick E. Maser and H. T. Maag (Philadelphia: The Historical Society of the Philadelphia Annual Conference, 1969), pp. 27–35. For half a century St. George's was the largest Methodist church in America. Cf. John J. Tigert, *A Constitutional History of the American Episcopal Methodism*, 2nd ed. (Nashville: The Publishing House of the Methodist Episcopal Church, South, 1904), p. 54.

4. Asbury, *Journal and Letters*, 1:4.

5. Thomas Ware, *Sketches of the Life and Travels of Thomas Ware* (New York: T. Mason and G. Lane, 1832), pp. 184.

6. Robert E. Cushman, "Theological Landmarks Of The Wesleyan Revival," in *Faith Seeking Understanding* (Durham, NC: Duke University Press, 1981), p. 53.

7. Asbury, *Journal and Letters*, 1:4.

8. *Hymns*, Preface, §4, p. 74; cf. pp. 73–5.

9. Cf. *The Doctrines and Discipline of the Methodist Episcopal Church* (New York: Emory & Waugh, 1828), pp. 33, 39, 48, 73, 166, 182, etc. See also *The Doctrines and Discipline of the Methodist Episcopal Church* (New York: Hunt & Eaton, 1892), Chapter II, "The General Rules," note to ¶26, p. 27: "The United Societies founded in this country by the apostolic Asbury and colaborers were, in 1784, organized into the Methodist Episcopal Church. But in this chapter and occasionally elsewhere in the *Discipline*, the words *Society* and *Societies* are retained as equivalent to the words Church and Churches, both as a convenience, and as a memorial to our early ecclesiastical life." This important admission of the ambiguity remained with ¶26 in the 1904 edition of the *Doctrines and Discipline*, edited by Bishop Edward G. Andrews.

10. *The Doctrines and Discipline of the Methodist Episcopal Church* (New York: Hill & Ware, 1812), §viii, pp. 36–39; ibid. (1843), §ix, pp. 36–39; ibid. (1852), pp. 55–58. Cf. *The Doctrines and Discipline Methodist Episcopal Church, South*, 1850 (Richmond: John Early, 1850), §x, pp. 57–60.

11. *Doctrines and Discipline* (1828), Part I, §I.1, "Of the Origin of the Methodist Episcopal Church," p. 7.

12. *Minutes of Several Conversations Between the Rev. Mr. John Wesley and Others, From the Year 1744, to the Year 1789*, Q.26, *Works*, 8:310. These are the so-called "Large Minutes."

13. C. H. Dodd, *The Apostolic Preaching and Its Developments* (New York: Harper & Row, 1964), pp. 7–35.

14. Nathaniel Burwash, *Wesley's Doctrinal Standards: For the Use of the Methodist Church of Canada* (Toronto: William Briggs, 1881), pp. xiii–x. Burwash observes of Methodism, as of Wesley himself, that "A church arising out of a great evangelistic movement quite naturally finds its standards in a grand norm or type of preaching; not out of dogmatic disputation, but out of the Apostolic and primitive form of standard." And he adds, respecting Wesley's *Sermons* and *Notes*, that Wesley "revived a form of doctrinal standard almost ignored by modern writers in symbolics." Cf. W. P. Harrison, ed., *The Conference Course of Study* (Nashville: The Publishing House of the Methodist Episcopal Church, South, 1891), p. 3, where an extended introduction took explicit notice of Burwash's views and reaffirmed the "Standard Sermons" (52 in number) of Wesley "as forming an important part of our doctrinal standards" and as "helps to the formation of a pure scriptural creed."

15. References to the Homilies of the Church of England are almost innumerable in Wesley's writings of all types. Examples are found in *An Earnest Appeal to Men of Reason and Religion* (1743), §59, *Appeals*, p. 68; ibid., §78, p. 78; *A Farther Appeal to Men of Reason and Religion* (1745), Part I, §II.1–8, *Appeals*, pp. 108–15; ibid., §V.25–26, pp. 167–70. Such references in his *Journal* appear

as early as September 30, 1739, and occur frequently thereafter into the 1740s; see *Journal*, 1:192.

16. Cf. *An Earnest Appeal*, §78, *Appeals*, pp. 77–8: "The Article mentions three things as essential to a visible church: living faith, without which indeed there can be no church at all, neither visible nor invisible. . . ."

17. Cf. Wesley's account of the founding of the Fetter Lane Society in London on May 1, 1738, *Journal*, 1:236. According to Tigert, *Constitutional History*, p. 65, the *Minutes of Several Conversations* (which were published by Wesley in three successive editions, 1753, 1763, and 1770) were those adopted by the 1773 Philadelphia conference of American Methodists and "became the original doctrinal and disciplinary basis of American Methodism."

18. *The Nature, Design, and General Rules of the United Societies* (1743), *Works*, 8:269f. Cf. *The Book of Discipline of the United Methodist Church, 1984*, ¶68, pp. 68–71.

19. Ibid., §2, p. 269.

20. Ibid., §3, p. 269.

21. Ibid., §4, p. 270. As the phrase "to flee from the wrath to come" is from Matt. 3:7, so the reference to "fruits worthy of repentance" is from Matt. 3:8.

22. Cf. *The Doctrines and Discipline of the Methodist Episcopal Church in America, With Explanatory Notes by Thomas Coke and Francis Asbury*, 10th ed. (Philadelphia: Printed by Henry Tuckness, Sold by John Dickens, 1798), facsimile edition, ed. Frederick A. Norwood (Rutland, Vt.: Academy Books, 1979), p. iii. This declaration by Coke and Asbury was included in the Preface "To the Members of the Methodist Societies in America" in every edition of the *Doctrines and Discipline* for a hundred years.

23. *Minutes of Several Conversations*, Q.3, *Works*, 8:299.

24. J. F. Anderson, *The Methodist Dictionary: A Brief Work on Methodist Terminology* (New York: Eaton and Mains, 1909), p. 1.

25. William Watters, *A Short Account of the Christian Experience and Ministerial Labors of William Watters* (Alexandria, Va.: Snowden, n.d.). The Preface is signed by William Watters, Fairfax, Va., May 14, 1806.

26. Article XIII of the Twenty-Four Articles, *Creeds*, 3:810. Cf. Article XIX of the Thirty-Nine Articles, *Creeds*, 3:499. Wesley's abridgment of the Thirty-Nine Articles was provided to the American Methodists in 1784. The General Conference of 1804 added Article XXIII, "Of the Rulers of the United States of America," bringing the total number of Articles to twenty-five.

27. Cf. *An Earnest Appeal*, §76, *Appeals*, p. 77. It can be argued that here we do have a text in which Wesley makes the "essence" of the church "a company of faithful (or believing) people." This faith is defined in §78 (p. 78) by reference to the Homilies as "a sure trust and confidence in God, that through the merits of Christ *my* sins are forgiven, and *I* reconciled to the favor of God." In this, we are getting very close indeed "to Christ's ordinance, in all those things that of necessity are requisite to the same."

28. Cf. the 1888 edition of *The Doctrines and Discipline of the Methodist Episcopal Church* (New York: Phillips & Hunt, 1888), pp. 3–6, with the 1892 edition (New York: Hunt & Eaton, 1892), pp. 3–6. In the 1892 edition of the

Doctrines and Discipline, for the first time, the traditional "message" is altered, but not the advices and admonitions on doctrine and discipline.

29. Abel Stevens, *Centenary of American Methodism* (New York: Carlton & Porter, 1865), pp. 125–126.

30. *The Journal of the General Conference of the Methodist Episcopal Church, Baltimore, 1840* (New York: Lane & Tippett, 1844), p. 154.

31. See Moses M. Henkle, *The Primary Platform of Methodism; Or An Exposition of the General Rules* (Louisville, Ky.: Sold by The Southern Methodist Book Concern, 1853), p. 52: "These General Rules were adopted and respected, as of binding force in this country, from the first formation of Methodist societies. And when the Methodist Episcopal Church was organized, in 1784, they were received as the law of the church. . . ."

32. Cf. *The Character of a Methodist*, §17, *Works*, 8:346. Plainly, the phrase "revelation of Jesus Christ" comes straight from Galatians 1:12 and serves notice, as so often the case, that Wesley is committed to St. Paul's scriptural way of salvation.

33. Cf. *Journal of the General Conference, 1840*, p. 155.

CHAPTER 1: DOCTRINES AND DISCIPLINE IN EARLY AMERICAN METHODISM

1. Jesse Lee, *A Short History of the Methodists In the United States of America; Beginning in 1766, and Continued to 1809* (Baltimore: Magill & Cline, 1810).

2. E. R. Hendrix, *The Creed of Ecumenical Methodism: Where Can It Be Found?* (Nashville: The Publishing House of the Methodist Episcopal Church, South, 1908; reprinted from *The Methodist Review* [April, 1907]).

3. Hilary T. Hudson, *The Methodist Armor; Or A Popular Exposition of the Doctrines, Peculiar Usages and Ecclesiastical Machinery of the Methodist Episcopal Church, South*, 9th ed. (Nashville: The Publishing House of the Methodist Episcopal Church, South, 1921).

4. *The Book of Discipline of the United Methodist Church, 1984*, ¶69, p. 78.

5. Cf. *Minutes* (American). As the preface to this volume plainly indicates, it was published at the initiative of John Dickens, chief Methodist publisher, who felt that while *Minutes* of some Annual Conferences had been published, a compendium of all the Conference *Minutes* between 1773 and 1794 should be preserved. How Dickens misdated the Philadelphia Conference of 1773 as in June, rather than July 14, 1773, remains unknown. I am grateful to my colleague Professor O. Kelly Ingram for use of this volume of uncommon importance and rarity.

6. Holland N. McTyeier recognizes John Dickens as founder of the original "Methodist Book Concern"; see *The History of Methodism* (Nashville: The Publishing House of the Methodist Episcopal Church, South, 1885), p. 310. Dickens, as preacher stationed in New York, received Thomas Coke on arrival November 3, 1784 and, as participant in the Christmas Conference made the motion to name the new church "The Methodist Episcopal Church." Cf. Ware, *Life and Travels*, p. 106.

7. *Minutes* (American), 1773 Conference, pp. iii and 5.

8. Ibid., p. 5. Italics mine.

9. *Works*, 8:299–338.

10. With the Philadelphia organizational Conference of July 1773 under Thomas Rankin, the policy was declared, according to Asbury's *Journal* for July 14, 1773, that "No preacher in our connexion shall be permitted to administer the ordinances at this time; except Mr. Strawbridge, and he under the particular direction of the assistant." See Asbury, *Journal and Letters*, 1:85. This exception, in the case of Strawbridge, was to prove the rule. He in fact remained insubordinate either to Rankin, or to Asbury, after the former's departure in 1777 when the rising demand for the sacraments occasioned a near schism of the American Methodists.

11. *Minutes* (American), 1780 Conference, p. 35.

12. Ibid., 1781 Conference, p. 41. Italics mine.

13. Ibid., 1782 Conference, p. 54.

14. Ibid., 1781 Conference, p. 43.

15. Ibid., 1784 Conference, p. 72.

16. For example, see the "Historical Statement" in the following editions of *The Doctrines and Discipline of the Methodist Episcopal Church* — 1912 (New York: The Methodist Book Concern, 1912), pp. 15–18; 1936 (New York: The Methodist Book Concern, 1936), pp. 5–7; 1940 (New York: The Methodist Publishing House, 1940), pp. 3–8 — and in *The Book of Discipline of The United Methodist Church, 1972* (Nashville: The United Methodist Publishing House, 1972), pp. 7–15.

17. Cf. John J. Tigert, *The Making of Methodism* (Nashville: The Publishing House of the Methodist Episcopal Church, South, 1898), chapter 8, where Tigert recounts the story with learning and perspicacity, and, I judge, correctly in balanced assessment of the available facts.

18. *Doctrines and Discipline* (1798), p. v.

19. Ibid.

20. Cf. Sermon 4, "Scriptural Christianity," *Sermons*, 1:159–80; Sermon 43, "The Scripture Way of Salvation," *Sermons*, 2:153–69.

21. See, for example, *Journal*, 1:208–10 (January 8–9, 1738), 1:213–16 (January 29, 1738), and 1:221–54 (February 1–June 7, 1738).

CHAPTER 2: A LITTLE BODY OF EXPERIMENTAL AND PRACTICAL DIVINITY

1. *Minutes of Several Conversations*, Q.27, *Works*, 8:310–313.

2. Lee, *Short History*, p. 29.

3. Ibid., p. 29–36.

4. *Hymns*, Preface, §4, p. 73–4.

5. *Minutes of Several Conversations*, Q.3, *Works*, 8:299.

6. *Journal*, 1:260 (July 6, 1738). Cf. *A Farther Appeal to Men of Reason and Religion*, Part I, §V.1, *Appeals*, p. 138f.

7. *A Farther Appeal*, Part I, §V.28, *Appeals*, p. 171.

8. *Minutes of Several Conversations*, Q.3, *Works*, 8:299.

9. Cf. *Journal* (Curnock), 2:321–2 (Nov. 25, 1739).

10. Cf. *Minutes of Several Conversations*, Q.13, *Works*, 8:305, and *Journal* (Curnock), 2:216–8 (June 11, 1739).

11. *Hymns*, #299:1–3, pp. 454–5.

12. *Hymns*, #29:1, 2, 6, pp. 116–7.

13. *Hymns*, #127:1, p. 238.

14. *Hymns*, #128:5, p. 239.

15. *Hymns*, #136:6, p. 251. Cf. also *Journal* (Curnock), 2:185–6 (April 29, 1739), and 2:201–5 (May 20–26, 1739).

16. *The Sunday Service of the Methodists in His Majesty's Dominions: With Other Occasional Services*, 4th ed. (London: Frys and Couchman, 1792); bound with *A Collection of Psalms and Hymns For The Lord's Day* (London: Published by John and Charles Wesley, 1791), Psalm CXXX, p. 21. Taken together the two titles provided a service book for British Methodists following the death of John Wesley. This version is virtually identical to its American counterpart, which was in fact published first: *The Sunday Service of the Methodists in the United States of America: With Other Occasional Services* (1st ed. 1784), also bound with *A Collection of Psalms and Hymns for the Lord's Day* (1st ed. 1784). See Richard Green, *The Works of John and Charles Wesley: A Bibliography*, 2nd ed. (London: C. H. Kelly, 1906), #376, #378, and #390, for a discussion of these works and their publication history.

17. *An Earnest Appeal*, §11, *Appeals*, pp. 48–9.

18. *Journal*, 1:246-7 (May 24, 1738, §9). Cf. *An Earnest Appeal*, §71, *Appeals*, p. 75.

19. *Minutes of Several Conversations*, Q.13, *Works*, 8:304.

20. Ibid., Q.26, p. 310. Italics mine.

21. Cf. Sermon 85, "On Working Out Our Own Salvation," *Sermons*, 3:199-209, and *Journal*, 1:246–7 (May 24, 1738, §9).

22. Cf. Wesley's Preface to his "Sermons on Several Occasions," §5, *Sermons*, 1:105.

23. See the Thirty-Nine Articles, Article VI, "Of the Sufficiency of the Holy Scriptures for Salvation," *Creeds*, 3:489.

24. *Hymns*, #93:1, 4a, pp. 195–7. Cf. #153, p. 272; #157, pp. 276–7; #195, pp. 325–6; and #197, p. 328.

25. *Journal*, 1:248–9 (May 24, 1738, §§12–13).

26. Ibid., pp. 249–59 (§14). The italicized personal pronouns are all Wesley's.

27. Ibid., pp. 246–7 (§9).

28. Ibid., pp. 233–4 (April 22, 1738).

29. Cf. *A Farther Appeal*, Part 1, §30, *Appeals*, pp. 173–4. It is of no small importance that in his sermon "Promises Obtained Through Faith," Richard Watson plainly recognizes and propounds the mutuality of "saving" or justifying faith with the truth of Scripture. The latter is realized or verified in faithful experience together with its concomitants, i.e., life empowered by the Holy Spirit, deliverance from love of the world, victory over temptation, and going on to perfection. The "promise" of Scripture is verified in experience. See Watson's *Sermons and Sketches of Sermons*, (New York: Lane & Tippett, 1845), 1:290–291.

30. *Journal*, 1:241 (May 19, 1738).

31. *The Character of a Methodist*, §5, *Works*, 8:341.

32. See The Thirty-Nine Articles, Article XII, "Of Good Works," and Article XVII, "Of Predestination and Election," *Creeds*, 3:494, 497–9. For the text of Wesley's abridgment of the Thirty-Nine Articles into the Twenty-Four Articles, see *Creeds*, 3:807–13.

33. *Hymns*, #92:6, p. 195.

34. Homily 4, "A Short Declaration of the True, Lively, and Christian Faith," Part 1, *Homilies*, pp. 33ff. This sermon is to be compared directly with the chapter on "Justification and Faith" in the *Loci Communes Theologici* of Philip Melanchthon; see *Melanchthon and Bucer*, ed. Wilhelm Pauck (Philadelphia: Westminster Press, 1969), pp. 88–109. The position here taken both in the Homilies and in Melanchthon's *Loci* reflects the famous words of Luther's commentary on the First Commandment in *The Large Catechism*: "The trust and faith of the heart alone makes both God and idol." See *The Book of Concord: Confessions of the Evangelical Lutheran Church*, edited by Theodore G. Tappert (Philadelphia: Fortress Press, 1959), pp. 365. In company with Luther, Melanchthon, almost for the first time, is trying to say how and why "justifying faith" alone is true and saving faith. This is so, not only because it is a gift of God, a work of Grace, but because it bestows forgiveness of sins and liberates the justified sinner to bring forth "good works" suited to "newness of life." Like Luther and Melanchthon, Cranmer is attempting in the Homily to distinguish the faith that justifies or saves from faith considered simply as assent or adherence to propositions on the authority of Holy Church, or tradition, or Scripture. Such is the faith of orthodoxy. This John Wesley came to understand also in the spring of 1738. Instead, the faith that saves, *fides salvifica*, has become an immediate transaction and renovation of relation between God the Father and penitent humanity through the mediation of the Holy Spirit on condition of the acceptance of God's acceptance in Jesus Christ and his righteousness, i.e., St. Paul's "righteousness of God through faith in Jesus Christ for all who believe" (Rom. 3:22). See Wesley's own abridgment of Cranmer's Homilies, *The Doctrine of Salvation, Faith and Good Works, Extracted from the Homilies of the Church of England*, in *John Wesley*, ed. Albert C. Outler (New York: Oxford University Press, 1964), pp. 123–33. Cf. Green, *Bibliography*, #9.

35. Cf. *The Augsburg Confession*, Part I, Article 22, "Of Good Works," *Creeds*, 3:20–26.

36. Homily 4, "Of Faith," Part 1, *Homilies*, pp. 34–5.

37. Ibid., Part 3, pp. 44–5.

38. *Loci Communes*, in *Melanchthon and Bucer*, p. 90.

39. *Journal*, 1:247 (May 24, 1738, §11).

40. Cf. *A Farther Appeal*, Part I, §I.1–2, *Appeals*, pp. 105–6, where Wesley speaks of justification as "present forgiveness, pardon of sins, acceptance with God." He continues: "I believe the condition of this is faith [Rom. 4:5]: I mean, not only, that without faith we cannot be justified, but, also, that as soon as anyone has true faith, in that moment he is justified. Good works follow this faith, but cannot go before it. . . ." For faith as the condition of justification, cf. Homily 3, "Of the Salvation of Mankind," Part III, *Homilies*, p. 29: "Only faith

justifieth us; meaning none other thing than St. Paul meant when he said, Faith without works justifieth us."

41. The Thirty-Nine Articles, Article X, "Of Free Will," *Creeds*, 3:493–4. Richard Baxter in his tract *The Life of Faith* makes the remarkable statement that "the work of faith is much promoted by the spiritual experiences of believers. When they find a considerable part of the Holy Scriptures verified in themselves, it much confirmeth their faith in the whole." See Baxter's *Practical Works*, ed. William Orme (London: J. Duncan, 1830), 12:14. While Wesley published *An Abstract of Mr. Richard Baxter's Aphorisms of Justification* in 1745 (cf. Green, *Bibliography*, #67), there is no reference elsewhere in Wesley's writings to Baxter's *The Life of Faith*, nor was it included in *The Christian Library*. Wesley did include extracts of Johann Arndt's *True Christianity* in *The Christian Library*. Arndt (1555–1621) shows evident dependency upon Melanchthon's teaching on the nature of "living faith" with an important discussion of the contrast between "historical and opinionative faith" and "living, saving, and experimental faith." This distinction also finds prominence in Wesley's writings. There is, moreover, for both Baxter and Arndt, a common source in Melanchthon's *Loci Communes*. For John Wesley that source is mediated by the Homilies of the Church of England and is echoed in Henry Scougal's *The Life of God in the Soul of Man*.

42. *Minutes of Several Conversations*, Q.4, *Works*, 8:300.

43. *Journal* (Curnock), 2:275 (Sept. 13, 1739). Wesley later published an abridged edition of Scougal's notable work *The Life of God in the Soul of Man* in 1744; it was reprinted in 1748, 1756, 1777, 1790, and 1797. Cf. Green. *Bibliography*, #51.

44. Cf. *Minutes of Several Conversations*, Q.51, *Works*, 8:325, and Q.56, 8:328.

45. The Thirty-Nine Articles, Article XII, "Of Good Works," *Creeds*, 3:494.

46. Ibid., Article IX, "Of Original or Birth-Sin," *Creeds*, 3:492–3.

47. See Wesley's Twenty-Four Articles, *Creeds*, 3:807–13.

48. *Journal* (Curnock), 2:220 (June 14, 1739).

49. Cf. *A Farther Appeal*, Part 1, §23, *Appeals*, pp. 163–5.

50. Cf. Sermon 4, "Scriptural Christianity," *Sermons*, 1:159–80; Sermon 6, "The Righteousness of Faith," *Sermons*, 1:200–16; Sermon 7, "The Way to the Kingdom," *Sermons*, 1:217–32; and Sermon 8, "The First-Fruits of Righteousness," *Sermons*, 1:233–47.

51. *Minutes of Several Conversations*, Q.77, *Works*, 8:337.

52. Sermon 85, "On Working Out Our Own Salvation," *Sermons*, 3:199–209. I fully concur with Dr. Outler's assessment: "This must be considered as a landmark sermon, for it stands as the late Wesley's most complete and careful exposition of the mystery of the divine-human interaction, his subtlest probing of the paradox of prevenient grace and human agency" (p. 199).

53. *A Farther Appeal*, Part I, §III.10, *Appeals*, p. 130.

54. *Minutes of Several Conversations*, Q.4, *Works*, 8:300.

CHAPTER 3: JUSTIFICATION IN EXPERIENCE

1. *The Life of the Reverend Freeborn Garrettson: Compiled from His Journals*, ed. Nathan Bangs, 3rd ed. (New York: Emory & Waugh, 1832), p. 170. This letter of Wesley's to Garrettson, who had been assigned by the General Conference of 1785 to Nova Scotia along with J. O. Cromwell, was the first of several letters exchanged between them until 1790.

2. See Sermon 42, "The Scripture Way of Salvation," *Sermons*, 2:153–69. I agree with Albert Outler's judgment that this sermon "is the most successful summary of the Wesleyan vision of the *ordo salutis* in the entire sermon corpus" (p. 154).

3. Luke Tyerman, *The Life and Times of the Reverend John Wesley, A.M.*, 3 vols. (New York: Harper and Brothers, 1872), 1:184.

4. Ibid., 1:177–196.

5. *Journal* (Curnock), 2:267 (Sept. 3, 1739). The statement is followed by Susanna Wesley's personal witness: "Therefore . . . I never durst ask for it myself. But two or three weeks ago, while my son Hall was pronouncing those words, in delivering the cup to me, 'The blood of the Lord Jesus Christ, which was given for thee,' the words struck through my heart, and I knew God for Christ's sake had forgiven *me* all *my* sins." On this Wesley makes no comment, but the italics are his, which suggests two things: (1) that he sees here a recapitulation of his own experience of May 24, 1738; and (2) that he finds in this event an instance of his own view that the Lord's Supper may be a "converting ordinance" at any time.

6. Ibid., 2:267–8. Samuel Palmer remarks in his edition of Edmund Calamy's *The Nonconformist's Memorial: An Account of the Ministers Ejected by the Act of Uniformity, August 24, 1662* (London: Harris, 1775), that Samuel Annesley "was one who may be said to have been sanctified from the womb . . . that he knew not the time when he was not converted" (p. 104).

7. Cf. Tyerman, *Life of Wesley*, 1:32–40.

8. *The Nonconformist's Memorial*, p. 106. It is worthy of particular notice that the joint position filled by Samuel Annesley, beginning 1657, as lecturer of St. Paul's Cathedral and Vicar of St. Giles, Cripplegate, was a distinguished old post occupied at the start of the 17th century by Lancelot Andrewes.

9. *Journal* (Curnock), 2:267–8 (Sept. 3, 1739).

10. See John Calvin, *The Institutes of the Christian Religion*, §III.ii.6–7, trans. & ed. John T. McNeill and Fred L. Battles, 2 vols. (Philadelphia: Westminster Press, 1950), 1:548 ff.

11. *Journal*, 1:248 (May 24, 1738, §11).

12. Ibid.

13. Ibid. (§12).

14. Ibid., pp. 248–9. The italics are Wesley's. Note that the two points of his resolution reflect respectively Romans 3 and Part 2 of Cranmer's Homily "Of Salvation."

15. Ibid., p. 260 (July 6, 1738).

16. Ibid., pp. 260–61 (July 12, 1738).

17. *Journal* (Curnock), 2:185 (April 29, 1739). The quotation is from Rom. 8:32.

18. Ibid., p. 250 (July 31, 1739). Curnock identifies the author of *A Caution Against Religious Delusion* as the Rev. Henry Stebbing, D.D., Chancellor of the diocese of Salisbury and observes that his *Caution* "was considered more temperate than many of the attacks made at the time upon the Methodist clergymen" (p. 249, n.2).

19. *Sermons*, 1:106 (Preface, §5). Wesley's use of both John 7:16–17 and 1 Cor. 2:13 is of crucial importance since it shows Wesley's identification of "spiritual things" with those affirmed by a human will that has been conformed to the will of God by the intervention of the Holy Spirit. Faith had become for Wesley a "transformation" and "renewal" of the mind of the believer as in Rom. 12:2. Wesley's quotation of the final phrase of 1 Cor. 2:13, "comparing spiritual things with spiritual," follows the King James Version. The phrase is better translated in the Revised Standard Version as "interpreting spiritual truths to those who possess the Spirit." The latter spells out the import of the preceding v. 12, "Now we have received not the spirit of the world, but the Spirit which is from God, that we might understand the gifts bestowed on us by God."

20. *Hymns*, #87:1–2, 4, pp. 186–7.

21. *Hymns*, #85:1–2, 4, p. 185. Cf. #34:2, p. 123; #110:4, p. 220; and #369:3, p. 539.

22. The position here adumbrated is entirely congenial with Albert Outler's statement in his Introduction to Wesley's *Sermons* (1:75): "His basic idea of the 'order of salvation' — as the process of the restoration of the image of God — is obviously an adaptation of St. Irenaeus' famous doctrine of *anakephalaiosis* (i.e., the recapitulatory work of Christ as the ground of all salvation)." To this I would add that the theme of *recapitulatio* is already articulated in the Pauline epistles, particularly in Phil. 2:5. Outler's discussion of Wesley's "peculiar doctrine of perfection as *teleiosis* (perfecting perfection) rather than *perfectus* (perfected perfection)" is especially important in this connection (p. 74).

23. *A Farther Appeal*, Part 1, §I.4–5, *Appeals*, pp. 106–7.

24. Cf. Wesley's extensive commentary on this matter in *A Farther Appeal*, Part 1, §V.27–28, *Appeals*, pp. 170–2.

25. *Sermons*, 1:106 (Preface, §6).

26. *Letters*, 1:160.

27. *Journal*, 1:233–4 (April 22, 1738).

28. Ibid. Cf. *Journal* (Curnock), 2:180 (April 17, 1739).

29. *The Character of a Methodist, Works*, 8:340–347; cf. Green, *Bibliography*, #34. The closely related essay *The Principles of a Methodist, Works*, 8:359–74, was first published in 1742; cf. Green, *Bibliography*, #35. It is my view that these two brief essays, of 20 and 32 pages respectively in the original editions, supply most readily the sum of Wesley's experimental religion and divinity. Next to these in importance are the far more extensive doctrinal discussions of *An Earnest Appeal* and the three parts of *A Farther Appeal*.

CHAPTER 4: CHRISTIAN EXPERIENCE ACCORDING TO WILLIAM WATTERS AND OTHERS

1. See the discussion of early Methodist preachers and leadership in McTyeire, *History of Methodism*, ch. 22–24. Few historians of the period have matched McTyeire's grasp of doctrinal issues, which gives depth to his treatment.

2. Watters, *Short Account*, p. 17. Italics mine. This volume appears to be a "log" or journal written over many years, though it may be memoirs based upon earlier diaries or notes. It was almost certainly not written as an autobiography of the later years. It is one of the very few surviving primary sources of earliest Methodism in America.

3. Ibid., p. 18.

4. McTyeire, *History of Methodism*, p. 268.

5. Ibid., p. 265. Watters' *Short Account*, p. 18, names Robert Strawbridge, John King, and Robert Williams as the only Methodist preachers known by him to have preached in Maryland at the time of his conversion in 1771. Watters accompanied Williams to Norfolk, Virginia, in 1772. There is evidence that Williams came from the north into the Baltimore region, perhaps in 1771 or 1772.

6. Watters, *Short Account*, p. 26.

7. Ibid., p. 27.

8. McTyeire, *History of Methodism*, pp. 285, 288.

9. Watters, *Short Account*, p. 7.

10. Ibid., p. 7.

11. Ibid., p. 8.

12. Ibid., p. 9.

13. Ibid.

14. Ibid., p. 12.

15. Ibid., p. 13.

16. Ibid., pp. 14–5.

17. *Minutes of Several Conversations*, Q.4, *Works*, 8:300.

18. *Hymns*, #334:1, 4, pp. 490–1.

19. Ware, *Life and Travels*, pp. 54–7.

20. Ibid.

21. *A Sketch of the Life of the Rev. John Collins, Late of the Ohio Conference* (Cincinnati: Swormstedt & Power, Methodist Episcopal Church, 1849), pp. 72–73. John Collins (1769–1845), born in Glouster County, New Jersey, of Quaker parents, delivered the first Methodist sermon preached in Cincinnati in 1804.

22. Frances J. McConnell, *The Essentials of Methodism* (New York: Methodist Book Concern, 1916), pp. 11, 17.

23. Cf. Lee, *Short History*, pp. 29–36.

CHAPTER 5: EXPERIMENTAL DIVINITY IN EARLY AMERICAN METHODISM

1. Lee, *Short History*, pp. 36–38.
2. Ibid., p. 36.
3. Sermon 53, "On the Death of George Whitefield," *Sermons*, 2:331, 341–3.
4. Lee, *Short History*, p. 26.
5. Quoted in Lee, *Short History*, p. 28.
6. *Minutes of Several Conversations*, Q.4, *Works*, 8:300.
7. *The Doctrines and Discipline of The Methodist Episcopal Church* (New York: Hitt & Ware, 1812), §III, "Of the General Conference," p. 23.
8. *Minutes of Several Conversations*, Q.4, *Works*, 8:300.
9. *Doctrines and Discipline*, preface. While succeeding Methodist bishops signed it over the years, the introductory "Message" or preface remained unchanged until 1888.
10. Nathan Bangs, *History of the Methodist Episcopal Church*, 4 vols. (New York: Carlton & Porter, 1857), 1:359–360.
11. Ibid., 1:364–5.
12. Ware, *Life and Travels*, p. 107f.
13. *Minutes of Several Conversations*, Q.4, *Works*, 8:300.
14. *A Farther Appeal*, Part I, §V.29, *Appeals*, p. 172. Cf. *The Character of a Methodist*, §17, *Works*, 8:346.
15. The title of this book of discipline, first published in 1785 following the Christmas Conference, remained in use till it was superseded by the title *The Doctrines and Discipline of the Methodist Episcopal Church* in 1792, when also there was a major alterations of its arrangement and content.
16. Cf. *A Farther Appeal*, Part III, §III.10, *Appeals*, p. 296, where as early as 1745 Wesley says, in support of his lay preachers, that "I trust there is not one of them who is not able to go through such an examination, in substantial practical, experimental divinity, as few of our candidates for holy orders, even in the University . . . are able to do."
17. Quoted in John Atkinson, *Memorials of Methodism in New Jersey: From the Foundation of the First Society, 1770–1790*, 2nd ed. (Philadelphia: Perkinpine & Higgins, 1860), p. 63. Cf. Wesley in *An Earnest Appeal*, §10, *Appeals*, p. 48: "May not your own experience teach you this?" Joseph Bellamy (1719–1790), a Connecticut Congregationalist pastor, was both a friend and a disciple of Jonathan Edwards.
18. Cf. *A Farther Appeal*, Part I, §§V.1–23, *Appeals*, pp. 138–166.
19. Ibid., §I.2–6, pp. 105–8.
20. Ibid., §I.3, p. 106.
21. *The Character of a Methodist*, §1, *Works*, 8:340.
22. *The Principles of a Methodist*, §9, *Works*, 8:363. Cf. *Advice to the People Called Methodists*, *Works*, 8:352.
23. Cf. *A Farther Appeal*, Part I, §V.28, *Appeals*, p. 170: "Every good gift is from God, and is given to man by the Holy Ghost. . . . Have we any true

knowledge of what is good? . . . we can never discern them until 'God reveals them unto us by his Spirit.'"

24. Ibid., §VI.1, pp. 176–7: "I was equally ignorant of *saving faith*, apprehending it to mean no more than a 'firm assent to all the propositions contained in the Old and New Testaments.'"

25. *The Principles of a Methodist*, §4, *Works*, 8:362.

26. *A Farther Appeal*, Part I, §III.10, *Appeals*, p. 130.

27. *The Fundamentals: A Testimony to the Truth*, 10 vols. (Chicago: Testimony Publishing Co., n.d. [c. 1906–10]), contains essays from may contributors of note from several denominaitons in the U.S., Britain, and Canada. See George M. Marsden's comprehensive and balanced account of *Fundamentalism in American Culture: The Shaping of Twentieth-Century Evangelicalism, 1870–1925* (Oxford & New York: Oxford University Press, 1980).

28. See, e.g., *An Earnest Appeal*, §4–10, *Appeals*, pp. 46–48; §13, p. 49; §40, p. 59; and §59, p. 68–9.

29. *The Sunday Service*, A2.

30. Cf. *An Earnest Appeal*, §62, *Appeals*, pp. 70–1.

31. *The Character of A Methodist*, §1, *Works*, 8:340.

32. Philip Melanchthon, *Melanchthon On Christian Doctrine: Loci Communes, 1555*, trans. and ed. Clyde L. Manschreck (New York: Oxford University Press, 1965), p. 163.

33. Ibid., p. 164.

34. Ibid., p. 158.

35. Ibid., pp. 103–4.

36. Homily 4, "Of The True, Lively, and Christian Faith," Part 1, *Homilies*, pp. 33–5. This homily has been generally attributed to Cranmer, as have Homily 1, "Of Holy Scripture," and Homily 3, "Of the Salvation of All Mankind." Because a Second Book was added to the First and published in 1563 as part of "the Elizabethan settlement" — making at that time 32 sermons in all — the Book of Homilies has since carried the designation: "Appointed to be Read in the Churches in the Time of Queen Elizabeth."

37. Ibid., Part I, pp. 34–35. Cf. pp. 37–40: "All holy Scripture agreeably beareth witness that a true and lively faith in Christ doth bring forth good works: therefore every man must examine himself, to know whether he have the . . . true lively faith in this heart . . . which he shall know by the fruits thereof."

38. *Journal*, 1:225–6 (Feb. 18, 1738).

39. Homily 4, "Of Faith," Part I, *Homilies*, p. 35.

40. Ibid., p. 34.

41. *Journal*, 1:228 (March 4, 1738).

42. Homily 4, "Of Faith," Part I, *Homilies*, pp. 33f.

43. *Journal*, 1:192 (Sept. 2, 1737).

44. Ibid., pp. 233–4 (April 22, 1738).

45. Ibid., pp. 248–9 (May 24, 1738, §12).

46. Ibid., p. 234 (April 22, 1738).

47. Ibid., p. 250 (May 24, 1738, §14).

CHAPTER 6: ORTHODOXY, PARADOX, AND EXPERIMENTAL DIVINITY

1. *The Character of a Methodist*, §1, *Works*, 8:340. As was noted above, this essay, along with *A Plain Account of Christian Perfection*, was commended to all preachers by the American Conference *Minutes* of 1781 as sound doctrine for instruction.

2. *A Plain Account of the People Called Methodists*, §I.2, *Works*, 8:249. First published at Bristol and Dublin in 1749, the substance of a letter to Rev. Mr. Perronet, 1748.

3. *A Letter to the Right Reverend the Lord Bishop of Gloucester* [William Warburton] (1763), §III.(II).5, *Appeals*, 532. Cf. Green, *Bibliography*, #216. Wesley is here quoting from his earlier *Letter to the Rev. Dr. Conyers Middleton* (1749), Part VI of which was subsequently published as *A Plain Account of Genuine Christianity* (1753); cf. Green, *Bibliography*, #121 & #122.

4. *An Earnest Appeal*, §67, *Appeals*, p. 73. This statement is reiterated in several sermons, and elsewhere in Wesley's writings.

5. *Journal*, 1:233 (April 22, 1738).

6. Sermon 150, "Hypocrisy in Oxford" (written June 24, 1741), *Sermons*, 4:389–407. Archbishop John Tillotson and noted theologian George Bull, both of the late 17th century, are named. Wesley's 19th-century editors supplied the traditional title "True Christianity Defended" for this university sermon, which Wesley never actually preached. See Outler's introduction for the circumstances surrounding its composition.

7. *Journal* (Curnock), 2:274–6 (Sept. 13, 1739).

8. *Popery Calmly Considered*, §I.1–6, *Works*, 10:140–2.

9. Melanchthon, *Loci Communes Theologici* in Pauck, ed., *Melanchthon and Bucer*, pp. 104-105. The italics are mine, as are the words in brackets. The extent of Cranmer's personal relationship to the Wittenberg Reformers is manifest, though often ignored. The most explicit and thorough scholarly attention and observation given to the relation of Cranmer's Homilies to Melanchthon of which I am aware is J. T. Tomlinson, *The Prayer Book, Articles and Homilies: Some Forgotten Facts in Their History* (London: Elliot Stock, 1899), cf. pp. 237-239. See also E. Gordan Rupp, *The English Protestant Tradition* (Cambridge: Cambridge University Press, 1949), pp. 174 ff.

10. Ibid.

11. Homily "Of Salvation," Part 3, *Homilies*, p. 34. Italics mine. The reasons for the virtual eclipse of the influence of the Homilies until recovered by Wesley in 1738 are an interesting but untold story of Caroline Divinity, quite missed by Tulloch. Wesley's extracts from the Homilies comprise his *The Doctrine of Salvation, Faith, and Good Works, Extracted from the Homilies of the Church of England* (London: James Hutton, 1739), reprinted in Outler, ed., *John Wesley*, pp. 123–33. As Outler correctly affirms (p. 121), this was Wesley's earliest doctrinal manifesto after May 24, 1738, with, of course, justification by faith as the focus. Cf. *Journal* (Curnock), 2:101 (Nov. 12, 1738).

12. Ibid.

13. Richard Hooker, *Of the Laws of Ecclesiastical Polity*, §V.63.1, in *The Works of Richard Hooker*, 2 vols. (Oxford: Oxford University Press, 1850), 2:42. For Hooker's probable dependence upon Augustine in this language of faith as *agnitio*, "acknowledgment," see *De Trinitate* §XVI.8–11, and my essay, "Faith and Reason in St. Augustine," in *Faith Seeking Understanding*, pp. 20–21.

14. *An Earnest Appeal*, §58–9, *Appeals*, 68–9. Italics mine.

15. Ibid, §59, *Appeals*, 69. Italics mine. Cf. *Advice to the People Called Methodists*, *Works*, 8:352, and *The Principles of a Methodist*, §9, *Works*, 8:363.

16. *Journal*, 1:233–4 (April 22, 1738).

17. *An Earnest Appeal*, §60, *Appeals*, pp. 69–70.

18. Ibid., §71, p. 75: "More especially, we call upon those who for many years saw our manner of life at Oxford. These well know that 'after the most straitest [*sic*] sect of our religion we lived Pharisees,' and the grand objection to us for all those years was the being 'righteous overmuch'. . . ."

19. *Journal*, 1:248–9 (May 24, 1738, §12). The italics are Wesley's.

20. *An Earnest Appeal*, §59, *Appeals*, p. 69. Cf. ibid., §23, *Appeals*, p. 53, and *A Farther Appeal*, Part I, §II.3–8, *Appeals*, pp. 110–15.

21. *A Farther Appeal*, Part I, §V.28, *Appeals*, p. 171.

22. Cf. *Journal* (Curnock), 2:390 (Jan. 2, 1749). The full title of Middleton's book was: *A Free Inquiry Into the Miraculous Powers, which are supposed to have subsisted in the Christian Church, from the Earliest Ages, through several successive centuries. By which it is shewn that we have no sufficient reason to believe, upon the Authority of the primitive Fathers, that any such powers were continued to the Church after the days of the Apostles* (London: Manby and Cox, 1749). Wesley's *Letter*, published in January, 1749, shows that Middleton denies miraculous powers not only to the sub-apostolic church, as his title implies, but also to Christ and the Apostles. Cf. Green, *Bibliography*, #121.

23. *Letter to the Rev. Dr. Conyers Middleton*, §VI.ii.3, *Works*, 10:72.

24. Ibid., §VI.ii,5, p. 73.

25. Ibid.

26. Ibid., §VI.ii.6–7, p. 73.

27. *An Earnest Appeal*, §84, *Appeals*, p. 82.

28. *A Farther Appeal*, Part I, §IV.5, *Appeals*, p. 137. The italics are Wesley's.

29. Ibid., Part II, §III.8–9, p. 258.

30. Ibid., Part I, §I.4–6, pp. 106–8.

31. Ibid., Part I, §III.10, p. 130. Cf. *Letter to Middleton*, §VI.ii.3, *Works*, 8:72–3.

32. Richard Hooker, Sermon II, "A Learned Discourse on Justification, Works, and How the Foundation of Faith is Overthrown," §26, *The Works of Richard Hooker*, 2:627.

33. Ibid.

34. *A Farther Appeal*, Part I, §I.6, *Appeals*, p. 108. Full attention to this subject occupies §V of *A Farther Appeal*, Part I. In particular, see Wesley's anonymous use of John Pearson's authoritative *An Exposition of the Creed* (1659) on "the ordinary operations of the Holy Ghost," §V.23, pp. 163–66.

35. Hooker, "Discourse of Justification," §26, *The Works of Richard Hooker*, 2:628. Cf. §24, 2:621.

36. *A Farther Appeal*, Part I, §I.4, *Appeals*, pp. 106–7.

37. *An Earnest Appeal*, §71, *Appeals*, p. 75; ibid., §88, pp. 83–4.

38. Ibid., §84, p. 82.

39. Hooker, "Discourse of Justification," §26, *The Works of Richard Hooker*, 2:626. Cf. *Of the Laws of Ecclesiastical Polity*, §V.63.1, *The Works of Richard Hooker*, 1:42–43.

40. Ibid., §26, 2:620.

41. *An Earnest Appeal*, §67, *Appeals*, p. 73.

42. *Letter to Middleton*, §VI.ii.7–8, *Works* 8:73. Cf. *A Farther Appeal*, Part I, §IV.5–6, *Appeals*, p. 136–8.

43. *A Farther Appeal*, Part I, §IV.5, *Appeals*, pp. 137.

44. An Earnest Appeal, §84, *Appeals*, p. 82.

CHAPTER 7: EMMISARIES OF THE GREAT SALVATION

1. Lee, *Short History*, p. 351. The surprising use of the word "ordination" may reflect a viewpoint and sentiment of Richard Whatcoat, as relayed by John Atkinson, which it is known Jesse Lee did not share; namely, a "high view of the Episcopate, esteeming it not an office taken at pleasure, but an order of God." This "high view," says Atkinson, "was shared by Asbury." See John Atkinson, *A Centennial History of American Methodism* (New York: Phillips & Hunt, 1884), p. 97.

2. Thomas Coke and Henry Moore, *The Life of the Reverend John Wesley* (Philadelphia: John Dickens, 1793), Volume 3, chapter 3, provides an account of the New England Puritan "religion" to the Great Awakening, including the work of both Edwards and Whitefield, as the setting for the revivals under the Methodists in Maryland and Virginia. These were known at first-hand by Joseph Pilmore and George Shadford, 1772–1777, who were possibly sources for this account, although there were others.

3. *Journal of the General Conference, 1808*, in *Journals of the General Conference of the Methodist Episcopal Church*, Volume I: *1796–1836* (New York: Carlton & Phillips, 1855), p. 87. Cf. *The Memoirs of the Reverend Jesse Lee*, edited by Minton Thrift (New York: Bangs and Mason, 1823), p. 310. Thrift states that "Sometime previous to this [May, 1808] he had contemplated publishing *A History of the Methodists in America*, and had actually commenced collecting and arranging materials for the publication of the work." It is further hinted by Thrift (p. 311) that, by his trip in New England in 1808, Lee had in view advancement of this *History*. Following the adjournment of the General Conference on May 26, Lee started northward immediately on his extensive several month's tour of the New England Methodist Societies, many of which he had founded.

4. *Journal of the General Conference, 1808*, p. 87

5. Ibid., pp. 90–91.

6. Ibid., p. 87.

7. *Minutes* (American), 1773 Conference, p. 6.

8. *Journal of the General Conference, 1808*, p. 87

9. Ibid., p. 92.

10. Ibid., pp. 92 and 89.

11. Cf. *Journal of the General Conference, 1808*, p. 94. The motion was lost. It is not stated or known whether the recommendation of the Committee of Review, disapproving the manuscript in question before it, in fact concerned Lee's manuscript; viz., *A History of the Methodists in America*. This is altogether probable in my view, but with the observation that the manuscript was surely lacking an updated account of New England Methodism.

12. Nathan Bangs, *A History of the Methodist Episcopal Church*, 4 vols. (New York: Carlton & Porter, 1839).

13. Ibid., 1:6. Nathan Bangs had indicated already that the manuscript of the first volume of his own *History* had been "consumed by the disasterous fire that had consumed the Book Room [of the Methodist Publishing House in New York] and its valuable contents" in 1836 (p. 4). Now, in a footnote on page 7 he observes that Jesse Lee's "manuscript journals, which were quite voluminous, were also consumed" by the fire. It was an irreparable disaster for Methodist historiography of the first generation, for there was nothing else comparable, as time was to prove.

14. Ibid., 1:5.

15. Ibid., 1:6.

16. Ibid., 1:6.

17. For the doctrinal provenance of the Great Awakening, and particularly of the Tennants, see Sydney Ahlstrom, *A Religious History of the American People* (New Haven: Yale University Press, 1972), p. 269. Here Ahlstrom notes that William Tennant, Sr., ordained in the Episcopal Church of Ireland, fostered in his sons, William and Gilbert, but also Samuel Blair, "a very 'experimental' form of evangelical Puritanism." The elder Tennant became a Presbyterian minister and served long in Bedford, New York.

18. *Journal* (Curnock), 2:83–84 (October 9, 1738) Wesley, of course, refers to Jonathan Edwards' *A Faithful Narrative of the Surprising Work of God in the Conversion of Many Hundred Souls in Northampton and the Neighboring Towns and Villages* (1737), of which he published an extract under the title *A Narrative of the Late Work of God at and near Northampton, in New England* (Bristol: Felix Farley, [1744]). Cf. Green, *Bibliography*, #54.

19. Sermon 53, "On the Death of George Whitefield," §III.5, *Sermons*, 2:343.

20. Joseph Pilmore, *The Journal of Joseph Pilmore*, edited by F. E. Mason and H. T. Maag (Philadelphia: Historical Society of the Philadelphia Annual Conference, 1969), p. 24.

21. Ibid., p. 33, n. 1.

22. Sermon 53, "On the Death of George Whitefield," §I.2, *Sermons*, 2:331. Italics mine.

23. Ibid., §I.3, p. 331.

24. Ibid., §III.5, p. 343. In these things we may suppose that Wesley was affirming the truth he could attest without openly declaring that, on the matter of holiness and the "living sacrifice" in the likeness of Christ, and the renewal of the "image of God" by sanctifying grace, Whitefield was held back by Calvinism and "imputed righteousness." To equivocate on this, however, was to relinquish half the gospel, i.e., Christian perfection, the fullness of ex-

periential religion, and the "Scripture way of salvation" in the view of the Wesleys.

25. Pilmore, *Journal*, pp. 25; cf. pp. 222, 226, 230.

26. Ibid., p. 26.

27. Ibid., pp. 140, 180.

28. Ibid., p. 138.

29. Ibid., pp. 149, 157, 158.

30. Ibid., p. 169. Italics mine. Cf. Wesley's *The Character of a Methodist.*

31. Ibid., p. 193.

32. Wesley, *Journal* (Curnock), 2:275 (Sept. 13, 1739). Cf. *A Farther Appeal*, Part I, §I.3, *Appeals*, p. 106; and *The Principles of a Methodist*, §20, *Works*, 8:367.

33. Asbury, *Journal and Letters*, 1:6–7.

34. Pilmore, *Journal*, pp. 27–28.

35. Ibid., p. 23, n. 23.

36. Wesley, *Journal* (Curnock), 2:185 (April 29, 1739).

37. Asbury, *Journal and Letters*, 1:8.

38. Ibid., 1:5.

39. Ibid., 1:12. Italics mine.

40. Cf. Wesley, *Journal*, 1:234 (April 22, 1738).

41. Asbury, *Journal and Letters*, 1:14.

42. Ibid., 1:14.

43. Ibid., 1:17.

44. Ibid., 1:17. Cf. *A Farther Appeal*, Part I, §I.6, *Appeals*, pp. 107–8.

45. Asbury, *Journal and Letters*, 1:59.

46. *A Farther Appeal*, §I.3, *Appeals*, p. 106.

47. Frank Baker, *From Wesley to Asbury* (Durham, N. C.: Duke University Press, 1976), p. 80; cf. pp. 70–83. Dr. Baker's rediscovery of Wesley's published text of Thomas Taylor's letter of April, 1768, is of first importance for history of Methodist origins, especially in the New York area. The letter pleads for assistance in "legal counsel, financial help, and qualified preachers," and supplies a contemporary sketch of the general situation attending Philip Embury's and Captain Webb's inaugural work in New York. Cf. Nathan Bangs' version in *A History of the Methodist Episcopal Church*, 1:52–58.

48. *Minutes* (British), 1770 Conference, Q.28, pp. 95–96.

49. *Minutes of Several Conversations*, Q.4, *Works*, 8:300.

CHAPTER 8: NATIVE AMERICAN PROFESSORS OF EXPERIMENTAL RELIGION

1. Thrift, *Memoirs of Jesse Lee*, pp. 343–344. Italics mine.

2. Cf. *Minutes* (British), 1770 Conference, p. 96.

3. *A Farther Appeal*, Part I, §III.10, *Appeals*, p. 130: ". . . faith alone is the condition of *present* salvation . . . [and] at what time soever faith is given, holiness commences in the soul." "*Present* salvation" means forgiveness of sins or justification by faith as a gift. But *full* salvation includes Christian perfection, or entire sanctification. Wesley speaks of this also at times as "*final* salvation."

4. Ibid., §II.8, p. 115.

5. *Minutes of Several Conversations*, Q.4., *Works*, 8:300.

6. *Minutes* (British), 1770 Conference, p. 96.

7. *A Farther Appeal*, Part I, §III.10, *Appeals*, p. 130.

8. *Minutes* (British), 1770 Conference, p. 96.

9. Ware, *Life and Travels*, p. 106. Ware adds: "Mr. Dickens was, in the estimation of his brethren, a man of sound sense and sterling piety: and there were few men on the conference floor heard with greater deference than he."

10. These statistics are derived, of course, from the *Minutes* (American), which alone, of all our sources for the period, preserve the roster of Conference membership. 379 persons were admitted to full connection in the years 1773–1794; by 1795, 30 had died, 74 had located, 12 had withdrawn, and 8 had been dismissed for cause, making a total of 124 removed from active service. This left 255 preachers in active service in 1795, with a membership role of 52,794 white and 13,814 black members. In 1774 there had been 2,073 members in the seaboard colonies.

11. Watters, *Short Account*, p. 2.

12. *Minutes* (British), 1768 Conference, p. 82. Wesley's abridgment of Edwards' *Life of Brainerd* was published in 1768; cf. Green, *Bibliography*, #253.

13. Freeborn Garrettson, *The Experiences and Travels of Freeborn Garrettson, Minister of the Methodist Episcopal Church* (Philadelphia: Printed by Parry Hall and sold by John Dickens, 1791) p. iv. The "second edition" of Garrettson's manuscript, having failed to meet the "deadline," was published in America by John Dickens rather than by Wesley in England, as certainly had been intended. The hesitancy of Garrettson continues to be evident in the subscript of the title page: "Hitherto hath the Lord Helped" [1 Sam. 7:12]. We know from an exchange of letters with Wesley, preserved by Nathan Bangs in his *Life of Garrettson*, p. 170, that Wesley's request came first to Garrettson in a letter directed to him at Halifax, Nova Scotia, dated June 26, 1785.

14. Bangs, *Life of Garrettson*, p. 170. Italics mine.

15. Garrettson, *Experiences and Travels*, p. iv.

16. Watters, *Short Account*, p. 109.

17. Thrift, *Memoirs of Jesse Lee*, p. 346f.

18. Ware, *Life and Travels*, pp. 107–108.

19. Watters, *Short Account*, p. 16.

20. Ibid., p. 14.

21. Ibid., p. 14. William Watters, in his *Short Account*, is so scrupulously modest as to mention almost no family names, such as those of his father, mother, or six brothers. Not even his older brother Nicholas (who was well known to Asbury and who was admitted on trial to Conference in 1776) is anywhere mentioned by name. Yet Nicholas served as an itinerant preacher, and died on mission in South Carolina in 1804. One must resort, therefore, to Asbury's *Journal* to identify the members of this important early Methodist family, which was centered, it appears, at Deer Creek in the Susquehannah Hundred, a subdivision of Harford County, Maryland, and not far from Robert Strawbridge. From 1772 onward Asbury was frequently "at home" at Deer Creek until at least 1810 [Asbury, *Journal and Letters*, 1:50]. Seven sons were born to Godfrey and Sarah Adams Watters at Deer Creek. Henry, perhaps the eldest son, lived at Deer Creek with his wife, Mary; he was perhaps the earliest

family convert to "experimental religion." This was evidently through the preaching of Robert Strawbridge and his "exhorter," Joseph Presbury, in the latter 1760s. It is surely through this brother, Henry, that William, Godfrey Jr., John (an elder brother much admired by Asbury), Stephen, and perhaps Harry, were introduced to Methodism. All of them had been baptized and reared according to the catechism and liturgy of the Church of England. It is plain that Henry was a power for Methodism in the area for two score years. Of the 62 references to the Watters family in Asbury's *Journal*, 34 refer to different members of the family and 28 specifically to William.

22. Ibid., pp. 15–17.

23. Ibid., p. 18. This reflects John Wesley's established views.

24. Ibid., p. 20. The word "Episcopal" is Watter's own. This was a parish church of the Church of England, but the latter was not "established" by law in Maryland as it was in Virginia.

25. Ibid., p. 27.

26. Ibid., p. 34.

27. Ibid., p. 58.

28. Ibid., p. 59.

29. Ibid., p. 57.

30. John McLean, ed., *A Sketch of Rev. Philip Gatch*, op. cit., 56. McLean, who was a justice of the Supreme Court of the United States, makes these comments: "The journal of Mr. Gatch is substantially copied from his own manuscripts [by Philip Gatch's son]. . . . Other parts, marked as quotations, were copied from manuscripts which were revised and corrected." Gatch names exhorters under Strawbridge as: Richard Owen, Sater Stephenson, and Nathan Perigau (p. 9). That Gatch does not mention Joseph Presbury, who was so influential upon William Watters, must be simply oversight.

31. Ibid., p. 14.

32. Ibid., p. 16.

33. Ibid., p. 7. Italics mine.

34. Russell's *Seven Sermons* were already widely read in the 1740s in the Hanover County Presbyterian parish of which Samuel Davies was pastor until 1751. The identity of Russell is not known but the volume of sermons clearly belonged to the Great Awakening. In *Revivalism in America* (New York: Charles Scribner's Sons, 1945), William W. Sweet provides a lead which I have not been able to follow. In calling attention to a painful awareness of the decline of religious vitality in the early 18th century by such New England divines as President Samuel Willard of Harvard and others, Sweet names among other "Annual Election Sermons" in Boston on that subject *The Decay of Love to God in the Churches, Offensive and Dangerous* by the Rev. William Russell, 1730 (p. 21).

35. Ibid., pp. 17–18. His experience of justification and sanctification was, it seems, in 1771.

36. Ibid., p. 56. This quotation could only have been used by Gatch after the publication of Watter's *Short Account* in 1806. This strongly suggests that the passage belongs not to Gatch's journal but to his later memoirs. He had moved to Ohio by 1798, where he was a pioneer Methodist preacher.

37. Bangs, *Life of Garrettson*, pp. 37–39.

38. Ibid., p. 169.
39. Ibid., p. 38.
40. Ibid., p. 39. Italics mine.
41. Ibid., p. 64. Cf. Watters, *Short Account*, p. 59.
42. Ibid., p. 67.
43. Ibid., p. 66.
44. Watters, *Short Account*, p. 59.
45. Bangs, *Life of Garrettson*, p. 67.
46. Ibid., p. 170.
47. *Minutes* (British), 1768 Conference, p. 79. Cf. §5 of the "Resolution for Union" of the 1769 Conference, ibid., pp. 88–89.
48. Bangs, *Life of Garrettson*, p. 168.
49. Jesse Lee, *A Short Account of the Life and Death of the Rev. John Lee* (Baltimore: 1805), pp. 9–10. John Lee was admitted on trial at the Conference of 1788, and to full connection in 1790. He located in 1791 after service in New York and New England under his brother, also named Jesse Lee, and died of a protracted illness on Oct. 6, 1801.
50. Ibid., p. 11.
51. Ibid., pp. 9–10. We have in these words the recognition of the parish as, by law established, part of the Church of England.
52. Thrift, *Memoirs of Jesse Lee*, p. 11. Cf. Leroy M. Lee, *The Life and Times of the Rev. Jesse Lee* (Richmond: John Early, 1848), pp. 27–28.
53. Leroy Lee, *Life of Jesse Lee*, pp. 27f.
54. Jesse Lee, *Life and Death of John Lee*, pp. 11–12.
55. Thrift, *Memoirs of Jesse Lee*, pp. 15–18.
56. Jesse Lee, *Life and Death of John Lee*, p. 12.
57. Thrift, *Memoirs of Jesse Lee*, p. 7. Italics mine.
58. Ibid., p. 8.
59. Ibid., p. 9.
60. Ibid., pp. 11f.
61. *A Farther Appeal*, Part I, §IV.5, *Appeals*, p. 137.
62. Thrift, *Memoirs of Jesse Lee*, pp. 12–13.
63. Bangs, *Life of Garrettson*, pp. 168–169. Italics mine. Having completed this slender account of these knights-errant of "experimental" or "heart-religion," who laid the foundation of American Methodism, I have belatedly come upon William W. Sweet's *Men of Zeal* (New York: Abingdon Press, 1935). It is long out of print, but pioneered a study which needs to be continued.

CHAPTER 9: EXPERIMENTAL RELIGION IN LOW PROFILE

1. Thomas à Kempis, *The Imitation of Christ* trans. from the Latin by Richard Whytford (London: Chatto and Windus, 1908), §I.1, p. 4. It is tradition that the first Latin edition of the *Imitation* was published in 1483. The Whytford translation was followed by two others in the 16th century. Wesley first used George Stanhope's English version, probably the 11th edition (London, 1726), but published his own translation in 1735 (reissued in 1750). An abridged edition, *An Extract of the Christian's Pattern*, appeared in 1741 and

was several times republished in Wesley's lifetime. The "Large Minutes" contain Wesley's observation that "Kempis ought to be in every house." Cf. Green, *Bibliography*, #19.

2. Cf. Philip Schaff's discussion of *The Articles of Smalcald* in *Creeds*, 1:255.

3. Sermon 53, "On the Death of George Whitefield,", §III.2–3, *Sermons*, 2:341f.

4. *Minutes of Several Conversations*, Q.4, *Works*, 8:300.

5. Ibid.

6. Bangs, *History*, 1:364.

7. Ibid., 1:26–28, 30, 33, 42, 76.

8. Ware, *Life and Travels*, pp. 131–132. By his use of the adjective "primitive" (which is the earliest Methodist usage I have seen) Ware seems, most likely, to refer to the early "irregular" or "regular" preachers of Methodism, after 1773 but prior to 1795, such as Robert Williams, William Watters, Richard Owen, or Caleb Pedicord, whose lives and ministries, as we have seen, were avowedly products of Wesley's experimental divinity. For usage of the words "irregular" and "regular," see McTyeire, *History of Methodism*, pp. 265–268.

9. D. W. Clark, *The Life and Times of Rev. Elijah Hedding, D.D.* (New York: Carlton & Phillips, 1855), pp. 61–63.

10. David Holmes, ed., *The Methodist Preacher: Containing Twenty-Eight Sermons on Doctrinal and Practical Subjects, by Bishop E. Hedding, Dr. Fisk, Dr. Bangs, et al.* (Auburn and Buffalo: Miller, Orton and Mulligan, 1854), pp. iii–v. Rev. David Holmes was a member of the Central New York or Genesee Conference at the time of publication of this symposium. He had been admitted to full connection in 1826 — a decade following the demise of Francis Asbury. David Holmes, Jr. (a son?), received conference membership in 1832. Cf. Bangs, *History*, Volume 4, Appendix 19 & 20.

11. Stephen Olin, *The Works Of Stephen Olin, D.D.*, 2 vols. (New York: Harper Bros., 1853), 1:59.

12. Wilbur Fisk, "On the Law and the Gospel," in Holmes, ed., *The Methodist Preacher*, p. 1.

13. Bangs, *Life of Garrettson*, p. 170.

14. Cf. Leroy Lee, *Life of Jesse Lee*, pp. 33, 37, 52.

15. Ibid., 31. See also Thrift, *Memoirs of Jesse Lee*, pp. 7–8.

16. Bangs, *History*, 1:365.

17. *Minutes of Several Conversations*, Q.26, *Works*, 8:310.

18. Ibid., Q.13, p. 306.

19. Ibid., Q.13, p. 304; Q.26, p. 310.

20. Leroy Lee, *Life of Jesse Lee*, p. 63.

21. *Minutes* (American), 1781 Conference, p. 43. Cf. chapter 1 above, esp. p. 30ff.

22. Ibid., p. 41. Italics mine.

23. *The Character of a Methodist*, §17, *Works*, 8:346.

24. D. W. Clark, *Life of Hedding*, pp. 63–67. Joseph Mitchell's pioneering ministry fell in the decade 1794–1804 and coincided in part with the work of Jesse Lee in the New England seaboard states.

25. Bangs, *History*, 1:269. The use of the phrase "experimental and

practical religion" is so widespread in the first volume of the *History* that it becomes in its usage a general descriptive phrase, almost, it appears, equivalent with the unfolding Methodism which Bangs relates.

26. *The Character of a Methodist*, §4, *Works*, 8:341.

27. Ibid., §4, p. 341; §18, p. 346.

28. Homily "Of Faith," Part III, *Homilies*, 44.

29. Ibid., p. 45.

30. *The Character of a Methodist*, §17, *Works*, 8:346. Italics mine.

31. Ibid. Italics mine. In this essay, first published in 1742, Wesley is on the defensive against sundry criticism from churchmen who charicature rather than truly characterize the Wesleys and their doctrine. Wesley's answer in *The Character of a Methodist* is to truly characterize and to show that, in both "principles" and "practice," the real Methodist simply conforms to "the common principles of Christianity." These, of course, Wesley is aware were often abandoned silently by his critics.

32. *Minutes of Several Conversations*, Q.4, *Works*, 8:300.

33. *The Character of a Methodist*, §17, p. 346. Italics mine.

34. *A Farther Appeal*, Part I, §I.3, *Appeals*, p. 106.

CHAPTER 10: DOCTRINAL STANDARDS IN EARLY AMERICAN METHODISM, 1773–1794

1. George J. Stevenson, "A Brief History of Methodism," in *Methodist Worthies*, 2 vols. (London: T. C. Jack, 1884), 1:22.

2. *Minutes* (British), 1769 Conference, p. 88. Italics mine.

3. Watters, *Short Account*, p. 81, provides the sole surviving eye-witness report: "In the morning, instead of coming off in despair of any remedy, we were invited to take our seats again in conference, where with great . . . praises to God, we on both sides heartily agreed to the . . . accommodation. I could not but say, 'it is the Lord's doing and it is marvelous in our eyes.'"

4. *Minutes* (American), 1781 Conference, p. 41. Italics mine.

5. Ibid., 1782 Conference, Q.19, p. 55.

6. Ibid., 1784 Conference, Q.21, pp. 72–73.

7. Ibid., 1782 Conference, p. 55.

8. Cf. Asbury, *Journal and Letters*, 1:207–224.

9. *Minutes* (British), 1769 Conference, p. 89. I have as yet been unable to determine whether Wesley responded positively to this request. Had he done so, we should have been supplied at the source with something of a summation of "the old Methodist doctrine" that I am not aware came to be.

10. *Minutes of Some Late Conversations*, *Works*,, 8:274.

11. *A Short History of Methodism*, §9, *Works*, 8:349.

12. *The Character of a Methodist*, §17, *Works*, 8:346.

13. *Minutes of Several Conversations*, Q.56, *Works*, 8:328.

14. *A Short History of Methodism*, §10, *Works*, 8:349.

15. Ibid.

16. See *Journal* (Curnock), 2:245, n.3; 2:248, n.2; and 2:304–305, n.2. Curnock identifies the writer of the letter as the Rev. Josiah Tucker of Bristol,

whose "Brief History of the Principles of a Methodist" occasioned Wesley's irenic response in *The Principles of a Methodist* (1742).

17. Ibid., 2:304–5 (Nov.1, 1739). Italics mine. On the subject of "living faith" as taught by Wesley, which chapters 3, 6, and 7 of this volume labor to clarify after long neglect, I judge this brief contemporary summation by Josiah Tucker to be he most discerning of any statement in the surviving literature, Methodist or extra-Methodist.

18. *The Principles of a Methodist* §9, *Works*, 8:363. Italics mine. The quotation, somewhat inexact, is from the Homily "Of Salvation," Part III; cf. *Homilies*, p. 34. See the same passage in Wesley's own abridgment, *The Doctrine of Salvation, Faith, and Good Works, Extracted from the Homilies of the Church of England*, in Outler, *John Wesley*, p. 128.

19. Ibid., §7, p. 362.

20. *Journal* (Curnock), 2:250 (July 31, 1739).

21. Ibid. The italics are Wesley's.

22. *The Principles of a Methodist*, §28, *Works*, 8:373.

23. Thrift, *Memoirs of Jesse Lee*, p. 7.

24. *Minutes* (British), 1769 Conference, p. 89.

25. *Minutes of Several Conversations*, Q.3, *Works*, 8:299.

26. Ibid.

27. For a comprehensive representation and account of the first eight editions of the *Discipline*, see Tigert, *The Making of Methodism*, pp. 102–109. Tigert's *Constitutional History*, Appendix VII: "On the First Discipline and the Large Minutes," indicates that the first American *Discipline* of 1785 carried the statement regarding "God's design for raising up the preachers called Methodists in America" (p. 535).

28. Tigert, *Constitutional History*, p. 533.

29. Baker, *From Wesley to Asbury*, pp. 167–172.

30. *Minutes of Several Conversations*, Q.77, *Works*, 8:337.

31. *Minutes* (American), 1773 Conference, p. 5. Italics mine.

32. Ibid., 1781 Conference, p. 41. Italics mine.

33. Tigert, *Constitutional History*. The reference is to Appendix VII: "The First Discipline and the Large Minutes of 1780," pp. 532–602. Here Tigert sets out in parallel columns the first Conference *Minutes* — those of the so-called "Christmas Conference" of the Methodist Episcopal Church (1784), which comprise the very rare first edition of *A Form of Discipline* (1785) — and the Wesleyan "Large Minutes" of 1780. So far as I am presently aware, a full exposition of and commentary on the substance of this parallelism, and an account of the unfolding deviations and alterations of the *Discipline* into the third decade of the 19th century, has never been published.

34. *Minutes of Several Conversations*, Q.3, *Works*, 8:299.

35. Ibid., Q.51, p. 325.

36. These texts are reproduced from Tigert, *Constitutional History*, Appendix VII, pp. 578–580.

37. *Minutes of Several Conversations*, Q.25, §11, *Works*, 8:310; cf. *A Form of Discipline*, Q.26, in Tigert, *Constitutional History*, p. 550.

38. *Rules of the Band-Societies*, *Works*, 8:272–273. These *Rules* were drawn up by Wesley on December 25, 1738.

39. Bangs, *Life of Garrettson*, p. 170.

40. *Journals of the General Conference of the Methodist Episcopal Church*, Volume I: *1796–1836* (New York: Carlton & Phillips, 1855), p. 89.

CHAPTER 11: THE METHODIST EPISCOPAL CHURCH: DOCTRINAL STANDARDS, 1785–1816

1. The statement of purpose is present in the first edition of *A Form of Discipline*, 1785. In the 1792 edition of *The Doctrines and Discipline of the Methodist Episcopal Church in America*, the Bishop's Address of introduction contained the statement of "God's design" in raising up the preachers called Methodists, namely, "to reform the continent, and spread Scripture holiness over these lands." In the 1896 edition, the word "evangelize" is substituted for "reform." The "Historical Statement" of *The Book of Discipline*, 1984 edition, acknowledges that a mark of "the true Church of Christ" includes, "to spread scriptural holiness" (p. 10).

2. Wesley's letter to Freeborn Garrettson, June 26, 1785, in Bangs, *Life of Garrettson*, pp. 169–170.

3. *Minutes* (British), p. 96; and *The Character of a Methodist*, §17, *Works*, 8:346.

4. Journal of the General Conference, 1840 (New York: Lane & Tippett, 1844), p. 154.

5. For examples, see the following: *Journal* (Curnock), 2:274–6 (Sept. 13, 1739); *An Earnest Appeal*, §35–71, *Appeals*, pp. 57–75; *A Letter to the Rev. Mr. Horne*, *Appeals*, pp. 441–58; "A Letter to an Evangelical Layman," *The Works of John Wesley*, Volume 26: *Letters II, 1740–1755*, ed. Frank Baker (Oxford: Clarendon Press, 1982), pp. 102–09, *The Character of a Methodist*, *Works*, 8:339–47; *The Principles of a Methodist*, *Works*, 8:359–74. Similar statements can be found scattered throughout Wesley's *Sermons*.

6. *The Doctrines and Discipline* (1792), pp. iii–iv.

7. *The Character of a Methodist*, §4, *Works*, 8:341.

8. Ware, *Life and Travels*, p. 105.

9. Quoted in Tigert, *The Making of Methodism*, p. 75.

10. McLean, *Sketch of Rev. Philip Gatch*, p. 56.

11. *Minutes of Several Conversations*, Q.3, *Works*, 8:299.

12. Ware, *Life and Travels*, p. 104.

13. Watters, *Short Account*, p. 102. Watters was the principal intermediary between a southern body of preachers in the years 1778–1780 who were adamant to administer the sacraments under a self-authorized presbyterial ordination and a northern group loyal to Asbury. He alludes in this passage to his personal correspondence on behalf of the southern body with John Wesley, appealing for his assistance in the crisis. He knows that Wesley's decision to ordain Coke and Asbury was Wesley's long-deferred solution to an otherwise insoluble problem. In this unpretentious and discreet account is lodged the most important surviving firsthand recording of the crisis that almost destroyed Methodism toward the close of the American Revolution.

14. Ware, *Life and Travels*, p. 105.

15. Ibid., p. 104.
16. Tigert, *The Making of Methodism*, p. 107.
17. See *The Sunday Service*, pp. 128–165, for the Orders for the Administration of the Lord's Supper, Baptism, Matrimony, Communion of the Sick, and Burial of the Dead.
18. Ibid., The Ordaining of Elders and Deacons, pp, 288, 298.
19. Ibid., The Ordination of Superintendents, p. 307.
20. Ibid., Order for the Burial of the Dead, p. 159f.
21. Tigert, *The Making of Methodism*, p. 107.
22. *A Form of Discipline* (1785), p. iii.

EPILOGUE

1. For a brief account of this important episode, see Wade C. Barclay, *History of Missions*, Volume III (New York: Methodist Board of Missions, 1957), p. 73.

2. Thus it is stated in §1, "Historical Background," of Part II of *The Book of Discipline of the United Methodist Church, 1972* (Nashville: The United Methodist Publishing House, 1972): "Despite continued and quite varigated theological development, there has been no significant project in formal doctrinal reformulation in Methodism since 1808" (¶68, p. 44). All references to the text of Part II are to this first published edition. The very few subsequent emendations are not explicitly implicated for this discussion.

3. Cf. *The Book of Discipline, 1972* n.1, ¶68, p. 39. For my analysis and critique of the report of the Commission on Doctrinal Standards, as dopted by the General Conference of 1972 to comprise Part II of *The Book of Discipline*, see *Religion in Life* 44:4 (Winter 1975), or my *Faith Seeking Understanding*, pp. 317-28.

4. From 1792 to 1846 "The Nature and Design of the General Rules of the United Societies" [*sic*] appeared as §1 of Chapter II of *The Doctrines and Discipline of the Methodist Episcopal Church*. Under it were ordered the work of the Classes, Band Societies, Privileges to non-Members, Marriage, Dress, Trial of Members, and Use of Spiritous Liquors. Cf. *The Doctrines and Discipline of the Methodist Episcopal Church*, 15th ed. (New York: Hitt & Ware, 1812), pp. 83-103. It is, of course, to be recalled that, until the mid-19th century, the concept and function of the old Methodist "Societies" were not replaced by that of the "Church" in American Methodism. Accordingly, the *General Rules* continued indispensable to Methodist self-understanding far into the 19th century, When, however, by 1888 in the Methodist Episcopal Church, "the classes" were virtually eliminated as to their former function (as had happened earlier in the South) the relevance of the *General Rules* became muted and their role in the way of holiness progressively forgotten. Wesley's interest, therefore, in *both* "inward" *and* "outward holiness" largely gave place to "outward holiness" alone. It became, thereafter, a struggle in Methodism between "moralism" on the one hand, and "humanitarianism" on the other, as accepted marks of the Christian life. Perhaps it remains so.

5. *Doctrines and Discipline* (1812), p. 23. The "Restrictive Rules" must be

understood in the light of the constituted powers of the General Conference, in particular, Number 5: "The General Conference shall have full powers to make rules and regulations for our church, under the following limitations and restrictions, viz." Then follows the First Restrictive Rule we have quoted and which, it should be observed, presupposes that both the Articles and the "standards" and "rules," or canons of doctrine, are already supplied and acknowledged; from them no departure is allowable by a General Conference. Does this signify that the General Conference of 1808 deems it the case that the General Conference of the Methodist Episcopal Church is empowered neither to make rules or canons of doctrine nor to alter those hitherto received and acknowledged? However strange it may seem, I believe it does so signify, and that it is congruent with Wesley's reliance upon 1 Corinthians 2:13: "And we impart this in words not taught by human wisdom but taught by the Spirit, interpreting spiritual truths to those who possess the Spirit." For Wesley this was the core meaning of the *analogia fidei*. Among other things, this meant that the truths of the gospel are not just the deliberations of human reason. To the contrary, they are "written not with ink but with the Spirit of the living God" (2 Cor. 3:3). To miss this point is to fail also to comprehend what "saving faith" meant to the original Methodists who were moved by Wesley's "experimental divinity."

6. Cf. chapter 10, pp. 159–60 above.

7. In 1825 there was published in London the first edition of a work entitled *Wesleyana: Or, A Complete System of Wesleyan Theology; Selected from the Writings of the Reverend John Wesley, A. M. And So Arranged as to Form a Miniature Body of Divinity*. It was the editorial work of the distinguished Wesleyan Methodist minister, the Reverend George Marsden, twice president of the British Conference, and once that of Canada. Four editions were published in London and one in Halifax, N.S., between 1825 and 1840. The first American edition by the Methodist Book Concern, under Mason and Lane, appeared in 1840 and had four reissues until 1852. As an anthology of Wesley's "experimental divinity," arranged by topics and selections from Wesley's *Works*, this publication is, so far as I am aware, the single effort after Wesley's death expressly to represent his body of experimental and practical divinity. There is other historical data to suggest that the mid-1850s mark a point of decline in America of early "canonical" Methodism. Because this work of Marsden's came to my attention only with the writing of this epilogue in the summer of 1987, it has not figured in the previous studies.

8. *Doctrines and Discipline* (1798), preface, p. iv.

9. *The Book of Discipline, 1972*, Part II, §1, ¶68, p. 40.

10. Ibid., ¶70, p. 70.

11. *The Character of a Methodist*, §1, *Works*, 8:340.

INDEX